Mexicans & Americans
Cracking the
Cultural Code

More early praise for Ned Crouch and
MEXICANS & AMERICANS

"Just when you think you've got it all figured out, Ned Crouch adds a new perspective to thinking about cultural differences. MEXICANS & AMERICANS is insightful, entertaining, and very helpful. Rather than diminishing the differences, the author accommodates and celebrates them."

—JOSEPH A. COOK, PH.D., SENIOR CONSULTANT
RHR INTERNATIONAL

"An entertaining and practical approach to help businesspeople navigate the cultural gaps between Mexicans and Americans . . . we learn to respect each culture while making interactions more authentic and effective . . . a great learning tool for professionals in HR."

—E. ARTURO FISHER, PRINCIPAL CONSULTANT
HEWITT ASSOCIATES

"Ned Crouch has always had wonderful stories about Mexicans that he shared with us and with General Motors and Chrysler at his dynamic seminars."

—BRENDA ARBELÁEZ-NOCK, PRESIDENT
PALS INTERNATIONAL

"There are lighter (and lesser) books with a similar focus on the market but only MEXICANS & AMERICANS leaves one with the basic blocks on which to build cultural fluency . . . You also help us gringos realize how negatively we are perceived when we behave 'normally' on Mexican turf! That startling discovery alone should be worth the price of the book for the unwary U.S. American about to embark on a Mexican business venture."

—DOUG STUART, TRAINING MANAGER USA
IOR GLOBAL SERVICES

"Extremely well written and very funny. You've got a hit on your hands. It should be required reading for all MBAs at Harvard Business School."

—I.C. BUPP, PH.D., FORMER PROFESSOR
KENNEDY SCHOOL OF GOVERNMENT,
HARVARD UNIVERSITY, AND AUTHOR OF
ENERGY FUTURE AND LIGHT WATER

Mexicans & Americans
Cracking the
Cultural Code

Ned Crouch

NICHOLAS BREALEY
PUBLISHING

LONDON
YARMOUTH, MAINE

Published by Nicholas Brealey Publishing in association with Intercultural Press in 2004.

Nicholas Brealey Publishing
3-5 Spafield Street
London, EC1R 4QB, UK
Tel: +44-(0)-207-239-0360
Fax: +44-(0)-207-239-0370
www.nbrealey-books.com

Intercultural Press, Inc., A Nicholas
 Brealey Company
PO Box 700
Yarmouth, Maine 04096 USA
Tel: 207-846-5168
Fax: 207-846-5181
www.interculturalpress.com

Printed in the United States of America

08 07 06 05 04   1 2 3 4 5

ISBN: 1-85788-342-X

Library of Congress Cataloging-in-Publication Data is available.

"We are going to be neighbors until this planet ceases to exist. Perhaps it's time to understand each other."

—Octavio Paz, New York, 1991

Contents

PART II Working with Mexicans

Acknowledgments

This book would not have been possible without the friendship and support of many people. Dr. Irwin C. Bupp has been my mentor throughout the process, sharpening my focus and raising the bar. Gary Simon, who has met the intercultural challenges of working in Mexico, provided generous encouragement at key points along the way. My friend Miguel Leaman, trade commissioner of Mexico, gave me the benefit of his astute perspective. Alex Thompson of Ohio State University brought the clear thinking of a talented scholar to the early manuscript. Judy Carl-Hendrick, managing editor with Intercultural Press, saved me from myself. Her knowledge of the subject and gift for organization made her contributions unique. Kati Boland and Sue Lena Thompson have also been most helpful.

My special thanks go to Patricia O'Hare at Intercultural Press and Nicholas Brealey Publishing for her initial response to my manuscript and for her generous spirit of assistance at every turn. There have been many other readers who have provided valuable feedback, and countless people in Mexico who have put up with me over the years. I am especially indebted to the real people—both Mexican and American—who are the subjects of anecdotes throughout the book. Finally, no one has been more important to the realization of this project—to helping me shape my ideas and polish my writing—than my wife, Elizabeth. Together we share a love of Mexico and its people.

Introduction

Of all the people in the world, only the Americans are so sure that there is a clear distinction between *yes* and *no*. We insist on black and white answers. We abhor contradictions. How many times in school, in business, or at home have we heard, "Well, will it or won't it? Are you with me or against me? Is it yes or no? Is it black or white?" This compulsion to resolve contradictions is usually punctuated by a fist to the table. The Mexicans, on the other hand, are much more accepting of life's crosscurrents. After all, the world is full of contradictions. Truth be told, there are lots of maybes and shades of gray.

When Americans are interfacing with Mexicans—and cultural differences run deep—a comprehensive analysis is needed. The U.S. style of doing business is often diametrically opposed to the Mexican approach, sometimes leading to discouraging and costly consequences. Too often American businesspeople go to Mexico, think they have a deal, and return home only to have their follow-up phone calls go unanswered.

I can't tell you how many times in the course of my international business career I've heard successful executives say that the "cultural thing" is the most difficult part of doing business around the world. If this is the case—and I firmly believe it is—then why are international departments often lacking in language skills and, more importantly, in *cultural fluency*?

How Americans respond to cultural differences can determine success or failure. I have seen people who swagger with the plumage of a peacock because they have "international" in their title but who couldn't order a Coca-Cola in a foreign country. At the other end of the spectrum is the seamstress from the mountains of North Carolina who has no degree and travels around the world teaching her company's methods of sewing. She is warmly received, making friends wherever she goes. Some people seem to succeed by dint of personality. Others scrape by despite their dispositions and because of the forgiving nature of the Mexicans. But everybody can use help. So the question becomes, how do you gain enough knowledge to manage intercultural relationships with Mexicans when you've had little exposure to the Mexican context? Clearly help is needed, but where do you turn?

There are the "dos-and-taboos" types of readings that instruct the aspiring internationalist in how to shake hands and how not to tell your Mexican host that his wife is pretty. But they never tell you *why*—other than it will get you killed. Since these books typically cover large regions of the world, they aren't deep. Business schools, on the other hand, offer a top-down academic approach to the study of cultural differences. Largely theoretical, this approach often lacks the reinforcement of real-life experience. Cultural anthropologists and behavioral psychologists can add to your overview of cross-cultural issues, but they rarely have experience dealing directly with business matters. On another front, there is much to be learned from successful businesspeople who have stories to tell about how they winnowed their way through cultural minefields. But businesspeople have not taken the time to analyze their experiences so as to provide a framework that students can carry forward.

Filling a need

This book is an analysis of culture, written by a businessman. While other books give prescriptive lists of dos and don'ts, this one tells you *why* people behave the way they do, and how people of different cultures can work together more effectively. The analysis goes further than others in explaining cultural attitudes toward work and in applying the lessons of cultural anthropologists to the real world. In addition, there is ample use of vivid war stories that are intended to stick with you. These anecdotes were gathered over many years of working in Mexico, and innumerable conversations and interviews. Finally, this book is intended for any reader on any level. It should be of interest to CEOs or to construction foremen.

Cracking a cultural code is much like cracking any code. When you first encounter a coded message, if you think you understand it, you're wrong. First, you have to figure out what ciphers are at work beneath the coded message, then you unravel how these ciphers operate within the system. Only then are you able to see how the components are put together to form a coherent message. The three distinct sections of this book parallel this process, emphasizing the different stages in a bottom-up approach.

Part I emphasizes cultural underpinnings, examining the profound differences between Mexicans and Americans and how these play out in a variety of business and real-life situations. It focuses on three phenomena operating beneath the surface that are key to understanding any culture and that vary greatly between Mexicans and Americans. These include the perception of time, the sense of space, and the construction and use of language—what I call *cultural set pieces*. Through comparisons, you will see how the deeply embedded influences of these cultural set pieces lead to sharp differences in approaches toward business. For instance, Chapter 5 discusses how the underlying construction and use of language affect the pace of business. To my knowledge, the language chapter presents a unique synthesis of linguistics and cultural anthropology. The fact that people speak different languages isn't necessarily what makes people different, rather it is the many ciphers and cryptic constructs contained in language that shape people's attitudes and set them to thinking in certain ways. Once understood, these features of language help break the cultural code.

Part II takes a nuts-and-bolts look at the opposing work styles of Mexicans and Americans. I have used the factory floor as a microcosm; within its four walls, work styles and working relationships reveal themselves clearly in an intensive environment. In studying work styles, you will learn how to cope with the inevitable problems that arise in business and in real-life situations. Insights into conflict resolution have broad application, since most often when Americans are interfacing with Mexicans, one of us will be working.

As we examine Mexicans through the lens of culture, we also turn the mirror on ourselves, asking why we work the way we do. A fuller appreciation of the differences between Mexicans and Americans, and the reasons behind these differences is key to exploring effective approaches to resolving conflicts and building relationships.

When first living or working in another culture, you often encounter attitudes and work styles that make no sense to you at all. You might assume that some people in other cultures simply don't know how to do things— that they've got it all wrong. Initially you might not understand the difference in individual orientation versus group orientation. Nor would you appreciate how their hierarchical outlook drives behavior quite different from Americans' egalitarian style. However, once these differences in work styles are revealed, you can begin to see how present and future orientation, for example, can be analyzed and measured. You can appreciate *why* people behave the way they do. You can devise strategies for communicating more effectively across cultural barriers in Mexico, as well as with Mexicans who are working or living in the United States.

Part III shows how achieving cultural fluency depends on building context. Context is an essential part of our study because work doesn't take place in a vacuum and because Mexicans are a highly contextual people. To appreciate the core values and self-concepts of Mexicans, Part III explores what I call "the archaeology of the Mexican mind." Then it looks at historic trends and current challenges in the Mexican political, economic, and social experience. These sections are not intended to be all-encompassing treatises. Rather, they are designed to offer a cultural perspective on aspects of daily life. Having seen how the cultural traits analyzed in Part I play out in the workplace, you now see their effects in society at large. Because this bottom-up approach extends to life on the street, this book should be useful not only for business and professional people, but also for travelers, tourists, retirees, and anyone with an interest in Mexico or Mexicans.

By learning to look through the lens of culture, you can avoid mistakes and frustration while building a bridge of communication. Without this understanding, you can fall into the trap of assuming that, underneath it all, things are much the same in Mexico as in the United States. With understanding, you can appreciate the value of adjusting your own thinking and behavior in order to be successful in your interactions with Mexicans.

Methodology

While attending Georgetown University School of Foreign Service, I was affected by the teachings of Carroll Quigley, whose seminal text—*The Evolution of Civilizations* (1979)—gave me an appreciation of the phenomenon of culture, and how cultures develop along different paths. I also studied comparative political and economic systems. While studying international business at the University of the Americas in Mexico City, I had an opportunity to get deeply involved in Mexican history, archaeology, and anthropology. While doing graduate studies at Michigan State University, I was impressed by the techniques of cultural anthropologist and sociologist Clifford Geertz.

His enlightening book—*The Interpretation of Cultures* (1973)—helped me hone my interviewing skills. Geertz imagines that culture is a screenlike material, a grid extending as far as you can see in every direction out to the horizon. Like a spider on a single filament, you drop down onto the screen, visiting individuals in the center of *their* universe. Over time, the opinions and observations gathered from this field begin to come together. The more people you interview, the more layered and cohesive the picture. Whereas Quigley gave me a framework for analyzing culture, Geertz showed me how to develop what he calls "thick description."

When you understand, as cultural anthropologists explain, that culture is a survival mechanism, you can accept that people hold onto their culture tenaciously. With this in mind, you don't have to waste your time trying to bring people around to *your* way of thinking. Instead, you can get right down to the business of trying to understand why people from other cultures act the way they do and how you can work more effectively with them.

Although this book has a methodology, the real lessons are in the war stories. Some of these are my own and have left some blood on my T-shirt. Other accounts were passed on to me by friends and associates who shared their victories and drubbings. I hope that the real-life experiences will be more informative than top-down cultural anthropologists or business professors can conjure. My intent is for you to come away with a truly invigorated appreciation of Mexican culture, no matter how much exposure you may have had.

Even though every culture is unique, the approach taken here should prove equally useful wherever you go—to China, Saudi Arabia, or France. First, you try to identify and analyze the key cultural differences operating beneath the surface. You observe how these play out in the workplace and develop strategies for improving communication and resolving conflicts. Then, using your cultural lens, you train your eye on the society at large. To build additional context, you interview cab drivers, academics, and company presidents until you can get a feel for their cultural set pieces at work. Also, reading histories, economic reports, newspapers, anything you can get your hands on gives you an opportunity to "interview" informed authors.

When you have acquired a level of cultural fluency in one country, you will find it easier to acquire in another. Coming to understand just one culture outside your own and learning to recognize your own assumptions and patterns of thought will prove helpful with whatever culture you approach in the future.

Dodging bullets

I did not come by cultural fluency as a result of my international business career. I have been dodging cultural bullets since I was six, and the experiences have left an indelible mark on my outlook. It was my early adventures in other countries that sensitized me to cultural differences. Intuitively, I learned to adapt. I began to see patterns. It wasn't until later in my business career that I started searching for a framework that would be helpful in analyzing culture and in making its dynamics more accessible to others. In a sense, I backed into figuring things out. But age six was when *Cracking the Cultural Code* began for me.

I never graduated from first grade. On April 9, 1948, a revolution broke out in Bogotá, Colombia, and the international community headed for cover. As the son of U.S. diplomats, I was shuttled from post to post, through Latin America and Europe, learning to survive in different cultures. I learned how to be a snob in Paris and how to be polite in Spain. In Barcelona, when the Franciscan friars marched my chums and me out to the playground to pledge allegiance to Generalísimo Franco and *La Pátria,* I stood at attention out of respect but refused to give a fascist salute. And when required to kiss the friar's hand, as a non-Catholic, I developed the art of the "immaculate kiss"—taking the friar's fingers in mine while piously smacking my own wrist.

It wasn't until I returned to the United States that I realized what a cultural oddity I had become. One weekend my boarding school roommate invited me to go home with him. Even at age fifteen, I was so formal his parents felt they should offer me a martini. "Thank you," I responded. But when I refused the martini they brought me, confusion reigned. I tried to explain, "In Spain, you say 'thank you' instead of 'no' because 'no' would be impolite." Eventually, they got it straight, but just to be safe they would always ask, "Thank you, *yes*?" or "Thank you, *no*?"

There were other problems. Why did my girlfriend and her mother giggle every time I came to call? Later they told me I was so proper they expected me to show up in a tuxedo. And because I wore pointy-toed shoes and carried a briefcase to class, it didn't take long for somebody to beat the hell out of me. I had to learn to be an American again.

In 1965, at age twenty-four, I went off to Mexico already speaking Spanish, if with a pronounced Castilian accent. As a young man living and studying among the Mexicans, I could put my academic tools to use. My Spanish affectations quickly disappeared as I learned the local ways and began to build an understanding of the people. Having been essentially Eurocentric, I was surprised at how fast and how thoroughly I became enamored with the history and culture of this five-thousand-year-old civilization. Not surprisingly, Mexico continued to be a focus throughout my years in international business while working for U.S. companies.

At the same time I was enjoying my corporate career, I also undertook archaeological expeditions in Mexico and Central America. Having dug the giant pyramid systems outside Mexico City when I was in college there, I can say that I have been down to bedrock with Mexicans. When you sweat all day in a hole with Mexican workers and you come out the same color, you understand their work styles and their connection to the past.

Regarding the text

I have used *he* and *she* in various anecdotes in this book with no intent to slight anyone. More often than not, *he* is used in the generic sense. My profound hope is that whatever your gender, race, age, or culture, I have shown you respect.

As for generalizations and exaggerations calculated to make a point, I apologize in advance to the subjects of this book on both sides of the border. Sometimes looking through a lens, objects appear larger than they really are. *Estimados mexicanos,* please forgive any exaggerations that are only intended to inform. As for my American brethren, I can be a bit harsh. As we say in the States, "Get over it!"

Of course, it's impossible to do justice to the Mexicans. I wish I could. But the more we learn, the better we'll do. And isn't it time we treat building intercultural relationships with the same level of attention and respect that we give to marketing, production, and financial matters? If we're going to succeed in our dealings with the Mexicans, we'd better make a serious effort to understand them, and, in the process, ourselves.

PART I

The Intercultural Thing

Recognizing the underlying differences in Mexican and American views of time and space, and in our construction and use of language, is essential to understanding who they are, who we are, and how we can work together.

The Meaning of Yes

The confusion arises innocently enough—out of a simple desire to please. Mexicans say yes or no because you say yes or no. "It will rain today, won't it?" Yes. "It won't rain today, will it?" No. "Well, will it or won't it rain today?" If God wills it, it will. If not, maybe.

Infusing the world with sunshine, the Mexicans are exceedingly polite—polite as in agreeable, agreeable as in telling you what you want to hear. Whether you're dealing with a banker in Guadalajara, a roofing contractor in Michigan, a supplier in Monterrey, or a government official in Mexico City, ask a direct question and you'll rarely get no for an answer. Why? Because Mexicans are never overtly contentious. Because no would be unco-operative, even offensive. So to avoid no, most Mexicans will naturally answer yes. But don't take yes for an answer. Ask yourself, What do they *really* mean—yes, no, or something in between? Never believe the first answer you get in Mexico.

Something as simple as yes and no can divide the world into two camps: those to whom yes means yes and those to whom yes means yes or no. And if this isn't maddening enough, there are subtle gradations along the yes/no scale. There are those to whom no sometimes means maybe. The yes/no phenomenon is operating at every level of engagement, in every arena of enterprise, in all matters of business or pleasure.

If you've ever vacationed in Mexico and planted yourself under a *palapa* along the beaches of Cancún, Ixtapa, or Acapulco, you have found yourself prey to a barefoot succession of indigenous vendors. Suddenly the alarm goes off on your tropical unwind. In your straightforward, gringo style, you set your piña colada aside, force a smile, and say no repeatedly, only to be pestered some more. Did you know that the vendors interpret no as meaning that you just want a better price? If indeed you want to say no and be left alone, say "Thank you" instead. *Thank you* means, "Thank you for bringing your wares to my attention, but I'm not interested." With this, the vendor will leave you alone and advance on some other gringo who has invaded his ancestral domain. (Mexicans assure us that *gringo* is a term of affection. But for some other Latin Americans the term is pejorative. For the purposes of this book, we will take the Mexicans' side.)

Or how about negotiating with a Mexican rental car dealership?

After working out of Mexico City for a time, I decide it would be fun to drive a Jeep out to Teotihuacán over the weekend to explore the ancient Toltec pyramids. The *Yellow Pages* indicate that across the Avenida Reforma from where I'm staying there is an agency that, among other things, advertises Jeeps. I enter the office. "Good morning, señorita, do you rent Jeeps?" "Sí, señor!" comes the confident, friendly, self-assured, even punctilious answer. "Are you sure?" "Sí, sí, señor!" she repeats with supreme confidence. I look into those innocent eyes, smile, and ask in a low voice, "Are you *really, really* sure?" Her chin drops, her head sways, and out comes "No-oo-oo." My prodding has plastered her soufflé into a hard crust, and she can no longer maintain a polite expression in the face of interrogation. Now she checks with the manager by phone. It turns out they have another agency in Acapulco and they use the same ad for both *Yellow Pages*. Sí, sí, they rent Jeeps—in Acapulco, just not in Mexico City. No problem. I rent a Nissan instead.

Had I believed the first answer, she would have been in a real bind. She had no Jeep, she couldn't get a Jeep, but I expected a Jeep. She can't say no, so she has only one alternative: tell the gringo anything. "Señor, the Jeep, it will be here this afternoon. I will call you when it is ready." Or a time-honored favorite, "Señor, the Jeep had an accident in which the owner's daughter was badly injured. He will get the Jeep to you as soon as he gets his daughter off the respirator." If I had gone back later to see if the Jeep had come in, the señorita would have been hiding under the counter.

In the olympics of rationalizations, Mexicans take the gold. Maybe because they've trained at altitude, no one can beat them at giving you a pleasant runaround. Long before the North American Free Trade Agreement (NAFTA), Mexico, with its unlimited reserves of creativity, was the world's leading manufacturer of artful sidesteps. So—you'll get everything but a Jeep or a simple no. You won't get a direct answer of any kind. How do you cope with such worrisome inconsistencies? As soon as you sense they are doing a fandango, give up! Don't put these agreeable, accommodating people between a rock and a hard place. Give them an out. Don't say, "But you said . . . ," and don't expect them to be like Americans. Don't argue and demand a Jeep. Balling up your fist won't get you a Jeep if there are no Jeeps. It's simple: they can't say no, and there aren't any Jeeps. Get a VW and a bottle of Tums. Smile and forget about the Jeep!

Does this example mean that you cannot negotiate with Mexicans? Absolutely not. It's just that as anywhere in the world, you have to negotiate within the realm of practical possibilities. The difference in Mexico is that they will not tell you there are no Jeeps. You have to coax the bad news out of them.

Yes . . . but

The more serious the business, the more unsettling the yes/no enigma becomes. Case in point:

I am navigating my way through what I thought would be a routine approval process with Mexican governmental officials. My American client is interested in purchasing a piece of property for his operations in a state in the north of Mexico. I have explained the approach we must take. But as we arrive for our first meeting, he insists that he is unwilling to plunk down a lot of money to buy property unless he can be assured *in advance* that his foundry process will be approved by the Mexican environmental protection agency. As logical as this seems to him, I warn him again: "In Mexico, you have to commit to a specific piece of property in order to get approval." I explain that the process starts with a soil use permit specific to the application. The Mexican "EPA" cannot deal with a request until you first show that permit. You must have at least a letter of intent to buy the property. Further, you proceed with nods along the way. You don't get environmental approval until the process is fully installed and you have met your plan. Then you get your operating permit.

An eager young representative of the state government takes us to the Mexican "EPA," interpreting the concerns of my agitated client into Spanish. I listen carefully. Even if you are fluent in Spanish, it's a good idea to weigh each word in context to understand what is really being said. The conversation goes like this:

> State representative (in Spanish): The client wants to know if he can start the application process now, get approval for his foundry process, and then decide which piece of property he wants to buy.
>
> Mexican "EPA" official (in Spanish): Yes, he can fill out an application, but we can't do anything with it until he selects the property.
>
> State representative (translating to client in English): Yes.
>
> Client (to me): See, I told you.

Not wanting to contradict the state representative in front of others and lose his support, I wait until after the meeting to explain to my client what has actually transpired. He thought the Mexican officials said yes to proceeding with the approval, but what we actually got was a "yes ... but," which wasn't a yes at all. "You *still* have to commit to buying the property in advance," I tell him. Naturally he feels he's been had. I break it to him gently: "You have just been hit by the Mexican desire to please."

The meaning of no

The yes/no conundrum can take some curious twists. It is not frustrating just to Americans.

A French client, Jacques, is eager to get an affirmative response to his offer to buy a manufacturing facility in Chihuahua. Before meeting with the Mexican seller, I explain that he should not accept a yes as a yes—at least on the first go around. I further tell him with great confidence what I have told you: "You have to listen carefully. Usually you hear 'Yes, if God wills it,' or 'Yes, if . . . ,' or just plain 'Yes.' But, Mexicans never say no."

The meeting unfolds. Jacques makes an offer to buy the property, but the Mexican responds with a polite no. Disappointed in the answer, but delighted as only the French can be to pounce on a mistake (in this case mine), Jacques takes me aside privately, shaking his finger in my face. "See here! And you told me they never say no." After reflecting for a moment, I have the answer, "But monsieur, what they really mean is yes!"

The logic was clear: a no from a Mexican was not necessarily a direct answer either. A no is usually said in such a way as to leave the door open for further negotiation. So, a no in this case was not impolite. It was an invitation to continue the discussion. When accompanied by a wistful dropping and side-to-side sway of the head, with eyes staring off sadly, a no of this sort signals that he can be had. And sure enough, with a little sweetening of the pot, the deal was consummated.

Both clients above modified their intercultural communications a bit according to Mexican practices. I'm pleased to report that their plants were fully operational within a year, and the initial concerns about the sequence of events were long forgotten.

Manuel and the gun cabinet

Beyond the Mexican border, you will encounter the confusing yes/no factor when interacting with Mexican immigrants to the United States who are trying to please, or when working with first-generation Mexican Americans.

Frequently, when a Mexican is trying to please an American, he or she succeeds in creating confusion.

While visiting my friend Chip in California on a bright, sunshiny day, Manuel, Chip's carpenter, delivered a beautiful, handmade coffee table. Although Manuel is six feet tall, blue-eyed, and has lived in this country for years, he remains very Mexican. His English is not good, but he is very agreeable.

"When will my gun cabinet be ready?" Chip inquires. "Half January," comes the answer. Puzzled, Chip wrinkles his brow. Now Manuel, trying to please, proffers, "First January." Still unclear about Manuel's response, Chip elaborates, "Look, it doesn't really matter, but I'm going to be gone between December 20 and March 1, so if you can't deliver it by the twentieth, then it'll have to wait until sometime in March. Otherwise, I won't be here to receive it. Either before I leave or after I get back—it doesn't really matter—but I'd like to know."

With this, Manuel is completely thrown for a loop. He wants above all to please his customer, but is not getting a clear signal of what Chip really wants to hear. So he turns in frustration and asks plaintively, "But when do you *want* it!?"

After Manuel leaves, Chip throws up his hands, wondering out loud, "What the hell just happened?"

Here's my take. First, Chip thinks the conversation is about when the gun cabinet is going to arrive. Manuel thinks the conversation is about being agreeable. Second, by "half January," Manuel means January 15. This reflects a simple lack of linguistic precision—a mere technicality. But when Chip, unfamiliar with the expression, wrinkles his brow, Manuel, rather than attributing the reaction to a simple lack of understanding, thinks his customer is unhappy with that date. So he makes up a new one—"first January." Then

Chip really throws him a screwball with his "if . . . otherwise . . . either . . ." scenario. Manuel can't get beyond the "if." He doesn't know what to say to maintain his agreeable posture. What Manuel needs to hear is, "I want my gun cabinet on December 15." Then he would have said, "December 15. Yes sir!" But would Chip have received his gun cabinet by December 15? Probably not.

Unlike your run-of-the-mill, ripsaw, American carpenter—who would have grumbled something like, "December 15! You gotta be kidding. Hey fella, you'll be lucky to get it by the end of April!"—Manuel is upholding centuries of Mexican dignity and respect. He is earnestly trying to comply with what his "Anglo-Saxon" customer wants, which is, after all, the nice, polite, agreeable thing to do. ("Anglo-Saxon" is what other people call our culture. We will explain this usage in Chapter 2.)

To arrive at an accurate date, you, as the customer, would need to investigate further. "Is December 15 a reasonable time to expect delivery?" *If God wills it.* "Well, is there anything I, as the customer, can do to assure prompt delivery?" *Well, if the wood arrives . . . you see, I get the wood at a discount, but I have to wait until the supply house has a full truckload to send to Chino. So, when the wood comes in, it will take about three days after that.* Now you are getting closer to a serious answer by developing realistic alternatives. You're not dealing with a nail-driving gringo fitted out with a hammer on his belt. You're dealing with a Mexican and beginning to understand his mentality. You are setting yourself up for happy surprises rather than frustration. Now you know when your cabinet will arrive—maybe April.

While illustrative, the gun cabinet poses limited financial consequences. What do you do when the business stakes are high, and a lot of money is riding on a commitment?

Yes doesn't always deliver the goods

With most manufacturing orders in the United States, if you ask for delivery by a certain day you will either get it by that date or you will be told up front that it will cost you extra for a rush order. You expect a direct answer to a direct question, and you get it. Not so in Mexico. They'll agree with your date, just to be accommodating. But they will not tell you that a rush order will cost extra, because that would be setting up a possible conflict and be considered an affront. You have to *ask* if a date is reasonable. Then, and only then, you will find out that the date is reasonable if. . . . Next you have to follow up to ask if there is any way you can get it by that date, if indeed it is important to you. At that point, you will find out about the increased cost of materials. Now it's appropriate to put your agreement in a contract.

In essence, you have to invite the supplier to elaborate further on the delivery conditions. In so doing, you are signaling that it's okay to give you realistic news, such as an increased charge for a rush order. You are indicating that you won't kill him if the real date is a few weeks later.

Of course, you don't *have* to do anything. You can just sit back believing the stipulated delivery date, and when it doesn't happen, you can stoke your fire of resentment at lazy, shiftless Mexicans who never keep their promises. On the other hand, a minor adjustment in how you approach a supplier can help you succeed with intercultural communications. Eschew frustration, invite happiness.

Mexicans are just as capable as Americans are of learning a new system, adapting to a new standard, or meeting a deadline. Also, Americans are just as likely to run into delivery problems or cost overruns. We simply handle such situations differently in our culture. If you don't believe me, then you haven't yet learned some key intercultural communications techniques. I'm not suggesting that we have to accept their delivery date, their quality standard, or their price. They understand as well as we do that "the customer is always right." On the other hand, when operating within Mexican culture, we do have to understand the unwritten rules.

Throughout this book *we* and *Americans* refer to members of the Anglo-Saxon culture in the United States—English-speaking men and women including but not limited to African Americans, Asian Americans, U.S.-born Latinos, Native Americans, Jews, or Muslims.

Room at the top . . . for trouble

It's a common mistake to think that cultural misunderstandings occur only when dealing on unsophisticated levels. Challenges don't suddenly melt away when you enter a sleek Mexico City high-rise, get on the elevator, and step off into the upscale offices of a Mexican CEO who speaks fluent English and has a Stanford mug on the desk. Don't assume your troubles are over. And don't assume that mastery of just a handful of basics will automatically assure success. Some of our most talented, well-intentioned businesspeople come back from Mexico thinking they have made friends, cleared the cultural hurdles, and cemented a viable business deal, only to see their hopes crumble.

Promises and pitfalls

While there have been some spectacular pratfalls due to cultural misunder-standing, there are many success stories involving companies that have dusted themselves off and worked their way up the learning curve.

Big problems for Big Blue

Everything has been patched up now, but a few years ago American IBM execs were indicted by the Mexican federal prosecutor when the all points bulletin system they sold to the Mexico City police department crashed. At the heart of the problem was American insistence that the system would work and Mexican reluctance to say that IBM had not adequately trained the users. IBM suffered a nosebleed, but today they continue to have prof-itable manufacturing operations in Mexico, and PCs are everywhere.

Delphi goes native

Delphi began setting up plants in Mexico in the 1960s. The company started in Chihuahua, training locals to do as much of the management as possible. By selecting young engineering graduates from the University of Chihuahua and instructing them in the Delphi way of doing business, it created a bilin-gual, bicultural management pool. Today, Delphi is the largest foreign-owned employer of Mexicans in Mexico. But that's not the end of the story. As operations grew, Delphi had thirty-four Mexican production and plant managers around the world. At this writing, there is a team of eight Mexican managers setting up the Delphi plant in China. What traits positioned Mex-icans so well for Delphi? According to their director of North American operations, it is their talent as engineers and their willingness to learn. I would add that Delphi gave them a chance.

Hooters gets knocked

The restaurant chain, the one that doesn't care if you keep your eyes on your fries, tried to put their failing Mexican franchisee out of business. It seems that people weren't buying warm beer and cold burgers. The Mexican fran-chisee went to court to protect his rights, arguing that he was performing according to his contract and complying with the wishes of the American owners. The Americans contended that the Mexican "just didn't get it." But the Mexican court did not buy that argument. The court ruled in favor of the Mexican franchisee, observing that the U.S. management had failed to stay with him long enough to help him work through the food and beverage service process. Evidently, the American once-over—that is, a quickie explanation based on the assumption that everybody should know what *we* know—and the Mexican nod of assent resulted in a lack of intercultural communication. American management had failed to recognize that a Mexican will not tell you he does not understand because that might be tantamount to saying, "You did not explain things adequately." Now, the U.S. management pays more attention to how it instructs its franchisees and is operating very successfully.

Wal-Mart's big oops

Many people are quick to assume that a company as big as Wal-Mart knows what it's doing. But with the subtle machinations of international business, this is not always the case. Despite the Mexican lawyers' mild warnings, Wal-Mart put hundreds of products on the shelves of its flagship store without appropriate standards approvals. Standards include such things as nutritional information, electrical safety testing, chemical warning labels, and the like. Mexico has its own system of consumer protection, but Americans are not always sensitive to others' regulations. A combination of U.S. management hubris and Mexican deference left Wal-Mart under a threat of closure by the Mexican prosecutor's office. Scrambling to come up with a resolution, Wal-Mart temporarily pulled scores of articles off the shelves. The Mexican government was anxious to expedite the approval process in response to the needs of the marketplace. The government first allowed testing to be done in non-Mexican (such as United Laboratories) facilities. Then, they compared norms and allowed U.S. standards to apply for some other items. But the mix-up could have been avoided with careful listening. When the Mexican lawyer says, "You might consider local standards," interpret that as meaning, "If you don't comply, you may die."

DeSoto's revenge

When Lee Iacocca, former chairman of Chrysler, was pleading to the U.S. Congress for a bailout and selling off the company's tank division, Chrysler de Mexico, S.A., was making money. Since Chrysler de Mexico was operating outside the U.S. economy, in the enclave of Mexico, it was free of the forces that affected the U.S. mother ship, and continued to contribute to the bottom line. At the time, Chrysler had only two Americans on staff in Mexico. The operation was managed entirely within the Mexican context by Mexicans.

The one-way gringo mentality

The most intractable, underlying factor that consistently gets Americans into trouble in other countries—certainly in Mexico—is what I call our one-way gringo mentality. Much of the world sees this trait in Americans as something they simply have to put up with. We are not known for our subtlety of thought. We speak in declarations. We preach when we could teach, and we teach when we could learn. We talk when we should listen. Recognizing these tendencies is the first hurdle on the road to cultural fluency.

It should be no surprise that Mexicans know more about the giant they sleep next to than we know about them. The Mexicans have necessarily learned to deal with us, even if we are slow to understand them. They will break their necks to give us what we want. We don't have to change our standards to please them, but we do have to get used to the idea that there are two ways of doing everything. Theirs is no worse than ours. They are not more foolish. They are not lazy. We are not superior. We are not always realistic. They are rarely liars.

What do Mexicans think about us privately? They say we are over-competitive, impatient, prickly, disagreeable, and often rude. We seem to get angry about nothing. We worry too much about nothing. Mexicans who have learned to live with us appreciate, to their relief, that we don't mean to kill them.

Like it or not, our success in international business is directly tied to how we come off. Sometimes modifying our behavior just a little bit can pay big dividends. For instance, when we insist that "In Chicago we do it like this," most Mexicans, and people in much of the rest of the world, will nod assent but think privately, "You're not in Chicago, güero." Because others don't openly disagree, we think we've made our point. In fact, we've just confirmed their stereotype of us. (Güero is a term of endearment referring to lighter skin, though it can be used for any young person with social status.)

Selling them short

Largely because we haven't taken the time to get to know Mexico, we are guilty of constantly underestimating its people. But make no mistake; Mexicans are competitive, intelligent, long-suffering, and resourceful. They are also extremely industrious. I have heard many international manufacturers comment that Mexicans are among the hardest working people on the planet. In 2001, Mexico had the ninth largest economy in the world. They have a thriving, young population (average age just over fifteen) that is dedicated to learning and achieving. In the last thirty-five years, their annual gross domestic product (GDP) growth has exceeded 5 percent. But the Mexican road to modernity has been much harder than ours.

In the minds of our Mexican friends, Americans have had it easy. We're still very young and relatively inexperienced. Our country is just a little more than two hundred years old. We settled on a land of abundance. With no preexisting institutions to restrain us, we had the wind at our backs. By contrast, Mexico suffered a clash of civilizations when Hernán Cortés attacked the Aztec Empire, bringing with him smallpox, which wiped out more than 80 percent of the native population in the first generation after A.D. 1519. Mexico has been invaded by Spain, France, and the United States. Cultural accommodation has been a means of survival.

Because Americans have been so dominant economically and politically in the past one hundred years, it's difficult for us to accord the proper value to other peoples' points of view. In order to prosper, we haven't had to be as flexible as our neighbors. Compared to Americans, Mexicans are less absolute. Often they are fatalistic. Constantly reminded of the hurricanes that have jostled them in the past and the earthquakes and floods that are sure to come again, they are resigned to the inevitable. While they believe that gringos have created much to admire and want to emulate the best parts of American business, they are thinking, "We Mexicans have our own problems and must seek our own solutions."

So how do we improve our working relationships with Mexicans? Understanding the meaning of yes is an important first step. However, there are deeper and more complicated cultural undercurrents to explore. But first, will the Mexicans ever learn to say no—and mean it? Will they ever give us the bad news up front? I keep trying to explain to Mexicans that being direct with an American is not an affront; it's what we expect and hope for. I've asked some sophisticated people about this issue. Their reaction? "Yes, we know we are too polite. We are like children sometimes. We know that we should be more direct. Sometimes we are indirect to a fault. Often we are misunderstood." So I ask, "Can we agree that being direct is good?" "Yes."

It's All about Culture

If American business leaders treated cultural challenges with the same degree of seriousness that they bring to the rest of their operations, they could avoid a lot of frustration and even failure. Typically, managers they assign to international projects are either facilities types, knowledgeable about setting up plants in the United States, or experts in some critical area of manufacturing, service, or sales. Such project leaders may not have any training or experience abroad, and therefore don't appreciate that understanding culture is just as important as locating materials, importing equipment, or setting up the proper distribution chain. One international vice president in the automotive industry told me, "We can solve the technical stuff; it's the people thing we can't figure out."

In the United States, management assumes that the multicultural workforce, which may be comprised of Asians, Hispanics, Eastern Europeans, and others, is obliged to learn from us, to adopt our methods and processes. We take that attitude with us to Mexico. While Mexicans are willing to learn and to follow our lead, it is unrealistic to expect that they can casually cast off the cultural underpinnings that shape their attitudes and influence their work styles. We Americans are bound by our own cultural approach as well. But when working with Mexicans in Mexico, we must take the first step toward understanding the Mexican culture. Both Americans and Mexicans have to be flexible, even though giving up cultural assumptions can be difficult. Our failure to take the first step toward understanding each other's cultures can impede a successful working relationship.

When confronting the culturally unfamiliar, all people feel a mixture of xenophobia (fear of foreigners), bewilderment, and vulnerability. But

Americans' fallback behavior can be ugly. We ratchet up our rhetoric and dig in our heels. After disaster hits, we tell our side of the story to headquarters and wait for management to help us out. Help usually comes from the human resources department. But HR people can help only if they have an understanding of the cultural dynamics at work. Otherwise, they may do more harm than good. Taking Mexican workers off the line, for example, to teach them the American version of "teamwork" is likely to prove counterproductive, as we will see. What may be needed instead is a job coach who understands both cultures—someone who can teach the project manager how to work more effectively with the Mexicans.

Curiously, many corporate executives who wouldn't dream of sending a salesperson into the field without proper training have few qualms about throwing a manager into the international arena without adequate preparation. That working in "international" requires a discreet set of skills and experiences, as does engineering, accounting, or marketing, simply hasn't occurred to them. But there are skills to be acquired and lessons to be learned. And it's not enough to take Spanish lessons, though that helps.

Corporations that are truly international are deeply aware of the need for developing cultural fluency. A Swiss company assumes that the people they hire will speak three or four languages and will have prospered in at least one other country. The reason is clear: Switzerland is a small country with three official languages, nestled in among other countries that have been at war with each other off and on for centuries. In a sense, Swiss businesspeople take cultural fluency for granted.

The Dutch have been fabulously successful in international business. As recently as 1980, the value of imports and exports to and from Holland was greater than that for all of Latin America. The Dutch know that no one but the Dutch speak Dutch. They have adapted to the rest of the world. Why don't Americans follow their lead? For one thing, we're a big, isolated superpower, so we haven't had to adapt. Furthermore, we don't think internationally because of our one-way gringo mentality. We don't understand other cultures, and expend little effort in trying to figure them out.

It's so easy to give that "culture thing" lip service and think we have adapted. We know it's politically correct to show respect for other people, but generally we don't have a grasp of the components of managing intercultural relationships or the depth of commitment needed. Too often we think, "It's my way or the highway!" Cultural fluency does not come naturally to many Americans. We tend to learn by the numbers, but understanding another culture requires analysis, intuition, and insight.

We are convinced that our logic is good enough for the rest of the world. In the accounting department, if a report doesn't foot and balance, everyone sees the problem. We assume that international challenges are just as easily resolved. But the real challenges of "international" are below the usual radar screens. Sales skills can be learned. Those in sales learn FAB (Features, Advantages, and Benefits) and go through a logical sequence, never proceeding to closing the sale until they have built trust and answered all the objections. Other professions have learned approaches by rules or by the numbers. If a doctor doesn't have a good bedside manner, there are techniques that can be learned. Lawyers learn to go through the steps in developing an argument so that it obeys the rules of evidence and sways the jury. Similarly, the international project manager or supervisor of a Mexican workforce can improve the odds of success by acquiring the skills to achieve cultural fluency. But in order to learn these skills, we must first examine the human forces that are at work beneath the surface.

Popping jellybeans

Acquiring cultural fluency is often confused with diversity training and political correctness (PC)—how to get along with subcultures in the United States by changing the words we use to denigrate them so we won't get sued. In the typical diversity training lecture, students are taught that white people are just another flavor of jellybean in a bowl full of different colors. This is a nice way of saying that there is a spectrum of color in the U.S. But if we're serious about dealing with cultural challenges, the first step is clearing up the confusion that often exists between culture and color. We need to understand that among preferred references to groups of people, there are geographic, cultural, and racial categories.

What color is Hispanic?

Brown? No. The term *Hispanic* is a cultural reference—a way of identifying people that is neither racial nor geographic. I heard a young woman argue with a baffled fellow traveler. She insisted that he couldn't be Hispanic because he was black. But what color is Hispanic? People with Hispanic culture can be black, as in the Dominican Republic, or white, as in Argentina, or of mixed white and native brown genes, as in Mexico.

The terms *Hispanic* and *Anglo-Saxon* define their respective cultures by reference to their respective languages. *Hispanic* comes from the Greek meaning "Spanish." And the word *English* is derived from the *Anglo* in Anglo-Saxon, where the language was once referred to as Anglish. Most of the rest of the world refers to the English and Americans as having an Anglo-Saxon culture, though there are some differences between Americans and Brits.

Culture is not color

Anglo does not refer to genes, rather to culture. An African American going to Mexico takes along Anglo culture. A Minnesotan with a Spanish surname who considers himself Hispanic may vacation in Mexico without realizing just how culturally Anglo he is. In the eyes of Mexicans, we Americans are all Anglos, because they see our culture more clearly than they see our color. In fact, it's easy to mislabel people who fall outside the usual frame of reference. When an African American visited Mexico's Copper Canyon, one of the shy Tarahumara Indians commented, "That is the blackest white man I have ever seen."

Especially in the case of Mexico, definitions can be confusing. For clarification, Mexican culture is Hispanic, but more properly, Mexican. Their race is predominantly *mestizo,* meaning "mixed." But a black man born and raised in Veracruz (and there are many) is black, not African American; nor is he any less Mexican or Hispanic by culture. A tall white man with blue eyes and a German surname in Monterrey (and there are many) is no less Mexican than his chestnut-hued colleague or his brown friend named Herrera.

Getting it right

Because culture is one of, if not *the* most important means of identifying groups of people, shouldn't we get it right—not just out of respect, but out of commitment to achieving a fuller understanding of our fellow travelers throughout world?

Culture is not geography

When cultures collide in the same geographic area, there is usually a blending of the two cultures, but one culture tends to dominate. The Spanish

---

Points to ponder

- Racially, most Mexicans are correctly referred to as *mestizos*, meaning mixed blood—specifically native (Aztec and other indigenous peoples) and Spanish.
- The term *Mexican* can properly be used as either a geographic or a cultural reference. While it is not incorrect to refer to Mexicans as Hispanics, they generally prefer to be known as Mexicans because of the distinctive nature of their culture within the Hispanic world.
- All Mexicans are Hispanic, but not all Hispanics are Mexicans. *Hispanic* is a cultural reference to people from any Spanish-speaking country, except (you're going to hate me) Spain. The Spanish insist that they are Spanish, and not Hispanic.
- *Latino/a* is a cultural reference, more or less interchangeable with *Hispanic*.
- Black Mexicans are called *negros* or *negritos*. In Spanish, *negro* means simply "black." It has none of the pejorative implications currently associated with the same word in English. *Negrito* is a wholly nonoffensive and affectionate term. It's akin to calling *mamá* your *mamasita*.
- The word *Indian* is generally viewed as pejorative in the States. Once we get beyond the observation that the word is based on Columbus' mistake about where he landed, we have to deal with what words we use to describe an important group of people. In the States, we have decided that *Native Americans* is more correct and more respectful. But that is not the case in Mexico. The word *indio* (Indian) is not a racial slur. It is, however, pejorative in the sense that it implies that one is uncivilized. Mexicans eliminate that stigma by using the term *indito*. What most people do not realize is that beyond the names, our "Native Americans" and the Mexican "inditos" come from the same gene pool. They are the same people.

---

conquered and occupied Mexico from 1521 until independence in 1820. Spanish is now the dominant language, and among the literati, business leaders, and politicians, Spanish dress and business practices predominate. Yet, under the surface the Aztec culture, with its own attitudes and ethos,

---

In case you didn't know

- If you call yourself American, some people will say, "I'm from Canada, Central America, or South America, so I'm American too." A valid point.
- If you say, "I'm from the United States," a Mexican who wants to be playful will say, "I'm from the United States too," because the formal name of Mexico is *Estados Unidos Mexicanos*, or the United States of Mexico.
- If you say, "I'm a North American," a Mexican might say, "Since NAFTA, we consider ourselves North Americans too."
- Once we get beyond the "who are *we*" issue, the Mexicans call us Americans. That's shorthand for "people of Anglo-Saxon culture who live in the U.S.A., who speak English, who may be of many colors and religions, and who are in a big hurry."

---

remains. Southern California, Arizona, New Mexico, and Texas—the four states that border Mexico—were once Mexican. Today, Anglo-Saxon culture dominates in these states, yet many people still speak Spanish and maintain Mexican ways.

Cultural deficit

When assessing our ability to live or do business abroad, we tend to blame our troubles on poor linguistic skills. But achieving cultural fluency is more important than speaking Spanish.

I would argue that many of us barely understand our own culture; and we are unnecessarily defensive about our linguistic ability. An American can travel three thousand miles and still order a cheeseburger, fries, and a Coke in English. No wonder schoolchildren have balked at conjugating foreign verbs. By contrast, Europeans turn on the TV and hear broadcasts in five languages. Mexicans are bombarded with programs in English. As for our linguistic talent, we are just as capable as they are; we simply have not been compelled to learn. Adding to our inexperience, most of us have not had to operate in contexts in which we are in the minority. Circumstances have not compelled us to become culturally or linguistically fluent. When we do acquire these traits, we recognize the survival implications of culture, and are more tolerant of others.

What is culture?

Having given a couple of clues as to what culture is *not*, we should define culture for the purpose of this analysis. Culture consists of layers of behavior that groups of people wrap themselves in for purposes of identifying friend or foe. Culture protects us from those who are not like us and who might do us harm. It binds people together in common defense and for common economic good. To those near us, culture communicates that we are part of the same group and therefore that we understand the same rules and rituals. Culture is as much a survival mechanism as is our ability to make weapons or to take flight from danger.

As *observers* of culture, we tend to see only the visible. In this sense, looking at a culture is like viewing an iceberg. We visit another country but see only the obvious 10 percent, with 90 percent of the substructure remaining out of view. We see the buildings and clothing. We hear the music and the voices. We smell and taste the food. But because we are experiencing only the top fraction of what is truly going on, is it any wonder that we are frequently so wrong when we make judgments about another culture? We say of Mexicans, "I don't understand why these people can't govern themselves" or "I don't understand why they ride so many in one little truck." We interpret the Mexican political system through our context and assume that they are in chaos. We jump to the conclusion that Mexicans crowd into pickup trucks because they can't figure out how to organize a trip to the market. When we make such value judgments, indeed *we* don't understand. We are indulging in superficial comparisons between the two cultures, failing to consider what lies beneath our different patterns of behavior. Without connecting the visible culture with the underlying cultural phenomena, we fail to see the system as a whole. Moreover, we allow our own cultural biases to color our views.

As *members* of a culture we are like termites in a petri dish. One, two, three, or twelve termites are just that—so many termites. But at a certain critical mass, termites switch into gear and start eating the lab table. Cultural anthropologists tell us that at a critical number of, say, one hundred, the same phenomenon occurs in humans. We begin to communicate on a different level, using an unwritten code based on a spectrum of possibilities. It is when this critical mass is achieved and people begin to work together that we see the gestation of culture. Work styles grow into a corporate culture, or by extension, a national culture. To know how a country works, understand how the people work.

To better understand the dynamics of belonging to a culture, it is useful to picture three concentric circles or spheres of activity. The innermost circle is, in effect, the petri dish, where individuals communicate by common language as well as nonlinguistic means. Humans in the same colony share unarticulated views of their place in the world and a common sense of urgency, as well as reactions to the environment. As humans, we use language as a primary tool to interpret our views of the environment and then to collectively effect changes in our surroundings.

The middle circle of the human cultural world is the sphere of organized work and living relationships. When our numbers achieve 100 or more, whether referring to a company or a country, we humans organize our work according to the cultural standards that we develop. Individuals in one culture may work better independently, as we do in the United States. In another culture, such as Mexico, people may work better in a *group-dependent* mode (more team-oriented). One culture may reject hierarchical organization while another greatly respects hierarchies. For the most part, groups fall into a pattern of behavior unaware that there are other options, or that people in other cultures work quite differently. Nobody in the work group goes around saying, "I'm *group*-dependent" or "I respect hierarchies."

The third, outermost circle encompasses the visible or concrete aspects of a culture. This is where society organizes to deal with economic, political, and social challenges; where intellectual ideas find expression. This is the sphere in which culture prints its hard copy. It is in this sphere that cultures collide and where we make erroneous judgments about each other—unless we understand the hidden background.

In analyzing another culture, we examine each of these three spheres. *First,* we identify key unwritten assumptions that exist among groups of individuals. What are their collective, if unarticulated, views of personal and group space? Do they share the same sense of time—linear or circular? How do they construct and use their language to communicate information that is vital to their survival? *Second,* we look at how individuals organize themselves for work, because work reveals how people cooperate for the common good and how they react when there is a change in or threat to their environment. Are they individual- or group-oriented? Proactive or reactive? Future-

or present-oriented? *Third,* we study the broader aspects of a culture in the outer circle—intellectual, political, economic, social—in order to understand the relationship of this sphere to the notions, patterns, and dynamics of the inner circles.

To return to the iceberg analogy, after completing these three steps, we can begin to understand the visible 10 percent of a culture as a direct expression and coherent extension of the underlying cultural structure.

Having analyzed the underlying factors, we are more enlightened readers about Mexican politics and more able to digest economic reports. We read anthropological studies or novels that reveal their social structure to our more informed eye. Now when we study other people's religion, self-concepts, art, and music, we have a keener sense of why they feel, see, and react the way they do. We understand how two people can look at the same thing but, based on our respective cultures, see something quite different. All of this enhances our working relationships. In the case of Mexicans, we understand that they are not lazy or incompetent. We know how and why they get to work and travel as they do. Consequently, we are also able to ask why *we* feel, work, and behave the way we do.

What culture are we, anyway?

It may come as a surprise that with all of our recent social introspection, in the United States we don't recognize that we have a culture and that it has a name. Our own dominant culture—the culture that all Americans share regardless of race, religion, or national origin—is called Anglo-Saxon by other cultures. As noted earlier, whether you are black, white, Asian American, or other, you're operating within an Anglo-Saxon culture. English is the dominant language. Despite differences among individuals, our Anglo-Saxon culture is a means of communicating shared values, of understanding, and subsequently of shaping our environment.

In spite of our myriad strains of immigration, our number of subcultures, and our geographical diversity, Mexicans see one dominant culture—Anglo. For our part, despite many regional variations in the United States, we all get along as one nation, with one common language, and with common institutions. Perhaps our own hegemony lures us into thinking that differences with Mexicans can easily be glossed over. A little extra smile, a friendly slap on the back, a peppy *"hola mano,"* and we've conquered that "culture thing."

Often our one-way gringo mentality leads us even further astray. When interacting with Mexicans, we assume that if we merely show them how *we* do things, they will understand and respond favorably. We even tell them how to behave. Frequently, I hear Americans tell Mexicans, "You should be more direct . . . we like to hear the bad news first." But this goes against all Mexicans' instincts to be pleasant. Our suggestion that they change is tantamount to saying, "You should trust us. Get naked and lie down, and we'll treat you nice." Is it any wonder that Mexicans put in this position are more likely to make superficial concessions than to disarm entirely?

Safety net

Those who fail to see the depth of cultural influences will say that all you really need to do in Mexico is to make some technical adjustments to Mexicans' behavior, and they will act and perform just the way we do. Don't be fooled. It is not uncommon for Mexican managers to learn what the gringo president wants, then to appear to be conforming to his boss's wishes while continuing to do business the same old way behind the scenes. That's not duplicitous, it's practical.

By the same token, don't expect a Mexican immigrant to act like a gringo just because he has lived in the U.S. for a number of years and wears a Dallas Cowboys sweatshirt. On the contrary, Mexicans bring their culture with them. It is their safety net. It is their shelter in a storm, protecting them from a frequently hostile environment. Most often, Mexicans working in the U.S. develop a bicultural approach to survival. They act one way on the job but revert to their native culture when they go home. A white American has more trouble understanding this than an African American does. White Americans are the majority and don't change their Anglo-Saxon manners at home. African and Hispanic Americans are more likely to leave the Anglo-Saxon affectations at the office or factory. The Cowboys sweatshirt is visible, all the rest is operating out of view but very real.

The Mexican American's sense of cultural identity is unique. Charley Trujillo writes in *Soldados: Chicanos in Viet Nam* (1990) that so long as he was working in the cotton fields of California as his parents, grandparents, and an uncertain number of generations before him had done, authorities considered him Mexican. But when the Vietnam War broke out, the draft board considered him American. After the war, he was working in the fields again, and the Immigration and Naturalization Service came calling. Once

again he was Mexican: "Could we see your papers?" "Here are my papers," he
responded with a wry smile, popping out and holding up the glass eye covering his combat loss. In reality, Charley is Mexican, American, and hero.

Scratching the surface

Typically, Americans visiting Mexico think that if we just scratch the surface
of a mestizo Mexican's skin, we'll find that there's really someone underneath
just like us. Wrong. In his illuminating book *Distant Neighbors* (1985), Alan
Riding develops a theme previously presented by Carlos Fuentes, alluding to
a series of masks. As you get to know a Mexican better, he takes off first one
mask, and then another, and another. This metaphor is extremely helpful in
understanding that the real Mexican is a blend of historical ancestry—a mixture of Aztec and Spanish blood and experience. When you scratch the surface, you find that the outer being is playing a role—the role he or she thinks
you expect. Peel off one mask and you will reveal the Spanish persona and
courtly Spanish social rituals. Underneath that layer, you discover the true
culture: the fatalistic Aztec who can go blindly into the boxing ring and fight
with a numbing detachment—a detachment that feels no pain, even if you
cut out his heart with an obsidian blade.

Underneath all the superficial descriptions, you will find a person of
piety who is energetic, innovative, and respectful; a person who works best
in a team setting, responding to personal goals rather than arbitrary deadlines. You will find a person who is often subject to irrational jealousies, and
who actually believes, at some level, that wrestling on TV is real. You will
find a person who can be aggravatingly passive on the one hand but willing
to stop a bullet for you on the other. You will find a human being who has
exerted superhuman effort, all the while knowing that he will fail because
nature will ultimately win. He makes the effort because it is his destiny to do
so. He knows no hell or heaven, just the here and now and a nether space
that is dark, but not evil. Good and bad are here and now. He wants to do
good, but if, because of circumstances beyond his control, he can't do good,
he will do bad—very bad. He becomes a soldier to get the only good pair of
boots he will ever own. But, having become a soldier, he would rather be a
lover than a fighter. If forced by circumstances to kill, he will do it without
the blink of an eye, without care for your family, your friends, your politics,
or your love of Mexicans. For instance, during the Mexican Revolution,
a small group of Americans was caught between warring factions. "But

you don't understand," they pleaded. "We're from the U.S., and we're not involved." "You're here, and you're dead" might as well have been written on the bullets.

The same deterministic attitude is illustrated in a famous incident involving Pancho Villa. The bandit general was in the barber chair getting a shave. With razor in hand, the barber joked that he could cut the great Villa's throat. When finished, Villa got up, thanked him, paid him, and shot him between the eyes. While not really threatening Villa, the barber had violated his position and role in society by assuming that the general was really a peasant underneath and could joke around too. But Villa was wearing his fatalistic, "any-act-for-the-Revolution" mask, and the barber had to go.

So, as Alan Riding's metaphor of the masks helps us see, Mexicans can change remarkably depending on how many layers are stripped away. Are Americans capable of the same levels of emotion and behavior? No. We don't have the Mexicans' capacity for dealing philosophically with contradictions. They don't have our capacity for unwavering certitude. Our mentality is more restrictive, more rigid. We have neither their range nor their complexity. Sorry!

Mexico is unique among other Latin American cultures

I met with Sam, the CEO of a company in Kansas who wanted to set up a plant to make juicers in Mexico. Sam began our conversation about doing business in Mexico by instructing me: "All those goddamn countries are alike. I know. I used to be in charge of Latin America!" As I deftly talked him out of wanting to use my services, I wondered if he would ever be capable of overcoming his cultural drag.

In fact, "all those goddamn countries" are quite different in terms of culture, race, geography, and their distinctive development. Variations are also tied to size, settlement patterns, and history. The countries of Latin America (a cultural reference) or South America (a geographical reference) are very different from each other in terms of their visible attributes, such as politics, economics, social structures, religious influences, and intellectual outlooks.

As noted, Mexico is predominantly mestizo—Indian and Spanish— whereas Argentina is notably Western European—descendants of predominantly Spanish, Italian, and German immigrants transplanted onto a sparse indigenous population with whom they rarely mixed. Like Mexico, Argentina is Spanish speaking, or Hispanic, but most Argentines feel a closer tie to

Europe than to Mexico or other Latin American countries. Chile is also white European, but it has been historically isolated—only the bravest sailed through the Straits of Magellan to arrive at Chile's Pacific coast. For many years the English—being masters of the sea—visited Chile and influenced Chile's development even more than the Spanish who dominated Mexico. Peru is similar to Mexico in that it had a prodigious indigenous civilization (the Inca), but Peru was more influenced by Japanese settlers and experienced little influence from North America as was Mexico's fate. Costa Rica was settled by Spanish coffee growers who were kind to local inhabitants, whereas Mexico's Aztecs were conquered, killed off by smallpox, and made to wear stigmatizing white pajamas to work. Belize, formerly British Honduras, is delighted to be counted as part of Latin America if it means a grant from the Pan-American Union, but ethnically and culturally it is a combination of escaped black slaves, Mayan and Spanish-speaking refugees from the Maya Wars of Mexico, and Garifuna Creoles. The official language is English.

Then there is Portuguese-speaking Brazil—the second largest economy in Latin America, and the largest population—which isn't Hispanic at all. Brazil is behind only Nigeria in size of its black population. Unlike the rest of Latin America, Brazil never had a war of independence and feels firmly linked to Portugal.

Each country in Latin America takes pride in its particular local attributes. I can't tell you how many times I've heard young people from different countries wistfully cite some far-off competition—the details of which are irretrievably lost—in which *their* national anthem was adjudged "the most beautiful national anthem in the world." This pride of place is part of the phenomenon known as *patria chica*, or "little country." It is not unlike our "this is God's country" phenomenon. One way to raise hackles in Latin America is to say that they are all alike. Don't go down that road.

A brief overview of Mexican culture

Mexico believes, and the rest of Latin America agrees, that Mexican culture is truly unique. Compared to the other countries in Latin America, with the exception of Peru and its Inca heritage, Mexico has the deepest roots in pre-Colombian culture. The abundance of Aztec words enriching the Mexican language reflects the fundamentally mestizo culture. Names of animals, foods, and places are ancient Aztec words that may or may not have a Castilian synonym. In fact, we get a number of words in English from Nahuatl, the

Aztec language. Tomatoes, coyotes, and ocelots are native to Mexico, and the names for them have worked their way into our culture. (This does not include Spanish words that influenced our Southwest.)

Mexico's distinctive character is also apparent in its films, providing an excellent venue for understanding its culture. In films, Mexican sensibilities are unmistakable and are appreciated throughout Latin America. With his singsong speech, baggy pants, and hilarious antics, the beloved comic actor Cantinflas made the Hispanic world laugh with his logical improbabilities. In one episode, Cantinflas plays a police officer taking a report over the phone. With his eyebrows arching higher and higher, he repeats breathlessly, "You don't say? You don't say?? You don't say???" Upon hanging up, his fellow officers ask excitedly, "What happened?" With a soulful expression, Cantinflas replies, "He didn't say."

Vicente Fernandez is the quintessential Mexican actor and singer with handsome mestizo features. His melodrama builds to a crescendo until he simply has to break into a mariachi lilt. His songs have become hits throughout Latin America. These and other characters could come only from Mexico, just as Elvis could come only from the United States.

Mexican music is also distinctive. Mariachi music belongs to Mexico alone. During the French occupation of Mexico, it was the custom to hire a local band to play for special receptions. In fact, the word *mariachi* comes from the French *marriage*. With its cascading phrasing and borrowed Aztec animal yelps, mariachi music flowered into its own art form, unique in the Hispanic world.

Mexican muralists like Rufino Tamayo and Diego Rivera could never have come from any other Latin American country. Rivera's scale, colors, themes, social commentary, and rank atheism are one-of-a-kind products of Mexican culture.

Americans have some feel for these outward expressions of Mexican culture—the movies, art, and music—but this in itself can be deceiving. Because we've vacationed in Acapulco, eaten Tex-Mex, and boogied to "La Bamba," we may delude ourselves into thinking we know the Mexicans. But we're barely penetrating the "outer sphere," or the most visible 10 percent of Mexican culture. Typically, we are more willing to acknowledge fundamental cultural differences with the Tibetans than with our close neighbors. We know Taco Bell, but we've never had a "Yak Attack." We fail to appreciate that the Mexicans are culturally as different from us as are the Sherpas. Along with Mexico's Latin American neighbors, we may laugh at Cantinflas and hoot with the mariachi music, but enjoying the outward expressions of a culture doesn't mean that we understand its inner complexities.

One-way gringo meets two-way Aztec

One striking difference between Mexican culture and American culture is that Americans abhor contradictions, whereas Mexicans seem to revel in them. We want yes or no answers that mean what they say they mean. We want resolutions to such questions as, "Why did you tell me that there were Jeeps when there were no Jeeps?" "Why did you tell me it would rain when you knew that it never rains in June?" We dislike having people behave one way (wear one mask) when we meet them, only to behave another way (reveal another mask) later on. "What are you, a man or a mouse?" we ask. Truth is there are lots of men/mice in the world. But we want answers. Not only do Mexicans never ask the kind of impertinent questions we do, they enjoy the inconsistencies inherent in the world.

The following saying illustrates the Mexican penchant for dealing with improbable events:

Cuando el tecolote canta, el indio muere. No es verdad pero sucede.

When an owl hoots, an Indian dies. It's not true, but it happens.

When we discover that contradictions are a way of life, we learn to appreciate them too. Pete Hamill, who has written with great sensitivity about Mexicans, observes that the movie *Viva Zapata* with Marlon Brando "might be of limited use as literal history, but was absolutely true as legend" (*Piecework* 1997). This view reflects an appreciation of the Mexicans' it's-not-necessarily-true-but-it-happens version of reality.

Mexicans live with contradictions. To us, there is an obvious difference between good and bad. To the Mexican, good and bad are relative—two aspects of the same phenomenon.

Faster than a speeding bullet

We Americans aren't very good at seeing ourselves, and we have very little understanding of our own culture. One way we can approach our culture is through our superheroes. When a sixth-grade teacher asked the class to write an essay about their culture, some Anglos from Lincoln Elementary School complained, "That's easy for Otis and Pablo. But what are *we* going to write about?" Start with Superman, I would counsel them. One of our most enduring fictional characters, Superman fights for "truth, justice, and the American way." He's a white guy who flies around the world doing good deeds, bending steel, changing the course of mighty rivers, and making the world safe for everyone who accepts our values. He's even willing to do it anonymously—that is, so long as everyone knows he's doing it. (Just what kind of disguise is a pair of glasses, anyway?) Our superheroes tell us a lot about ourselves.

We have a superheroine, too. Wonder Woman also wears glasses as a civilian. She has a lasso that compels others always to tell the truth. Wouldn't that be convenient in this yes, no, maybe world!

Popular literature is a good starting point for understanding any culture. It is full of symbolism, and symbols are what readers try to live up to. Paul Bunyan and Johnny Appleseed are less than two hundred years old. They are enduring cultural icons because they represent how we choose to see ourselves. The traits they embody are found in virtually all our pop heroes: They are rugged and strong, but have big, soft hearts and do good deeds.

Send in the masks

Not surprisingly, the Mexican superheroes have a slightly different cast. There is the mysterious Aztec mummy, who staggers around the city, seeming to move with cement in his knickers. Nevertheless, he catches up with the bad guy and dispatches him. Like all Mexican folk heroes, you never see his face. By operating in anonymity, the mummy represents the masses and embodies the revenge of every wounded or wronged Aztec.

Another favorite is *El Santo* (The Saint) and his homologues—the masked and caped wrestlers who battle against all odds and win in the end because their cause is just. They pay the price, being soundly thrashed in the early rounds, but ultimately victory will go to the one who represents the people best. Like the Aztec mummy, the wrestlers are totally anonymous. Their faces will never be seen or even depicted in artists' renderings because to unmask them, even to contemplate what they look like, would be to divest these superheroes of the great virtue of their anonymity and thereby diminish the strength all Mexicans have invested in them. Never mind that the match is fixed, or that everybody knows the wrestling is fake. What is important is maintaining the mask and the values. They never show their faces because their strength lies with the faceless mass of Mexicans, rather than with the individual. The need for Mexicans to maintain their faceless countenance, which we will explore later, is as important to them as is our need to feel big, strong, and good.

Fake fake and real fake

Speaking of "fake," what about Mexican actors? Their *telenovelas* (soap operas) seem uproariously overdrawn to us. Here's why. Whereas we expect our actors to faithfully portray their parts, making us forget that behind their character, there is a paid professional, the Mexican actor allows us to see that he or she is wearing three masks. The first mask is that of the character being portrayed—let's say the outraged mother-in-law whose son has been wronged. The outraged look is highly exaggerated and worn like a Mardi Gras get-up. The second mask is that of the actor who is portraying a role; the third is that of the person playing the role of the stage actor and isn't taken off until the actor picks up her paycheck and drives home. Because the Mexicans' concept of acting is so different from ours, we shouldn't be shocked to learn that they don't think we're good actors either. They fundamentally do not appreciate method acting, in which the American actor gets in touch with his or her real-life experiences and feelings. To the Mexicans, that's real life, not acting.

What Mexicans call acting we call faking. For them acting is hyperreality. They reserve their most serious performances for the dramas of real life. And who could be more convincing at agreeing with you, while maintaining their myths, than the Mexicans? But that's not acting. Those masks are real.

THREE

Time and Time Again

Three phenomena operating beneath the surface of culture are key to understanding important differences between Mexicans and Americans. These are perception of time, sense of space, and construction and use of language. The influences of these features are so deeply embedded in our development that we fail to appreciate their impact.

We rarely talk about contrasting concepts of time or personal space. Yet these concepts cause us to view the world and our place in it in vastly different ways. Even with language, we have difficulty seeing beyond the obvious translation process to the underlying characteristics of use and construction that set us to thinking in certain patterns.

From the moment we're born, the specific notions of time, space, and language nurtured by those around us operate as *cultural set pieces,* producing underlying patterns of thinking and behavior that play out in nearly everything we do—certainly in the way we work. Paying attention to these operatives in another culture can make the difference between getting along or stubbing our toes. In this chapter, we'll look at time. In the next two chapters, we will examine space and language.

The windup

Americans are slaves to time and casually dismiss more relaxed attitudes toward the clock as convention, outdated tradition, or simple lethargy. But time is not merely convention. It is a cultural modality that influences a whole range of attitudes and behavior. The notion of time we carry around in our heads explains why Mexicans think we're anxiety-ridden and why we see them as laid-back; why we take the announcement of a 9:00 A.M. meeting as a mandate, and Mexicans regard it as a suggestion. Analyzing the differences in Mexican and American concepts of time is key to managing intercultural relationships.

The stuff of time

All humans have a sense of time. Time counts. We can't live without it. But because in the Unites States we are so conditioned to our own view, we plow ahead believing that everyone is working with the same assumptions as to "the stuff" of time. It simply doesn't occur to us that someone else might be operating according to a different notion. But throughout the world, there are two distinct views of time: time as an arrow and time as a circle. Americans, like most northern Europeans, follow a linear path, whereas Mexicans, like some Asians, southern Italians, Arabs, and Brazilians have the sense of a cyclical course.

In the United States, where time is fixed and measurable, and where we feel the seconds ticking away, we attach much significance to schedules. We measure our efficiency according to our ability to meet deadlines and cross off items on our checklist by the end of the day. Getting things done on schedule has a value in itself. "Don't put off until tomorrow what you can do today." Punctuality is rewarded. We have difficulty coping with a Mexican who agrees to deliver a package tomorrow but doesn't produce. We make derisive jokes about *mañana-land,* reinforcing the erroneous view held by some that Mexicans put off everything until tomorrow. Our one-way gringo mentality keeps us from seeing that to the Mexican, *mañana* doesn't mean "tomorrow," as we understand the word, it means sometime in the future, not today. Whereas we Americans lock on to the finish line, Mexicans regard deadlines as arbitrary. After all, mañana we will be doing the same thing, and the next day, and the following day. Mañana there will be another set of tasks, another checklist.

To understand our time differences with the Mexicans in greater depth, consider how the respective views of our cultures developed over thousands of years.

Time out for a brief history of time

The Greek philosophers gave our European ancestors their insights into the nature of time. Time, they said, is the lapse that occurs when an object moves from one place to another, as when an arrow flies from a bow to a target. It follows that you can measure this period in discrete packets we call seconds, minutes, and hours. Furthermore, argued the Greeks, time implies change. Everything changes with time.

What has come down to Western civilization, and particularly Anglo-Saxon culture, is the notion of time as an arrow, and what is more, time's a-wastin'. We have a limited amount of time to reap crops, chop wood, and store fodder for the winter. We feel an urgency about the lines we have drawn in time. Additionally, time to us is change and change is progress.

But is our view of time really scientific? The Greek philosopher Zeno (circa 495–430 B.C.) complicated matters. He laid out a paradox that called into question assumptions about the linear view of time. If a rabbit takes off from a starting point and a hunter standing five meters behind him shoots an arrow, the arrow, argued Zeno, will never strike the target. By the time the arrow gets to where the rabbit was, the rabbit has moved forward a bit. And by the time the arrow gets to *that* point, the rabbit has moved yet farther, and so on ad infinitum. According to Zeno's paradox, the arrow will get immeasurably closer, but never actually hit the target. In other words, what Zeno cautions is that you can't draw arbitrary lines in time; that doing so may lead to wrong conclusions. Therefore, to view time as an arrow divided into increments is fallacious.

How then do we reconcile Zeno's paradox with reality? Easy. We simply skip over the contradiction and come down with both feet on the side of insisting that lines in time are scientific, natural, obvious, rational, and correct—an international standard that everyone shares with no question. We see the target, and we're on our way. This is clear to us. But linear time doesn't adequately explain cyclical phenomena. It doesn't tell us why things seem to come back to haunt us, why what goes around comes around, or why history repeats itself.

Going around in circles

The Mexican circular view of time has its roots in the Mesoamerican (i.e., Maya/Aztec) view. The Mesoamericans were accomplished mathematicians and astronomers, with a calendar that was as accurate as ours in some ways.

The Aztec calendar was a series of circles within circles that rotated like cogwheels in a gearbox. At predictable intervals, the gears came back to the beginning point. Over centuries, Aztec priests observed celestial phenomena and adjusted the calendar according to the cycles of Venus. As a result, they were able to calculate the period of an Earth year to the fourth decimal point—365.2225 days. The result of their observations was the ability to predict more accurately the onset of the rainy season. In a climate that changes very little, unlike the North that goes from baking summers to ten feet of snow, it was of great value to have a calendar that instructed when to plant corn. The cyclical nature of the Aztec calendar proved to be an important economic tool.

Cultural advantages

There are two reasons to suppose that the circular calendar best suited the Aztecs. First, their climate changed much more subtly than the climate of the North Sea region, as just mentioned. So, as a practical tool, the circular calendar dialed them in accurately and indicated when a day repeated itself year after year. As a result, they knew when the rainy season would likely come.

Second, the Aztecs were obsessed with time. They believed that at some point, time would end and they would cease to exist. Circular time was a way of keeping hope alive. So long as time kept coming around, they were safe. Their calendar was developed over centuries, with records going back in circular time to A.D. 300. They had records of past celestial events such as solar eclipses. So, if a solar eclipse occurred again, they could accept it as a recurring phenomenon that was not going to kill them. Their circular view of time was firmly linked with survival. Absent environmental clues, the circular calendar became an object of economic importance and even reverence.

What has come down to modern Mexicans is a sense that there is a certain sameness about time. This Friday looks a bit like last Friday, and probably next Friday. There will always be another Friday, so long as God lends us life. There will always be another checklist and another objective.

Because modern Mexicans use a Western calendar and wear Casio watches, we Americans are easily fooled into thinking that Mexicans respond to time as we do. But for us, time is fixed, measurable, and inflexible—like a steel rod with internationally recognized standards embossed on it. For them, time does not have absolute measurements, but is flexible, like a coiled spring, subject to outside pulls and contractions. Circular time has a linear aspect—that is, it moves forward, but with varying periods depending on the push or pull that the coil spring is under.

Mexicans accept very readily that certain events *will* happen—the recession *will* end, and the construction industry *will* experience a downturn. What goes around comes around. But no one can predict or control *when* the events will occur. Cycles are subject to outside forces—the periods change. Time is elastic. And Mexicans believe they have to react to events when they happen.

Time isn't money, but it sure counts

Because the Mexicans don't share our sense of urgency about time, we are apt to think that they don't place a high value on time. They do. It's just that they value time spent with you but not schedules issued by bureaucrats. The intercultural misunderstanding arises when we make a comment like "Time is money," and our Mexican host nods enthusiastically—"Yes, time is money." On one level, everybody recognizes the monetary implications. When you get into a cab anywhere in the world and the driver flips the lever, you're charged by the click. But to a prospective business partner in Guadalajara, our favorite little bromide seems shallow. He won't say so because he is too agreeable. Maybe when he knows you better, he will impart his own bromide:

> Money is a very poor substitute for time. God gave us each a budget of time, and time is the only truly limited substance in the universe, whereas the amount of money each of us has can vary widely. Furthermore, I work to live; I don't live to work. My time spent for work takes away from my limited budget of time for the rest of my life. When I am not working, I prefer to spend my time with my family, partying, or at rest. Right now, I am at leisure, and work time will start again when I get to the office. Time is not money; work is money.

In light of the tremendous value that Mexican culture places on time, when a businessperson meets with you for an hour or two or three, it is the most precious gift he or she can give. To interrupt and say that you have to catch a plane is to reject this gift and to leave the impression that business with him is unimportant. Or, if you are in a meeting and inadvertently look at your watch, you are sending the signal that this meeting is not worth your time. A small gesture, ignored in this country, may be perceived as an insult in Mexico. Time spent at dinner or socially is also a generous exchange. Because time is of great importance to the Mexican—more limited and more important than money—use it wisely.

Culture on cruise control

You land in Mexico City. You're ushered out to the next available official taxi and sped out of the pick-up area. The cab caroms around the *Circuito Interior* at sixty MPH, cutting to the right to pass a dump truck, and jogging to the left to cut off an '86 Dodge Diablo full of nuns. Then you're passed by a blue and white VW bus with a papaya juice logo on it. You're in the back seat sliding on the vinyl bench, holding onto the overhead strap with one hand and your briefcase with the other. The taxi driver is telling you a joke about how he wants to die in his sleep like his father, not screaming like all the passengers in his father's cab. At least, between the altitude in Mexico City and all the ambient noise, you think that's the gist of it. So if Mexicans are never in a hurry, why is driving in Mexico City like a lemming stampede on Dexedrine? And there's a corollary question: Once they've hurried out of Mexico City, why do they drive so slow on the back roads and country two-lanes?

It gets more bizarre. Mexico has long stretches of good two-lane highways in the high desert area, where you can go for a hundred miles without seeing another car. As a typical retiree motoring toward Puerto Vallarta, you put the Caddy on cruise control and click off seventy-two miles each hour for three hours steady. Suddenly, a green conversion van looms up in the rearview mirror going ninety-eight MPH and descends on your rear bumper. With a friendly wave, he pulls around and speeds over the horizon. Fifteen minutes later, you come up on the van. Now, he's going forty, has the windows down, and is singing "*ay, ay, ay, ay, canta y no llo'res.*" Later, here he comes again, steaming around you and off in the dust. Still later, you find him loafing and pass him again. Then, you both stop in Matehuala. He's ordering a four-course lunch. You take your sandwiches and go, hoping that your steady seventy-two will rid you of this nuisance for good. But two hours later, the green dot in your rearview mirror starts to expand again.

How do we cope with such driving? In the States, we have epithets for people who go slower than we do, and other epithets for people who drive faster. But this guy is all over the place. What do we call him? *Hermano.* "Brother." He is a Mexican on elastic time. He is not in a hurry. It's just that he sees you and wants to go faster than you. Then, later he doesn't see you and wants to go slower. Or maybe his driving has nothing to do with you at all. In fact, he has trouble with a steady pace because he does not see clicks, ticks, and cruise control the way you do. And it's not as though he has a fixed time to get to his destination.

Driving gives us insight into the Mexicans' sense of time. It is not a matter of planning your trajectory and metering out your time. It is a process, like a river—a flowing toward a destination. And, like a river, sometimes you go fast, sometimes you go slow.

River madness

People who spend a lot of time in Latin America often find themselves slipping into a more laid-back state of mind. This mood can be infectious. After a two-month project in Mexico, followed by an extended period in Brazil and Venezuela, I returned for a brief visit to the States. Still under the spell of circular time, I went to a busy airport in the Midwest to take my next trip. A couple of noisy gringos barrel up behind me joining the long line at the ticket counter. They sputter and cuss, "Look at this goddamn line." Fuss, fuss. Fume, fume. Even though I am a full-blooded, type-A, driver-driver, impatient gringo, it hasn't occurred to me to be upset about the wait. Why this inner calm? Then it dawns on me: I am still in Mexico, on circular time.

Never had the gringos with their wagging tongues and tightly wound faces looked so wretchedly linear and squinched. Their arrow had been loosed. Their lives were ticking away in discrete units. Their destination was waiting. But before they could even get on the plane they were stopped dead in their tracks. To these Americans, each person standing in front of them was a line drawn in space, a click, an impediment to acquiring their target. A Mexican would not have perceived the situation that way at all. He would probably have said to himself, "We are all going in the same direction. We will all get there at about the same time, so why worry?"

American saying: You've gotta get there firstest with the mostest.

Mexican saying: *No hay que llegar primero, sino hay que saber llegar.* (You don't have to get there first, you just have to know how to get there.)

Here's how our different attitudes toward "getting there" play out when Americans and Mexicans meet. We appear to be in a hurry; they are willing to sit back and wait. We get impatient with their lack of urgency; they wonder what all the fuss is about. We want to get there first; they think we want to get there first, but are unwilling to ask how to get there. In our view, they will never achieve their target because they show no signs of pressure about the time factor of the mission. In our view, they don't care if they get there or not. In their view, we may not get there because we shoot off like a cannon without knowing where we're going.

A Mexican family standing in the same line at the airport has no compunctions about darting in and out of line. At first they may present only one obstacle to the two gringos getting onboard. Then suddenly one family member, one impediment, morphs into a mob of clicks, all of whom are in your way. Our impatient American travelers suddenly feel that their arrow is flying backward. The Americans want to step in, assign numbers, and direct the women and children into the waiting lounge. Meanwhile, a Mexican standing behind the Americans isn't fazed at all. If an American brings his or her concern to the attention of the other Mexican in line, he will smile and agree. But if he knew you well, he would say, "Yes, the children are darting in and out, but that is what children do. It won't change when we get to our destination."

Jose Narezo is an established artist in Michigan, who was born in Mexico. He discovered just how anglicized he had become when recently he went back to visit family. Stopping in Nuevo Laredo to register his car for the trip into the interior, he stood in line for hours, sweltering under the tin roof of the customs patio. But the line of Mexicans in front of him kept growing. Adding to his frustration, he wasn't certain he was even *in* the right line and wouldn't know until he got to the window. As the file ahead of him continued to swell, Jose's acquired Anglo temperament finally erupted into a compulsion to take charge. Commandeering paper and pencil, he began handing out numbers.

Mexicans who remain inoculated against the linear time itch simply don't see delays the same way we do. It doesn't occur to the Mexican *papá*, whose family slipped into the line ahead of you, that you are anxiety-ridden. If he thought you were—and that he had it in his power to make you feel better—he would get his family out of the line. He will do it to please you, without fully understanding why you are turning purple. It's not that Mexicans never get upset or anxious. They generally won't get antsy until they are on final approach, and a half-hour late, and think they may miss Aunt Gloria. Why get upset at the beginning of the trip, way back in Guadalajara? Mexicans get anxious over a missed personal contact, not a missed deadline.

Which train are you on?

In his colorful book *Yesterday's Train* (1996), author Terry Pindell recounts the following incident in his extensive travels throughout Mexico:

> When we arrive at the station to catch our southbound train out of Zacatecas, we are surprised that there is no crowd waiting, as there usually has been. The ticket window is closed, and a chalkboard beside it has a time scribbled on it—six hours from now. We explore the seemingly deserted place till we find a rail employee nodding at his desk in a back room. "Is the train six hours late?" we ask him.
>
> "Which train are you ticketed for?" he asks.
>
> Confused, we tell him we thought there was only one train, due to stop here in about a half hour.
>
> "There is only one train," he answers, "But is your ticket for today's train or yesterday's train?"
>
> "Today's, of course," we answer.
>
> "The train listed on the chalkboard—that is yesterday's train. It will arrive tonight, but your ticket is not good for that train."
>
> "When will today's train arrive?" we ask. He shrugs. He has no idea. Nothing has been heard from it yet. And so, our hopes dashed again, we trundle off to the bus station to catch a ride to Aguas-calientes.

Americans wonder how the Mexican can tolerate such a contradiction. How is it possible that yesterday's train is arriving today? The Mexican may receive our barrage of questions politely, shrug, and make his excuses. But he questions why anyone would be so worried about whether you call it "yesterday's train arriving today" or "the train that is arriving today that is a day late." He wonders what the fuss is all about. If you give him half a chance, he will gladly change your ticket so that you can get on yesterday's train today.

At the crux of the confusion in the train station is the clash between the linear and the circular views of time. For the Mexican stationmaster, it is not at all illogical to refer to yesterday's train in order to distinguish it from today's train. Given his view of the circular nature of time, his description is perfectly appropriate.

Being a seasoned traveler in Mexico, Pindell simply trundled off to the bus station. The uninitiated American in this situation would probably have bristled and stormed off with a shower of epithets.

Doubling up

When dealt with separately, our cultural differences seem pretty manageable. But what happens when you get a couple of issues hitting you at the same time? A classic example is the layering of the time issue with the yes/no enigma.

You remember the Chip versus Manuel and the gun cabinet incident? Fundamentally the issue was time, but it was also about being agreeable. Where there was a potential conflict over time, Manuel's response was to be agreeable. If Chip had asked for his gun cabinet by March 15, would he have gotten it? No. Would Manuel have said yes? Yes—at least at first. But he had to get through the initial response and the indirect speech just to find out what the issue with time really was. This double cultural conundrum—time and yes/no—is especially common in Mexico. Moreover, Manuel failed to appreciate Chip's concern with a specific deadline. Manuel didn't draw lines in time, and neither did his mother or father or a procession of ancestors before him. He simply cannot conceive of someone else's compulsion to do so. While time is extremely valuable to him as a Mexican, the difference between January 15 and February 15 becomes important only when it is directly tied to the more important goal—pleasing the customer.

Attitude toward time is an important cultural set piece that drives our living and working behaviors, as we will see in Part II. For now, keep the following three guidelines in mind when it comes to the time component of intercultural relationships.

First, remember that most of the rest of the world is not driven by the clock. If people are not driven by time, then by what? More often than not, individuals are motivated by a personal aspect of an upcoming event. In a work setting, for example, when urging Mexicans to accomplish a task by a certain target, don't announce that the schedule must be met by Friday. Explain that we want to make schedule by Friday because that's when the customer is visiting, and we want to show the customer how well we do our jobs. Friday is arbitrary, but the customer's visit is real. In shifting the focus from time to people, you reinforce the idea that impressing the customer will reflect well on all of us. You have personalized the challenge and made it more meaningful.

Just-in-time suggestions

- Take off your watch. The natural tendency to glance at your watch will be viewed by Mexicans as a signal that you don't value your time with them.
- If asked to go to dinner, say yes. If you really can't accept because your flight leaves at 6:00 p.m., first say yes. Then follow up with, "Can your secretary please help me with my plane reservation?" Being no strangers to indirect messages, they will respond appropriately and let you off the hook, knowing that you still love them.
- When in Mexico City, you can get in seven business meetings a day—the same as in the U.S. The difference is that some of these meetings will include breakfast, lunch, and dinner. The Mexican workday can be much, much longer than ours. If business isn't completed, be flexible enough to change your plane reservations and come home a day late.
- Always thank people for their time, and give every signal that you are willing to take the time required to get to know them. Go out to dinner? Sure. In the next city? No problem. Go for it. Say, "My time is your time." Don't say, "Well you know, I gotta get to sleep by 9:30 because we agreed to meet at 8:00 A.M. tomorrow."
- On business trips, several days before your departure, begin to get into a relaxed mode. Do all your preparations ahead of time so you can cruise into the trip unburdened by fretfulness. You will land in Mexico in a frame of mind much more conducive to succeeding in business. In short, eliminate frustration. Embrace the success that will come from their hard work and your patience.
- When meeting with your Mexican workforce in Saltillo or Indianapolis, unplug the phone and relax. Give them the signal that you have all day to listen to their suggestions. They will return the favor by not wasting your time. But, you can blow it by telling them you are in a hurry. They will think you don't give a damn.

Second, don't take a proffered date as a commitment to a schedule. Until you have interviewed the Mexican supplier and negotiated a reasonable delivery date, he will not feel the same level of commitment that you perceive.

You have to invite bad news and give a signal that it is all right to disagree. Otherwise, you will get the answer the supplier thinks you want to hear, not the date he intends for delivery. For Manuel in our prior example, or for a waiter, a ticket agent, or a mechanic, being agreeable with you is more important than scratching a date in wet cement. If you do not take their flexible attitude toward time into account, you will be disappointed. And you will blame the Mexicans.

Finally, remember that time is a gift to all of us. How we invest our own time shows the level of commitment we are willing to make. Whether dealing with Mexicans in the U.S. or in Mexico, if they come to you with a concern or an idea, show that you have time for them. Put your calls on hold, and put your papers aside. Then look them in the eye as if to say there is nothing more important to you than meeting with them. In the U.S., taking time to make such a person-to-person statement would be refreshing. In Mexico, personal communication of this kind is essential.

In summary, when you recognize that there is fundamental disagreement on something as basic as the concept of time, and you are willing to make adjustments, you are on your way to achieving cultural fluency. You make an appointment with the Mexicans, they playfully ask, "*¿Hora mexicana o hora americana?*" which means, "Mexican time or American time?" They recognize that their view is flexible. You agree on dinner at 8:00 that night. But you know that for them time is elastic.

CHAPTER
FOUR

A Different Sense of Space

It's Sunday morning. You're up extra early so you can beat the crowds, get down to the beach, commune with nature. You want to recharge your batteries so you'll be your usual go-getter self come Monday. What could be better? The sound of the surf, a cup o' hot coffee, not a living soul in sight—nobody, that is, until a Mexican plunks down right beside you.

Crossing five hundred feet of unoccupied sand, he greets you with a polite, *"Buenos dias!"* Then he shouts excitedly to his whole family, motioning for the nursemaids and the dog to come join you.

You say, *"Buenos dias"* rather politely, but your body language betrays your displeasure. You wait a few moments so that your next action isn't too obvious. Then—knowing you're going to come off as a tight-assed gringo, but not caring—you pick up your cup and towel and head back to the hotel. You're thinking, "A half mile of beach in either direction, and they have to pick on me! What's with these people? Can't they see they're invading my personal space?"

The answer is no. No they can't. This isn't how they see it at all. Mexicans have a different sense of space. They sit down beside you because "that's where the people are." It doesn't occur to them that this is objectionable or impolite. On the contrary, it's the natural, friendly, obvious thing to do. Unlike Americans who prefer to spread out, Mexicans tend to congregate.

If another gringo had come along, he would have settled about halfway toward the horizon to the south. Intuitively he would understand that both you and he want space and tranquility. If a third gringo had arrived, he would have gone halfway toward the northern horizon. According to our sense of space, we tend to seek the maximum convenient distance between

45

one another before the inevitable crowd arrives. We draw a circle around ourselves—a circle as big as circumstance will allow. It shrinks as conditions dictate, until we feel agitated and claustrophobic.

The Mexicans look disappointed as you leave, and quietly, very quietly, the señora asks papá what happened. "I don't know. I must have done something wrong. I can't imagine what it is. Or perhaps he does not like Mexicans."

Mexicans are quick to pick up on any show of irritation or impatience and assume that they have caused the displeasure. But they are also aware that some of us don't like them. They hear us complain about illegal immigrants, the oil slicks in the Gulf of Mexico, losing jobs, drugs. We blame it all on them. They have seen our police beating them on TV. They know that we can be prejudiced and they're thinking, "Maybe it's our brown skin."

Somehow a moment of solitude on the beach has turned into an international racial incident. You're feeling violated; they're feeling discriminated against. While you're asking why they are so intrusive, they're wondering what it is about them that you don't like. But the real issue is not lack of manners or skin color. It's space.

Bumper to bumper

I pull into the parking lot of the Hispanic Center in Michigan with my brand new car. Wanting to avoid dings in my doors, I deliberately park three rows away from the building in an area sixty feet from any other car and ninety feet farther from the front door than the closest available parking slot. As I am getting out of my car, a woman swings through the entrance, around the median, and parks right next to me. How do I know she's not an Anglo? Could it be that she parked next to me because that's where the people are parking now?

In keeping with their sense of space, Mexicans tolerate a high compression factor. An American manager sent to Mexico was concerned because his wife had invited about thirty couples to their small apartment in Monterrey. When the guests started showing up with their children, there was hardly room to breathe. Much to his surprise, no one seemed to mind. In fact he noted that as the rooms became more crowded, his guests seemed to relax and have more fun. This is the Mexican's sense of space in action.

Social orientation

Our sense of space is directly tied to how we perceive our connection to other people. Whereas we Americans draw circles around the individual,

Mexicans draw circles around the group. Most of the world is closer to the Mexicans in this regard. We—plus some western and most northern Europeans— are the exceptions. People from Latin America, the Middle East, Africa, and Asia tend to be more group-oriented and are less sensitive to individual space needs.

Differences in our sense of space undoubtedly contribute to the impression held by most Mexicans that Americans are somewhat cold and distant. Space becomes a big issue on trains, on planes, and in cars. Travel is definitely more uncomfortable for those of us in cultures where the sense of personal space is tighter. Our natural instinct is to feel stress when we are crowded onto a small commuter plane in Mexico, where passengers carry on a year's worth of luggage and cram themselves into smaller seats.

We Americans will always be more comfortable being separated; Mexicans will always be more comfortable being part of a group. We will always resist being crowded; they will always want to get closer. It's not personal. It's not prejudice. They don't know it, but on that Sunday morning at the beach, you would have gotten up and left if another gringo had sat next to you—only faster.

Because the Mexican and American notions of space are so deeply embedded, it is unrealistic to think that either is going to change. Nor should we expect change. Both senses of space are natural and not insensitive.

When we draw circles around ourselves, we are inside the circle looking out. Since Mexicans draw a circle around the group, they are constantly looking inward toward that group. Figuratively speaking, the Mexican family surrounded by the walls of their house look inward toward one another. We, on the other hand, are inside the house looking out through the biggest picture window we can afford, hoping that nobody will build within sight of us—a markedly different social orientation.

In the United States, our sense of space begins to develop from the moment we are brought home from the hospital in a bassinet. From that moment on, the American child develops an expectation of privacy. He or she begins referring to "my room" and "my toys." The walls are going up. Children begin to feel more comfortable with a private space that they can crawl off to for insulation against pressure. This is quite different from the Mexican experience. We Americans become territorial about our half of the dorm room at college. We set up separate shelves in the community refrigerator. We want a den in our dream house where we can put our feet up and think about what we should have said today and mentally project what we will do tomorrow—all without interruption from the family. Not so in Mexico.

Mexicans' closer sense of space is related to the way they have been raised, living much closer together in the home and looking inward to each other for support and nurturing. Physical closeness goes along with closer families and less sibling rivalry. Each child does not get his own room. Boys and girls are not necessarily divided until a more advanced age, and then only if resources allow. There's nothing inherently better or worse about either the American or Mexican approach—although Mexican children sure do get along well, both among themselves and with others. When passing playgrounds in Mexico, I'm always struck with the pleasant sounds. No taunting, teasing, or squabbling.

There is a story about a Mexican worker who came to the States for training. His supervisor asked a coworker to take Javier home to show him how Americans live. The American coworker took him through his house. "This is the entry hall where we take off our snowshoes. Here's the living room, but we spend more time in the den over there where the TV is. This is the dinette next to the kitchen. Here's Bertha's and my room. Here's the boys' room. Here's where little Martha sleeps, except when Grandma and Grandpa visit and she sleeps in the den." Javier was delighted with the tour and said, "You know, it's exactly the same in Mexico—except for the walls." This story is not intended to be derogatory in any way. It is instructive.

Don't fence me in

Although Mexicans are less concerned than Americans about defining individual space, they are generally more concerned with sharply demarcating one family's living space from another family's. This usually means having a wall between houses. When Mexicans visit the United States, they often marvel at the open lawns between homes. The Mexican wonders, "How do they know where their property stops and their neighbor's begins?" Americans know. We know exactly where to mow, don't we? To construct walls between houses seems to run counter to something in the American spirit. "Something there is that doesn't love a wall," wrote Robert Frost in his quintessentially American poem, "Mending Wall." The Mexican's feelings run just as deep on the other side. For them it is important to define family space. This is because the family and its space are a final refuge from the chaos and uncertainty of life outside their walls. The home is the one place where, with all the gods playing their ungodly tricks, they can finally feel in control. Protecting the group space is paramount.

When we Americans observe Mexicans, we see them piled onto a train with families, chickens, goats, and a whole menagerie. We wonder how they can fit so many on a bus. We observe clusters of family members moving around Sears in unison. We make jokes about crowding into a pickup truck. But we are observing only the top 10 percent of a cultural phenomenon that rises above the surface. What is going on underneath the surface is a clash in our opposing sense of space.

There is a strong correlation between sense of space and behavior. We Americans have a definite sense of individual space and we carry a protective shell around our individuality. Our sense of individuality goes with us wherever we go. We act independently, whereas Mexicans see themselves as part of a group. They act as a group, looking to each other for direction, approbation, and survival. When they are in their group space, they behave according to what that space is dedicated to. If they are in the receiving hall outside the mayor's office, they wait for the mayor like dutiful citizens. If they are in the polishing department, they see themselves as polishers. When they are in the home, they act like a family. As Americans, we too adjust our behavior and shift gears depending on what is required of us. We cooperate with the team and blend into the choir, but we don't shed the circle around ourselves. Typically, we see ourselves as discrete individuals operating within the group, whereas Mexicans are *the group*.

Whether working in the United States or in Mexico, Mexicans working on the factory floor of a large manufacturing entity perceive the walls of their department as enveloping their circle. In this setting, they have their backs to the wall and relate to the group. By contrast, when Americans visualize the overall operation of a plant, we see a continuous production line cutting through all departments. We draw little boxes for machines and little circles for operators performing specific tasks. Mexican workers, on the other hand, relate primarily to the inner circle of their department and secondarily to the larger space where the entire company team works together.

Another difference in our respective senses of space is that Americans feel threatened if our personal space is invaded, whereas Mexicans are alarmed if their group space is invaded. We feel as though our person is being violated. They feel that their group identity is being threatened.

Here's looking at you

What happens when you enter their space? Both Mexicans and Americans have rituals for approaching another person's or group's space. But our respective rituals are very different.

In her novel, *Stones for Ibarra* (1984), Harriet Doerr writes about a local man visiting the house where the author and her husband were living in a remote Mexican village. The local was looking for work. He didn't want to disturb the American couple needlessly, so rather than knock on the door, he went around the house, window to window, looking in to see if they were there and if they were busy. Had they been in the kitchen sipping coffee, he would have gone to the back door and announced himself. Had they been in bed, he would have left quietly to return the next day. Within the context of his peasant Mexican culture, he was behaving perfectly properly in the way he approached the author's space. He was being polite. It was jarring to the writer, however. What if Harriet and her husband were in an intimate embrace? What if they were naked? How can someone just come up to your window and look in?

From the Mexican peasant's perspective, his actions were innocent and nonthreatening. (This may be one reason Mexican city dwellers put walls all the way around their houses.) Had he seen anything of a personal nature, he would have averted his eyes and returned later. As for the nakedness, well, it is as natural as can be and nothing to get excited about. He would have been confused if the gringos had come out screaming and shooing him off. It would not have computed. He would not have understood why the gringos were so hostile.

Other aspects of Mexicans' behavior within their workspace—regarding individual versus group work styles—are discussed in Chapter 7.

Backing off

You probably don't recognize that Americans routinely behave ritualistically, but we do. Imagine that you want to borrow a rake from your neighbor. First, you knock on his screen door, then quickly back up. If nobody comes, you knock again, this time yelling to the upstairs window. Did you peer in through the screen? No. Did you walk around the house looking for the rake? No. Somewhere along the line we picked up cultural cues about personal space that tell us how to approach the neighbor's house. We have learned that there is an acceptable, nonthreatening way to get the attention of a neighbor whom we consider vulnerable because his doors and windows are open.

Ritualistic practices also help us cope with confined spaces, such as crowded elevators. As we get on, we lower our eyes, turn toward the buttons, and press our floor. We face front and say nothing. If we must, we say, "Out please," or "Excuse me," with our Yankee penchant for economy of words. It's different in Mexico. They get on an elevator and say, "*Buenas tardes,*" to everybody. It is not unusual to hear chatter among the strangers. They ask permission to get off—"*Con permiso.*" The others respond, "*Propio*" (*of course*). Or they may insist that you go first.

There is a different ritual in Mexico for entering shopping spaces. We Americans go into a store and immediately put up our defense shields. If forced to speak, we say, "Just looking around." Mexicans go to a store and, recognizing that they have entered the shopkeeper's space, immediately proffer a "*Buenas tardes*" to the owner and staff. There is nothing more out of place than the woman in Bermuda shorts and Rockports who says, "*Nada mas mirando*"—a lame translation of "just looking," which to the Mexican means absolutely nothing. In Mexico the clerk will follow you around the store quietly—not uttering a word. We feel crowded by her presence. Is she checking up on us? No. She's there, close to you, in case you have any questions. Be aware that we think we're shopping, whereas they think we have come for a visit. This is their space, and we will get better service, when the time comes, if we act as though we are invitees rather than dispassionate purchasing agents.

Correct distance

Americans' individual space is quite well defined, though most of us don't realize it. The correct face-to-face distance between American men is one arm's length, less the hand. The distance woman-to-woman is a bit closer than man-to-man. If you are a man, the next time you're at a cocktail party or convention, try moving one half step closer to the man you're talking to. You will see him avert his eyes, shift his feet, turn sideways, and finally take a half step back. He won't be conscious of his own actions. You then take another half step closer. He will repeat his backward shuffle. Keep it up, and you could waltz him around the room and out the door.

Understanding the different boundaries of personal space is important when doing business. In the United States, if a woman were to move a little closer to a man, he may interpret the narrowing of space as an invitation to flirt, which would be taboo in the workplace. If a Mexican woman stands closer to an American male, however, it is not a come-on. In fact, it means nothing of the sort. Her circle of personal space is simply smaller, or less acutely felt than his. Men and women generally stand closer in Mexico. If you are showing a Mexican woman something on your computer screen, she will get much closer to you than an American woman would. She may stand with her legs right next to your arm or lean over your shoulder. American males should note that this is not a come-on.

In the States, the personal space between individuals remains the same, irrespective of status—whether speaking to the president of the company or the guy who sets up our AV equipment. In Mexico's more hierarchical society, there is a need to establish greater separation between the workers and the *jefe,* or "big man." The workers tend to operate together more closely than in the United States, but the president maintains more distance between himself and his accounting clerk. The Mexican boss will have an exaggeratedly large office and desk to emphasize the hierarchical distance between himself and his minions. This is his "power distance."

As an American operating with Mexicans, you want to be sensitive to the greater zone that surrounds the president of a company. But in the course of your dealings, when the president takes a step closer, puts his arms around you, and gives you an *abrazo,* or hug, he is indicating that he means to accept you as an equal. If you are a woman, the parallel behavior might be a pat on the arm and an "air kiss" (touching cheeks and smacking the void next to the woman's head), which acknowledges trust and confers respect. Whatever you do, don't pull back and blow it. In this context, the gesture signals that you have crossed into the Mexican president's circle and are trusted to work within his group. You must now maintain that relationship and build on it.

I explained the *abrazo* practice to middle management at Chrysler Motors. "Hold on a minute," one man interjected. "In sensitivity training, we were told never to touch *anybody!*" I'm not suggesting you go hugging anyone unless you feel comfortable getting that close. On the other hand, be aware that men will hug men in Mexico, and it means nothing beyond friendship and acceptance.

Americans and Mexicans have been living next to each other for many years and have learned to appreciate each other's customs. I have a friend in

McAllen, Texas, named Mike Heap. (There is no more Anglo-Saxon name than Mike Heap.) Mike is a laconic Texan, a cowboy, and a former bronco-buster who is now on the rodeo circuit as a clown. He loves Mexicans, his girlfriend is Mexican, and like most Anglos in the Rio Grande Valley, he speaks Spanish. When he goes to Mexico, he gives his men friends *abrazos*. I too give and receive *abrazos* when I go to Mexico. But Mike and I would never hug each other.

According to street lore, the *abrazo* came into being as a means of "patting down" the person you greet to make sure he's not armed. But today it means, "Welcome to my space."

Group space

How should Americans adapt our usual business practices in response to the Mexicans' sense of space? Since Mexicans draw a circle around their group and focus inward, as previously mentioned, anyone entering their space makes a big impact. So in the business setting, how you enter a Mexican group's space is important. A proper greeting, avoiding flamboyant gestures, not shouting, and general circumspection are appreciated.

Most how-to books tell you how to greet and what to wear. But remember that in addition to proper manners, violating Mexicans' group space may be perceived as a threat to how they live and work. If we go into their group space and disrupt the harmony of the group, we are signaling to the group that we do not care about them. They may assume that they are the next to be transferred, fired, or shot.

When a gringo walks into a native cantina in a remote village, suddenly everything goes quiet. When they realize you are just there to throw down tequila, they relax and start talking again. We are clearly outsiders. But once we enter the group and behave, they accept us. If we buy one of them a drink and tell a good joke, the atmosphere turns to jubilation.

In the workplace, Mexicans can favor us with cooperation and the rewards of group effort if we are sensitive to the effect we are having on their space. By minimizing disruption when we enter their space, we indicate respect for their group and earn their support. The unfortunate corollary for us is that often once we leave their space, we may no longer exist to them. We have to be in their space to get the best results. Once in their group space, we have to spend time building relationships or else we will be "out of sight, out of mind."

Space tips

- Be attuned to the fact that you are entering *their* space. Always keep your antennae up. Consider what kind of space you are entering and behave accordingly.
- If a Mexican invades your sense of personal space, treat it as non-threatening.
- When waiting outside the mayor's office for your appointment, respect the mood of the space. If you huff and puff because your appointment is already a half-hour overdue, you will only succeed in making a pest of yourself.
- When you go into the mayor's conference room, you are entering a conference space—a space where a certain awe and dignity are supposed to reign. Don't put your briefcase, glides down, on the hand-rubbed conference table. You are not in a schoolroom.
- When entering a business conference room in Mexico, wait for someone to signal where you should sit. If you are the guest of honor, they may put you on their *jefe's* immediate right. But wait for a signal, don't just sit down. One Mexican chap I know made such a mistake, but recovered brilliantly when the boss came in. He simply said, with aplomb, "Señor, wherever you sit is the head of the table!"

The Deeper Meaning of Language

Along with time and space, the third and arguably most intricate cultural set piece influencing behavior is language. Over centuries, languages acquire unique, built-in features that affect the perspectives of their speakers. Language is the primary mechanism by which people interpret, transmit, and shape their culture. As such, it becomes fused with the culture itself. Comparing the construction and use, even the sounds of Spanish and English, helps us understand our differences with the Mexicans.

Gender gap

The Spanish language is constructed around the precept that everything has a gender and that gender matters. Inherent in the language is the assumption that the sun is masculine and the moon is feminine. Pots, pans, pajamas, potatoes—all "things" are gender-specific. *Book* ends in *o,* (masculine ending) but *machine* ends in *a* (feminine ending.) Such an issue never even comes up in English, because English is more inherently egalitarian, marking no gender. There is no difference in English between a female doctor and a male doctor, lawyer, or farmer. Of course, there are exceptions—*actor* and *actress.* But today, our female Hollywood stars (I didn't say starlets) insist on being called "actors." Apart from dower rights (legalese for the wife gets everything when the husband dies), using *she* for ships, and shouting "*man the life boats,*" there are very few ways in which English codifies gender into law, commerce, or daily discourse. Historically, we have added *man* to *post,* creating *postman.* But because there is no gender, we can easily concatenate two words—for example, *post* and *woman* or *post* and *person*—without

55

altering the language. In Spanish such change is far more cumbersome, requiring feminine pronouns, articles, and adjectives.

The Spanish gender difference muddles professional designations. *Lawyer, president, chief,* and *tortilla maker* are all masculine words. Trying to accommodate women by changing the endings of such words to the feminine letter *a* results in distortion and confusion. *Jefe* (masculine) means chief, but *jefa* just sounds funny. We all know what a tortilla is, but watch out for the change in gender when you go from a *tortillero*—someone who makes tortillas—to a *tortillera*—slang for lesbian. The limitations of a gender-specific vocabulary have reinforced the idea that the professions are male monopolies.

Out of respect

Whereas the "macho thing" is, to a degree, built into the language, Spanish speakers have a device for mollifying its effects. The use of titles confers respect and compensates for linguistic inequality. There is a difference in Spanish between the term for doctor and the title for a doctor. *Doctor* is *médico* (masculine). There is no such thing as a *médica* (feminized version). However, as a title, the terms *Doctor* or *Doctora* sound great.

In Mexico, even if you know *Doctora Sanchez* so well that socially you would call her Susana, you would address her as "Doctora" at the office, clinic, or in public places.

Giving respect for achievement is part of the Mexican linguistic blueprint. Titles such as *ingeniero* (engineer), *profesor* (professor or teacher), *licenciado* (attorney or other professional designation), and others are generously accorded. Other Spanish-speaking countries recognize Mexicans by their frequent use of titles. It's an art form that the Mexicans have retained after centuries of use—a linguistic tradition that other Latin American countries have abandoned. Since Mexicans are particularly sensitive to self-respect and its corollary, respect for others, they mitigate any unintended slights by lavishing titles. Introducing your associate as Licenciado Santana in Spain evokes a wry smile since it is viewed as a bit of overkill. In Mexico, it gets action. A Peruvian businessman and his associate were made to wait for a seat at a restaurant, until he snorted that he was Licenciado Reyes. Immediately they were ushered to a table. The Peruvian knew how to play the game.

In an inverse linguistic ploy, Mexicans can demote themselves in our presence. *Su servidor* (your servant) is a common expression. It is part of

Mexican ritual to elevate another while diminishing one's self. If you call out a Mexican worker by name—"José!"—he may answer "Servidor!" Can you imagine my Anglo friend Mike Heap doing that?

Any possible unintended sting of cultural, material, or racial reference is often reduced by adding the affectionate *-ito/-ita*. An Indian becomes an *indito*. Black becomes *negrito*. Brown becomes *morenito*. The word for mother, sometimes being associated with a longer term of sidewalk art, is lovingly embellished with the diminutive suffix and becomes *mamasita*. The endings *-ito* or *-ita* confer a cuteness to the subject that makes its reference acceptable.

Passing participles

Mexican businesspeople use an elevated Spanish that reinforces their position in a class hierarchy. They revel in pomp, sprinkling phrases with formalities, compliments, and indirect references—a process that involves many rules governing word usage and body language. A person's position in society is defined by his ability to manipulate these factors. So Mexicans with limited education find it harder to move up the social and professional scale. Integrating into the mainstream is especially difficult for those who come from the country and are more adept with their indigenous language. They may misuse an irregular verb such as *romper* (to break), saying *rompido* instead of *roto*—the correct form.

When passing the butter, a gentlewoman will say "*Se la paso*," observing the necessary gender agreement between the impersonal pronoun *la* and its implied antecedent *mantequilla* (feminine). The maid, not guided by such formalities, may say "*Se lo paso*." Anyone can make a mistake in any language and be judged accordingly. What makes Spanish different from English is that such mistakes can impede communication. If a Spanish speaker asks for "it" (feminine) and someone responds, "I will pass 'it'" (masculine), the speaker is left wondering what it is that he is going to receive. *It* (masculine) could be a knife, a glass, a ladle, or a nutcracker, but not the butter. Basic miscommunications relegate people to the status of hired help.

Conversely, political and social power go to the eloquent. A true leader is the person who can command his environment with tact and correct posture. With its numerous complex rules, including unwritten art forms, more traps are set for the uneducated. A social hierarchy is imposed and maintained through Spanish language construction and usage.

In addition to being more sensitive in their use of words, Spanish speakers are keenly aware of the sound of their voices. Businesspeople, especially, tend to modulate their tones. The goal is to sound elevated—*bien educado*—whereas we try to sound democratic and down-to-earth. Given a choice, we will use Anglo-Saxon root words rather than longer Latin/French root words that grace our language. In daily discourse we won't say *revenue, royalty, reimbursement,* or *recompense,* we say *money* or *bucks.* Why say *conference* or *convocation* if a simple *meeting* will do?

While we go to a language lab to study the construction and use of Spanish, let's put on a set of earphones and listen to the English language to see what we can learn about our own way of communicating.

English is EZ

Compared to Spanish, English is extremely forgiving and creates a more level playing field. English has few rules; we have no verb conjugations of consequence. "If I were you" is correct or standard English, using the subjunctive to connote an element of improbability. But if we say, "If I *was* you," our listener would probably let it pass. Our nouns, pronouns, and adjectives are supposed to agree with each other according to number, but how many times do you hear, "There's a lot of people who. . . ." It's as if *there's* is a separate part of speech that need not agree with the noun it refers to. (The correct version would be "there *are*" or "there*'re* a lot of people who. . . .") A foreigner searching for a rule that allows us to say, "There's a lot of people who . . ." will be frustrated beyond pity because he cannot find any such rule. Is it any wonder that the French or Spanish, or those from many other parts of the world, come to the United States having learned our grammar better than we have? It is common to hear an American say "with you and I." This is grammatically incorrect, but we get away with it. Native speakers of Romance languages say "with you and me," which is correct. That is because they *must* use the correct objective pronoun in their language or the meaning will be totally lost. They transfer their own precision to our language, where we conveniently concentrate on substance, not formality.

English is inherently more forgiving, so much so that we make mistakes with few consequences. For Americans, what we say is more important than how we say it. For Mexicans, the belief that how they say something is as important as what they say tells us something about them.

The English language has fewer traps to expose mistakes. Of course, it is an unmistakable fact that as soon as someone opens his mouth, someone else judges him. Americans, just like anyone else in the world, have a bottomless well of epithets to impart to others we consider to be less perfect than we are. When people misuse standard English, we mark them as less intelligent, underclassed, or quaintly bucolic. But there is a difference between misusing a language and having stigmatizing traps inherent in the language. The English language has fewer such impediments and is less likely to inhibit social or economic progress.

Our language says it all

The way we talk reveals just how flat-thinking Americans are. English is, at bottom, Anglo-Saxon. The grunts, huffs, easy words, and country wit were part of the Anglo-Saxon's wordbook in A.D. 900. So are words like *I, you, he, she, it, we, you,* and *they,* as well as *and, but, for, or,* and *nor.* Basic words like *water, land, woods,* and *sky* are Anglo-Saxon. Basic verbs like *go, come, stay, sit, stand,* and *look* are too. Anything you can do to a tree is Anglo-Saxon. You can *go up* a tree. You can *cut down* a tree. You can *crash into* a tree. You can *hang your neighbor from* a tree. All these things and more are Anglo-Saxon. This whole aforementioned string of thoughts has been writ with Anglo-Saxon root words only, and you had pictures in your mind's eye about these words when you read them. These words have in them the soul of our wit and the bulk of our thinking. These are the nickel words.

Today in English most of what we say is in nickel words. We farm and raise cows, pigs, sheep, and horses using nickel words. We go to work, earn our keep, and spend it foolishly. We eat lunch and call it a day. We go home and put our heads down on the bed and try to forget how dumb the boss is. We do all that with nickel, or Anglo-Saxon, words. Nothing fancy. These too are all Anglo-Saxon words.

It wasn't until the French conquerors brought another language onto English soil in A.D. 1066 that our language became more complex. They spoke the elevated language of the rulers. As a result, hierarchy was superimposed on our basic Anglo-Saxon tongue. The French imported boatloads of abstract expressions we use in administration, finance, jurisprudence, philosophy, and ethics. *High-minded* (Anglo-Saxon) became *sophisticated* (French). *The way we talk* became *proper language.*

From 1066 on, we have had two sources of vocabulary—one improper, or Anglo-Saxon, the other proper, or French, in origin. Our four-letter words are Anglo-Saxon, and we chuckle at their rough, down and dirty tone—some unfit for womenfolk's ears. Further, *cow* was okay for the barnyard, but *roast beef* (*rôti de boeuf*) was what the conquerors ate. It's *pig* on the hoof, but *pork* (*porc*) on the table. The French terms are five-dollar words. Suddenly "I have to pee" (not considered vulgar by Anglo-Saxons) became "Pardon me, where are the facilities?"

The French had come to rule, and their language gave us new ways of expressing complex, erudite forms of domination. There were legal words and terms, such as *constitution, institution, administration, pursuant, regard, judge's chambers,* and *license. Land* became *real estate* (*l'état du roi*—the land of the king), adding political insult to the stigma of not speaking an elevated language. *Declaration, conference, attorney general, absolution, punishment,* and *sentence* were all French origin words of hierarchy that the Anglo-Saxons learned to hate. There was privilege, or private law, for the French and common law—law for the commoners—for Anglo-Saxons. The French had come to England to dominate the Anglo peasants, and their sophisticated words helped them do the job.

Drunk, or disorderly, or both . . .

Because the Anglo-Saxons didn't understand the French words at first, many dual concepts were born. You had to *swear* (Anglo-Saxon) and *affirm* (French) that you were not *drunk* (A-S) and *disorderly* (F) when you *signed* (A-S) and *sealed* (F) your *will* (A-S) and *testament* (F), so it would not be *null* (F) and *void* (A-S.) That is, to the best of your *information* (F) and *belief* (A-S.)

Expressing philosophical concepts proved clunky in "Anglish." But with the addition of French vocabulary, our English language flowered. The *again bite of in-wit* (Anglo-Saxon) became the *remorse of conscience* (French). Our language became bifurcated—or, in Anglo-Saxon, it went down two roads at the same time. Whereas we deride the French for sitting around and talking all the time and never actually doing anything, we pay our respect to them by copying their words for abstractions.

We instinctively understand the difference in spirit and feeling between the Anglo-Saxon words of simplicity and the French words of hierarchy. While we draw freely on both, we remain, at heart, much more comfortable with the simple. Today, when a lawyer waxes on in legalese, we pull her down a peg, telling her to speak English. We abhor people who use pretentious language to say what could be said more simply—we call them snobs, snoots, and other good ole' Anglish words. Only geeks know the word *aphorism*, after all. Why do we hate the overuse of French root words? That question lies at the heart of our egalitarian outlook. It's difficult to say which came first, language or attitude, but the fact is, we are that way. It is one of our cultural set pieces. When we talk, it's for content, not for effect.

In addition to language per se, we express egalitarianism in our body language. We slouch, walk with a bob and a weave, put our hands in our pockets, rest our feet on the desk, and generally try to show the world that we do not consider ourselves above the common man, as we perceive the common man. The common man is kind of aw-shucks, easy-goin', more interested in Indiana basketball than Shakespeare down-to-earth. The common man is also a woman with a master's degree in immuno-something who nevertheless greets visitors to her house with a "c'mon in," drinks water out of a plastic bottle, goes to the supermarket in her sweats, and answers to "hey you." A new twist on the American common man is not American at all. Arnold Schwarzenegger's *Terminator* is tough, but he has a big heart. *Ahnold* made 150 million bucks using very few words—"*Hasta la vista*, baby." Never mind that they are uttered with an Austrian accent, mostly in Spanish!

Keeping it simple

What, then, is the connection between language and culture? We Americans are driven to simplify. We go for practicality, not pretense. We have a passion for nickel words and resist five-dollar words. An American lawyer is pulled off her pedestal when she uses terms of art. This is most unfortunate and unfair because many of the centuries-old words she uses have evolved meaning through case law. But we make her give it to us in Mark Twain monosyllables. Conversely, the Mexican businessperson is respected for his scholarly grasp of the past as evidenced by his use of elevated vocabulary.

Generally speaking, Americans are more concerned with meaning than with eloquence. We dislike those who get their knickers in a twist trying to state simple facts. We might say, and in saying it make the point, that English is a user-friendly language. English both reflects and reinforces our egalitarian sensibility.

Conversely, the Mexicans are steeped in the emotive quality of the language itself and search for ways to get more meaning or feeling out of each phrase they utter. If one word isn't good enough, they will use more words, and yet more, until they have fully enveloped you in their meaning and style. When a Mexican offers you a compliment take it, or else you may find yourself in an endlessly mushrooming bouquet of floridity leaving both of you gasping for respite. If a Mexican says you speak Spanish beautifully, say, "Thank you." It is even appropriate to say, "Yes, thank you." Why? That politely cuts off debate. If you take the usual Anglo-Saxon tone of shrinking from higher forms of language, you will say, "Aw, naw, I just barely get by." This leads the Mexican to think he has not stated his appreciation with enough grace. He will respond, "No, certainly, if I could confer upon my poor English the liquidity with which your Spanish flows, I would be the host of all the creatures of the forest." To which you might say, "Aw, naw, I just barely get by." To which he gasps and thinks, What more can I come up with to convince this fellow that I mean to compliment him? Just say, "Thank you."

Traditional versus adaptable

The simple grammar that we derive from the early Anglo-Saxons has benefited us in ways that they could not have anticipated. Those who speak English are better able than most to adapt their language to new technology. When we invent a fax, immediately it rings up in our dictionaries as a noun, an adjective (a *faxed* message), or a verb—I *faxed* it to you yesterday; I *am faxing* it to you right now; I *will fax* it to you tomorrow. Spanish speakers finally gave up on trying to use *telephone* and *fax* as verbs. Trying to fax someone in the subjunctive doesn't connect. "*El quería que yo le faxease*" sounds weird. Instead, they fell back on the time-tested verb *mandar*, meaning "to send." Today you *mandar un fax*.

Unlike English, Spanish is filled with peccadilloes that scream to be resolved by some legally sanctioned linguistic authority. When I lived in Colombia in the late 1940s, the literati were still trying to decide if *radio* was masculine or feminine. Years later it was determined that the device is masculine, but the radio industry—a grander concept—is feminine. The gender dilemma arose again when television was introduced. Since all words that end in *-ion* are automatically feminine, the word *televisión* came to describe the industry, with *televisor* invented for the apparatus. English is simpler: *television*. And if that's more than you can pronounce, *TV*.

Frequently the purists among us rail that we are too quick to use nouns as verbs, verbs as adjectives, and so on. But flexibility is one of the beauties of

English. Watching a football game you may hear John Madden say that the quarterback *audiblized* the signal. *Audare* is the verb "to hear" in Latin. *Audible* is an adjective, and adding *-ize* makes it a verb again. Boom! Point made. In the interest of efficiency, we tend to go with whatever works—whatever is doable and passes the sniff test. Without batting an eye, we can substitute a transitive verb for an intransitive verb and sound supercompetitive and efficient. We can *grow* a company. We can build a ship and we can *ship* something to you. Or if that isn't fast enough, we can *fax* it, *FedEx* it, or *UPS* it overnight. We can even turn a company name into a verb—*Xeroxing* a copy. And with electronic speed we can integrate *e-mail* into the language, knowing instinctively how to use it as a noun, an adjective, or a verb.

The ease with which we take company names or brands and turn them into generic terms is an unending concern to the owners of those trademarks. By making generic words of them, we dilute the strength of their trademark. A trademark is supposed to inform the public of the source and therefore the quality of the goods. But if everyone refers to all tissues as *Kleenex,* then Delsey loses. If you ask for a Coke, meaning any brown fizzy drink, that dilutes Coca-Cola's trademark. Because of a lawsuit, today's waitstaffs are instructed to say, "We have Pepsi. Is that OK?" Xerox, FedEx, Formica, and many others have rued the fact that English is the world's leading hijacker of words.

This is not a problem in Spanish. None of those marks are in danger of being hijacked to be turned into generic words or verbs by the Spanish-speaking world. By being less adaptable than English, Spanish has much more of a tradition-binding effect on the culture. The language itself is less ready to absorb new modalities and technologies. It tugs at its users to stick with the past. To get around many of these limitations, Mexicans—reluctant to change their language—simply adopt the English term or expression as the best possible. One favorite adaptation in Mexico is to end new words with *-azo*. *Telefono* becomes *telefonazo* (telephone call). *Avion* (airplane) becomes *avionazo* (plane crash). These are new nouns made from old nouns. Still no verbs.

Eloquence without pretense

The rigor with which Mexicans protect their language is nothing compared to the French. Since the mid-seventeenth century, the Académie Française has appointed scholars to codify and purify the language, keeping foreign words out. While maintaining its eloquence, Spanish is more straightforward. Mercifully it is spelled exactly the way it sounds. If you have an inkling of how to pronounce a Spanish word, you cannot misspell it. The French added an *x* to some plural words simply because it looked more elegant when scratched out by a quill. Where the French want their culture to remain French, not influenced by foreigners, Spanish is not so pretentious. The Spanish language promotes formality and eloquence within the culture, but not at the expense of accessibility.

Spanish is not particularly adaptive to new technology, because a new verb has to be conjugated into sixteen tenses. Nouns are not quite so difficult. For example, the names for all the parts of an automobile exist in Castilian Spanish, in Spain, where English has much less influence. But the Mexicans find it more convenient to use *cloch, brekes, mofle,* and *wayín* (station wagon). This doesn't mean that we are smarter because we invented all the terms that they use, nor are we necessarily better mechanics or engineers. It's just that they have more linguistic hurdles to jump. So, in the north of Mexico and the south of Texas, you will hear conversations that include many English words. "*Yo voy al* shoe store *para comprar unos* sandals"—"I'm going to the shoe store to buy some . . . ," you've got it.

Formal versus informal: hey "you"

Spanish also makes a distinction between the familiar and the formal forms of *you*. No matter who you are, or what the setting, there is no simple answer to how I address you. Spanish requires a distinction. You must choose between the formal *Usted* (always capitalized) that comes from *Vuestra Merced,* meaning "your mercy," or the informal *tú,* usually reserved for friends, equals, pets, and children.

In Mexico, the answer to which form of *you* to employ when a young police officer pulls you over for speeding is wrapped in hierarchical ritual that even takes into account what kind of car you are driving. As a means of addressing many nuances of hierarchy and avoiding insult or slight with regard to age, status, and authority gaps, Spanish speakers have developed an indirect manner of speaking. More on that later.

In doing business, you will find that the formality of Mexico's Spanish heritage remains in full force. And nowhere is traditional etiquette more exhaustively on display than in the language of business letters. Not long ago, a correct sign-off was *Quedamos de Ustedes afectuosísimos seguros que estrechan su mano*. Literally, this means, "We remain so affectionately certainly yours, that we extend our hands." English translation: Sincerely.

The other side of this coin is that our informality can shock Mexicans. A Mexican would never refer to a bodily function or private part in business discourse. Conversely, some gringos don't think they are credible unless they throw in a "shit" for good measure. Not only will you find that, as a practice, "kicking ass" doesn't work, but saying that you are going to "kick ass" can bring work to a halt.

Sounding grrrr-uff

Echoing across the linguistic divide are marked differences in the actual sounds of English and Spanish. In contrast to the guttural, harsh, consonant-ridden syllables of English, Spanish is rich in soft, more mellifluous vowels. In a moment of rare directness, my Mexican personnel manager once told me that "rough draft" sounded to her like a dog barking. Because our language is replete with more abrasive sounds than the Mexican ear is accustomed to, it is important to compensate for the impression that we are gruff.

To put differences between English and Spanish into context, consider the following aspects of other languages. Okay, I'm going to pick on the French again. But what other culture has so studiously manipulated its language to distinguish itself from those who would pretend to be erudite? French pronunciation is an impossible combination of Frankish German, Parisian invention, and High Latin. Their *r* is a unique, back-of-the-throat, supra-glottal stop. Their *u* is impossible for an Anglo-Saxon to pronounce without feeling that he has crossed over into some bizarre sexual practice. However, speaking Spanish with the Mexicans does not require any facial contortions. The vowels are the same for the most part. And aside from an occasional, front-loaded roll of a double *r*, you're home free—even in Monterrey.

English is a consonant-rich language, and consonants, we now know, are processed on the left side of our brains, where analysis occurs. You might conclude from this that there is a difference in how we think based on whether our language is consonant-rich (left-brained and analytical) or vowel-rich like Spanish (right-brained and emotional). Linguists will tell you that there is something to that observation, though it's dangerous to oversimplify.

Around the world in eighty seconds

A quick sampling of what language reveals about other cultures puts our observations about Spanish and English into context. At the risk of inviting a United Nations armed force of *patois* police, we can generalize that Germans can be painstakingly precise and analytical. So is their language. Loaded with consonants, it is processed on the left, analytical side of the brain. Because nouns are concatenated, you can't have your car break down on the autobahn and simply ask for a "mechanic." They will look at you like you are an unwashed dolt. What kind of mechanic? There are *dieselmechaniche, feinmechaniche,* and an array of others. You must be explicit, or you are delivering only half of a thought. Your reaction to this overprecision may be to say, "To hell with it—gimme a screwdriver and I'll fix it myself!" They would reply, "Vat kinda shkrewdriver? Ve got shkinnybobsshkrewdriver, fatbobsshkrewdriver. . . ." They are not being difficult; the exactitude is required by their language. I would argue that this quality has fostered generations of superior engineers and machinists.

Italian, firing up the emotional hemisphere, is even more vowel-rich than Spanish. Furthermore, everything in Italian rhymes with *eh!* Is it any wonder they are lovers and singers!? (But don't be misled—a list of science magnates would not be complete without Fermi, Bernoulli, Galileo, and others.)

Chinese is a vowel-poor language. With a limited number of possible sounds, Chinese uses tones of voice to change the meaning of words. The sound *ma* has four meanings: "mother," "horse," "question," and "freckle." By changing the tone, you change the word. Is it any wonder they limit raising and lowering their voices when expressing emotions? You could end up insulting somebody's mother rather than going giddyap. In English, we add emphasis to change the meaning. For example, "*Where* did you get that?"; "Where did *you* get that?"; and "Where did you get *that?*" all use the same words but have different meanings. The Chinese language doesn't allow for this. As a result, Chinese is more suited to transmitting content than emotion. By contrast, the construction of Spanish facilitates the transmission of emotions. Moreover, the way Mexicans "sing" their Spanish expresses emotions on a unique level, even within the Hispanic world.

Words fail

The sonority of Spanish makes it especially well suited for conveying warm feelings. In fact, certain emotions can be expressed in Spanish for which we have no equivalent words in English. There is no true translation for *cariño,* with its sweet vowel sounds and softened *ñ.* The closest expression we have is "love gift," but it doesn't come close to *cariño* in melding feeling with sound. When Mexicans send someone flowers, they do it *con cariño,* or lovingly.

The sentiment of Spanish words is so wrapped up in sounds that Spanish/Mexican songs are impossible to translate into English without losing their emotional impact, just as you lose a lot translating Shakespeare into German. In Hamlet's soliloquy, "slings and arrows" (Anglo-Saxon words) contrast with "of outrageous fortune" (French root words), transmitting a cacophony that emphasizes Hamlet's angst. This linguistic trait is lost when Shakespeare is translated. Similarly, Mexican songs suffer from translation because the sonority is lost. "*Ya sola frente a la iglesia, Y llorando, Ante el Cristo . . . fui a implorar. Al contemplar mi tristeza, El crucifijo de piedra, También se puso a llorar*" is translated as, "There alone in front of the church crying before Christ, I began to plead, and upon seeing my sadness, the stone crucifix also began to cry." I cannot say for certain that because the Spanish version has fifty one vowels and the English version has thirty-nine vowels in the same number of bars, it proves that Spanish is more laden with emotion. But people who speak Spanish and English fluently will tell you that the Spanish language is better at expressing emotion, that songs in Spanish have more emotional presence. For them, the difference in emotional heft is striking.

Sonority is an issue when speaking. The Mexicans like the sound of a complete, well-rounded answer to a question. Whereas many Anglos are content to give and receive one-word responses, the Spanish speaker prefers a windup, a delivery, and a coda. Ask an American what time it is and she'll say "six." Ask a Mexican what time it is and she'll say the idiomatic equivalent of "The time is exactly six o'clock." The Mexican offers a full, circular response by including the question in the answer, unlike the American who goes straight for the one-word summation. Underlying the Mexican's response is a less hurried sense of time, a predilection for formality, and an unmistakable pleasure in using the language itself. In this sense, the Mexican's answer conveys more than information. It is worth noting that the pattern of circularity crops up again and again in Mexican culture—in the concept of time, the sense of space, and in the construction and use of language.

There are other ways in which disparities in our respective languages point to underlying cultural differences. For example, Spanish provides a nifty conjunction—*sino*—for handling either/or situations. There is no linguistic counterpart in English. "*La tienda no está abierta*, sino *cerrada*," means, "The store is not open (*rather, but, for now*) closed." Whereas conjunctions (*and, but, for, or, nor*) in English force us to resolve contradictions as we speak, and reinforce taking one-way gringo, black-or-white, all-or-nothing sides, Spanish enables the Mexicans to live with contradictions indefinitely. In English, it's either open or closed. In Spanish, it's closed, not open, for now. We need *sino* in the English language.

Spanish sometimes frees its speakers up in a way that English does not. There are tense changes in Spanish that indicate levels of probability. No such phenomenon exists in English. In English, we say, "If I had gone to the movies, I would have invited my friend John." There are two suppositions in that sentence. But both *gone* and *invited* are in the past tense. The native English speaker would have a response like, "Well, you didn't go to the movies, so you didn't invite your friend John. It's over." In Spanish, you would have a tense change from subjunctive to preterit. This linguistic trick highlights the different levels of hypothetical situations. A native Spanish speaker might be left thinking, "Well, you didn't go to the movies, but you might have invited your friend John if you had gone. So stay tuned."

In the Manuel and the gun cabinet incident, you recall that Manuel had trouble interpreting his customer's wishes because the customer used *if, otherwise,* and *either* all in the same breath. With no *sino* and no tense change such as he was accustomed to in Spanish, Manuel didn't know how to untangle the sentence. The customer was asking for a delivery date based on three key decision points. Manuel could not find the continuity in what appeared to the native English speaker to be a very logical request. So the construction of language affects our mental processing. If a concept is difficult to master linguistically, it is difficult to handle intellectually. In English we have no *sino*, and we have difficulty processing contradictions. Mexicans have more complex verb forms for handling hypothetical situations and have trouble with our insistence on choosing one definitive mood.

Family ties

As an integral part of the language, the free flow of honorifics in Spanish reinforces relationships. Nowhere is this more evident than in communication among family. Parents most frequently call their children *hijo* (son) and *hija* (daughter), rather than Jimmy or Jane. Anyone can call a child by name, but only two people in the world can say "son" or "daughter." In this way, the use of language strengthens the family unit.

Later in life come the affectionate appellations heard throughout Mexico—honorifics such as *joven* or *joven señor* (young man or young sir). A young woman is very keen to be called *Usted* (you, formal) instead of *tú* (you, the child.) Later in life she is *señorita* (miss) until she becomes *señora*. *Señora* has two translations in English. It means "Mrs." or it means something akin to "woman of respect." The latter use of *senora* is restricted to women of a certain age who have achieved a station in life—a forty-something shop owner, a female manager, or a pharmacist. But in any case, the *señora* may not be married at all. Such expressions as "*Usted, su servidor*" (your servant, meaning *me*) and *Don* (a title of courtesy) continue to be common. A longtime labor leader who has no meaningful professional designation may be called *Don Jaime* to distinguish him from the other Jaimes. We have no such titles in English.

In Colombia, at the age of seven, I was called a *caballero.* I knew it had something to do with horses, and, hearing it for the first time, I wasn't sure I liked it. When the meaning was clarified—literally "horseman," figuratively "gentleman"—I knew it was intended respectfully and it made me feel grown-up. It also distinguished me from the workers at the country club. Even then, I wasn't sure that was good. Just how was I being categorized? What was the deeper meaning? Nowhere is the power of language felt more acutely than when it affects one's sense of identity.

That great American "no ho"

Given the considerable differences between English and Spanish, what happens when we write and speak each other's languages? How does it change us? Generally, Mexicans do extremely well with English. But many difficulties in pronunciation stem from complicated spellings in English.

English was codified when William Caxton printed the first dictionary in England in the 1500s. He spelled words the way they sounded to him. For a time, his spellings remained the standard. But the language was pronounced differently from shire to shire, and vowel shifts that began in Old German have been carried down to current English usage. *Bakker* became *becker,* which became *baker*. Even today, *baker* is pronounced one way in Grand Rapids (a tight, short *a*) and another way in Biloxi (a loose, diphthong *eye-ai*.) Vowels became diphthongal and were a sliding mush that nobody knew how to spell. Today, we have a spelling that is deemed acceptable, but the standards are hard to find, which continues to make spelling a challenge in English. A simple expression like "know-how," which seems easy enough to pronounce and to spell—that is, if you speak English—is actually a problem for most foreigners. There is a diphthong lurking in each word: *know* is "no-u-w", and *how* is "h-a-o-u-w." I once heard a German patent attorney, eager to use his English, pronounce it "now how." And then there was the Mexican engineer who complimented Americans on their "no ho."

One woman's cushions are another man's . . .

And how do we Americans do with Spanish? If you are strongly analytical like my left-brained wife, you may have trouble getting your Spanish vowels right. While setting up our house in Mexico, she had the upholsterer, *Señor Picaso,* re-cover some sofa cushions—*co-ji-nes*. When she went to pick them up, she asked how he was doing with the *co-jo-nes* (Spanish vernacular for testicles). *Sr. Picaso* turned crimson. One innocent little vowel mistake almost cost the poor man his life. A little imp on my shoulder told me to make my wife's existence a living hell. To further confuse her, I told her that the word for "dresser drawers" is *ca-jo-nes*. A few months later when *Sr. Picaso* came to the house to pick up a loveseat along with some throw pillows that I had put in the dresser drawer, my wife resorted to sign language. To this day, she avoids talking about certain household items.

The following are four points about our respective languages that provide additional insight into Mexican culture.

1. In English we derive words for objects or actions from the sounds they make. Saying "bang," "crash," and "boom" are reiterations of the sounds, not definitions like "explosion," "collision," and "implosion." We use such sounds (onomatopoeia) liberally. Mexicans rarely do, and certainly not in business meetings. Such expressions are the stuff of barroom chatter.

2. Mexican Spanish differs from Spanish in Colombia or Spain in its use of many local Nahuatl (Aztec language) words. I traveled to Mexico once with my Spanish friend, Theo. He tried to order a sandwich like one he had enjoyed a few days earlier, but he didn't know the Mexican words. Much to his dismay, I had to intercede. Here's a sophisticated Spaniard who can't even order a sandwich. Turn it around and you see that Mexicans don't exactly appreciate how the Spanish speak either. It can be a mistake to assume that if you hire a Colombian, Chilean, or Argentinean to manage your sales office, he or she will be successful by virtue of being a native Spanish speaker. In fact, the Spanish in particular don't mix well with the Mexicans, expressly because of their language use. Although Mexicans love the "mother culture," the Castilians, with their noses in the air, their lisped z's and c's, and their more extreme brand of formality, actually irritate the hell out of the Mexicans—and that's hard to do.

3. As delivered in Mexico, Spanish often has a singsong quality. Unlike any other Spanish-speaking country, Mexicans—especially lower-class people in the South—sing their language. You have heard this in caricature in the Speedy Gonzalez cartoons. Sometimes Mexicans will add syllables just to complete the song. "*Que hay?*" ("What's up?") becomes "*Que hubo?*" and then becomes "*Que hubole?*" just to make it sound more musical. In the North, this quality is generally seen as déclassé.

4. There is a general distinction in the Spanish-speaking world between cosmopolitan and rural usage. Businesspeople from Mexico City, Bogotá, Barcelona, Santiago, and other major metropolitan areas have little trouble understanding each other, though some words are different. But once you get outside the metropolitan areas, among the working class, the language becomes more remote, devolving into local usage and references. It is very difficult for a Spaniard from Cuenca to communicate with a Mexican from Jojutla. This, too, is a function of education and exposure.

What kind of pond?

The following example illustrates differences in how Americans and Mexicans use our respective languages. It also reflects how Americans can scuttle the language when it suits our purposes, whereas Mexicans uphold the precision of language to a fault.

I took Tom, facilities director for a multibillion-dollar U.S. company, to an industrial park outside of Querétaro to hear a sales pitch. The Mexican sales manager spoke English well. "Of course, we have a good drainage system," he assured Tom. "So what's your coverage requirement?" Tom asked. (Industrial park restrictions usually let you build on 50 percent of the land you buy. Use more and you create a rain runoff problem for your neighbor.) "Here, it's 70 percent coverage," the sales manager said positively. "This means you can build on more of your land than elsewhere." Then, he added with a smile, "Of course you have to have a runoff pond." With this, Tom shot back abruptly, "I don't care about the f***ing pond. That's a no-brainer. We can put it anywhere. We always put in a f***ing pond."

At this point, the industrial park's chief engineer, who had been quietly standing by, spoke up cheerfully, "No problem." Then, in his best school-taught English, he added innocently, "You can put the *fawkeen pond* either in the front or the back." He had no idea what he had said. He was simply trying to please.

Direct versus indirect speech

One of the key language use differences between Americans and Mexicans involves direct versus indirect speech. The tendency of Mexicans to use indirect forms of speech puts our listening skills to the test. In case you can't explain to yourself where problems in communications arise, the answer frequently lies in these two distinct styles of expression. Gringos generally have a very direct style of stating things. Here's an easy example. An American says, "Oops, you got some salsa on your tie." Mexicans, on the other hand, tend to use the indirect approach: "Oops, your tie got some salsa on it," or "Oops, some salsa got on your tie." The way we put it, *you* are a dirty little boy. The way the Mexicans put it, the culprit is either the tie or the salsa. How many times have you said, "Jimmy, you got peanut butter on your shirt," only to have him deny it? Try this: "Son, your shirt got some peanut butter on it."

The gringo says, "Don't go near the water!" The Mexican hears a direct order and wonders, "Does the American think I'm too stupid to think for myself?" How would the Mexicans have put it? They would have stated the same concept more delicately and more indirectly: "Be careful of the water, it can be dangerous." Rather than imply that you can't think, they would choose to vilify the water. They learn this polite approach to deflecting any hint of blame at a very early age and transfer it to all kinds of situations. Everything in Mexico is ratcheted one click toward the more polite.

You'll begin to recognize the pattern. Someone asks, "Is George a good worker?" The American responds, "No, he couldn't do the job if his life depended on it." The Mexican is thinking, "If you slam him when he's not here, what do you say about me when my back is turned?" How might the Mexican have responded? Question: "Is he a good worker?" Answer: "He tries *very hard*." But the gringo has to listen carefully and read between the lines, because what the Mexican is really saying is that this poor fellow couldn't do the job if his life depended on it.

The American states bluntly, "I need this information, and it should be public anyway." This is like saying to the Mexican, "Where I come from, we do things right, so get off your duff and act like me." The more effective, indirect approach is, "This information would be most useful because the project is scheduled for launch in early May." In this way, you are trading information, not demanding a one-way gift. Exchanges are politely brokered in Mexico, not thrown at each other.

If we were raised using more *in*direct speech around the house, we would be better at picking up the true meaning of Mexicans' statements. But we aren't. That may be why we have to take courses on how to be good listeners.

A few more examples. Question: "Is he a dependable supplier?" The American would respond sarcastically, "Yeah, if quality, price, and delivery don't matter!" What he has conveyed to the Mexican is that you have to be a horse's keister to ask a question like that. Here's a better approach. Question: "If I were to use him as a supplier, what should I expect?" This will elicit a more honest answer from your Mexican friend. Answer: "You can expect him to be late most of the time. At first his quality will be good, but watch out later." If you ask the same question directly, your Mexican friend may say, "He is very sincere." "Sincere" in this context is the kiss of death, though the mean-what-you-say American may not recognize it. The message, while indirect, will be clearly understood by another Mexican.

Once you are attuned to the insights that language provides, you will discover endless connections with the culture on your own. The more you study the language, the better you will understand the people. Ultimately, however, it is not speaking, *sino* listening that determines cultural fluency.

The power of words

- Take your time. Feel free to talk all around a subject. You are not judged by how economically you can express yourself. On the contrary, taking time to roll out a complete thought is seen as an act of caring. If asked a question, don't answer "yes." Answer "Yes, I do love Mexican food, and I am always surprised by the regional variation." Or "Yes, we do make excellent propellers, but we try to make them with as little scrap as possible." Rather than being taken as unnecessarily loquacious, a Mexican would feel respected because you took the time to explain.

  Researchers have actually measured the words and syllables used in English and Spanish to express equivalent meaning, and Spanish requires 10 percent more words to convey the same meaning. The next time you unpack the instruction sheet with a purchase, compare the copy in English and Spanish, and I'll bet the Spanish will be longer. Expressing yourself fully in Spanish simply requires more words, so slow down and enjoy the process.

- Make your questions gracious and polite. You will hear Mexicans use expressions like *"no me explico porqué . . . ,"* which means, "I can't explain to myself why. . . ." This takes the onus off of the speaker for not making something clear. When we fail to understand, we are likely to tersely ask why. This leaves the Mexican feeling like he is at fault for not explaining himself adequately.

- Make use of the Spanish vocabulary you already have. Spanish shares Latin roots with a long list of English business, law, and administrative words derived from the French. In fact, virtually all words that end in *-tion* in English can be pronounced with a Spanish accent and be understood by Spanish-only speakers. Unfortunately, with our penchant for trashing five-dollar words, we miss a huge opportunity to communicate effectively with Mexicans. As an exercise, make two columns on a sheet. Put a simple word in the left column and an equivalent *-tion* word in the right column. Your lists may include: *ask/question; rain/precipitation; flying/aviation; bringing in/importation; country/nation; law/regulation; hope/expectation.* These may not translate into perfect Spanish, but the longer words will be understood. Further, in Spanish, all words that end in *-ción* are feminine.

Therefore, it's *la constitución, la nación, la absolución, la definición, la reconciliación, la declaración,* etc. In turn, any English, French, Italian, or Portuguese (i.e., Romance language) speaker would understand those Spanish words. There are some ten thousand such examples that you can use as building blocks.

- Sound relaxed. Mexicans tend to speak in a drawn-out fashion. Especially in business situations, Americans talk faster because we're more driven by the clock. We tend to engage in fewer overtures, to shorten everything, and to get right to the point, as in "Get it? Got it. Good." Because we feel hurried ourselves, we try to take as little of the other person's time as possible and to compact as much meaning into the shortest phrase we can. This pressure cooker style has contaminated our personal communications as well.

- Soften your tone. Typically, Americans are unaware of how they sound to others. Especially in business situations, we use language primarily to convey facts. Intentionally or unintentionally, we also convey that we are curt, tough, decision-oriented, and can get the job done. By contrast, our polite southern neighbors use language to convey their *willingness* to get the job done.

Putting It All Together

When you're out there in the trenches, you won't be dealing with cultural differences one at a time. They'll be coming at you as combination punches. And let's face it, you're going to be frustrated. In spite of all you've absorbed, you are still likely to think that your experience in Mexico will play out pretty much the way it would here. As a rule, don't expect things to go the way they would in the United States.

Ducks in a row

Let's say you're visiting Kokomo, Indiana, for the first time to set up an electronics plant that services the automotive industry. Operating within your own culture, you've got a logical game plan in your head, a realistic timetable, and a sense of how people will react. First, you get the name of an individual in the state government. Your Hoosier contact may call you with an update before your anticipated arrival. He has accomplished four of six tasks you have asked of him, and he hopes to have the rest done by the time you arrive. You prepare an agenda and send a summary of your project ahead of time so that your contact can prepare for your arrival with other appointments, data, and the like. You meet with the Indiana Development Authority, who puts some preliminary data in your hands. After your preliminary meeting, you visit the local government bookstore or library and pay $60 for some studies. You go to the county and get an aerial photo of a target property. You meet two Realtors for a windshield tour. You're done. Your ducks are in a row. You have binders of data that signal to everyone that you are a studious and analytical type with an ability to get things done.

The meaning of yes

Now here's what's likely to transpire in Mexico. You call the contact. He is very open and apparently eager to receive you. Graciously, he says that yes, he will be delighted to meet with you, and your summary of information will be most helpful. Sending it by fax will be fine. With eloquence and formality, he assures you in mellifluous English that yes, he will prepare for your visit and take care of everything—information, appointments, and the rest. You are confident that you will hit the ground running. Wrong. You arrive and nothing has been done.

The fax is buried somewhere under a pile. You are concerned and frustrated because you know that you have only five days in Monterrey, and it takes time to set up appointments. What will you do for the next two days? What went wrong? Why didn't your contact pull together the data he said he would? At least you could have read it by the pool. And why didn't he call you with an update? He confirmed the meeting, but he has done absolutely nothing to advance the purpose of your visit.

Okay, here's what happened. First, he said yes several times and you believed him. He agreed with you because he knew that his job was to receive you and pave the way for you. He was not lying. In his mind, he *was* paving the way. But he was really saying, "Yes, I will help you obtain information." By "information," he doesn't mean statistical reports or raw data, which, to him, are unreliable. He believes that he can only provide meaningful information after you are there, in person, when he has a better understanding of your project.

All the cultural set pieces of time, space, and language are operating beneath the surface: The lack of urgency—matters can wait until you arrive; the insistence on closeness of contact—action won't be taken long distance. Furthermore, your Mexican contact has been *indirect* in his method of telling you what he will do, and to add one more piece to the puzzle, he will not turn over anything to you until you offer something in return. In the real world, you will find a surprise in Mexico every day. This being only your fifth trip, you hadn't figured out until now that for the Mexican—and this is important—information is not processed, it is brokered.

In order to obtain data, first you have to meet face-to-face with the right person and explain your project. Then your respondent will reciprocate, not just with data, but with additional information of his own. For example, it's important for the Mexicans to know that you will need three hundred employees for the coming fiscal year, and that you will have to rent a facility that's 50,000 square feet. If you had pressed your contact as to what data he would pull together before your arrival, he would probably have responded that you should not worry, that he would take care of everything. But, you must understand what that means. You should plan on meeting with him first, allow a grace period of maybe two days to pass, and then follow up. Whereas we are satisfied with state-level data on Kokomo and feel that we can extrapolate the information we need, in fact, data on Nuevo León does little good without the insights that locals can provide. Data in Mexico is not always reliable. Moreover, Mexicans don't trust data unless they surround it with opinion and subjective observation. This stems from their cultural view that something has meaning only in context. (More on context and contextuality in Chapter 12.)

Typically, having spent the first morning meeting with your contact and reiterating what was already in your fax, he tells you that the person who can *really* provide the information you need is the director general of foreign investment for the state of Nuevo León. He calls to set up the appointment for later that afternoon. Meeting with some resistance, he schmoozes the secretary with a gentle "*no seas malita*"—don't be naughty—and she puts him right through. The meeting is set for 4:00.

You and your contact go to lunch. Lunch lasts three hours. You go to the director's office in the afternoon and wait another forty minutes. By now it's almost 5:00. The first day is done, and you have nothing to show for your time and effort. You lit the fuse back in Chicago, and now your brain is about to explode.

If you are patient enough, you will meet with the director, discuss the project again, and in about an hour you'll be on your way with the data you need, plus some other very useful information. You have gained an important contact and support at the highest level. In fact, you are further along the curve than you would have been in Indiana. In your gringo perception of lines in time, it took you forever to arrive at step one, and you worried the entire time as to whether you would get anything at all out of your efforts. Now you've achieved step two. After agonizing that Zeno's arrow would never reach the speeding rabbit, suddenly you're swaddled in fur.

The director general has given you a list of industrial parks, a copy of the federal labor law, and a copy of a wage and salary study. This is all very useful data to you. But it is merely data. To this he will now add his personal insights. Why? Because you have given him information about how many workers you will need. He values this exchange since he is interested in bring-ing jobs to his state. He wants your project to be successful. Not only does he tell you where workers live, but how far they are willing to travel to get to work. He advises you on how to cut through the red tape with the city gov-ernment. He adds to the published information he has handed you by dis-cussing company benefits that are not part of the wage survey. He suggests two or three good contractors to retrofit your space. He volunteers what hotels offer the best value and where the good restaurants are. He promises to put you in contact with other Americans who have done similar projects and to introduce you to two industrial park owners. He gives you the address and phone number of the private company that provides aerial photos. He tells you not to waste time looking on the west side of town because the water you need is not available there. You won't find out that tidbit from the water department. "No problem—we got water. Where do you want it?" All of this is most useful and will save you significant time downstream.

At the end of the day (not that 6:00 is the end of the day in Mexico), you have more meaningful information than you could have dreamed of in repayment for your patience and effort. During the process, you may have felt whipsawed, but ultimately going along with *their* approach at *their* pace has paid off splendidly. As your project moves ahead, you will see that you can set up a plant in Mexico as fast as you can in Indiana. It's just that the time sequence will be different. And yes never really meant yes, but you are on course . . . more or less.

The space and time thing again

So why can't you accomplish anything meaningful by fax or e-mail? Because in Mexico you have to enter their space. You have to establish a relationship. There is simply no substitute for direct contact. Initially, it's fine to make a phone call as a means of introducing yourself or making an appointment, then follow up with a fax. But if a piece of paper is all they receive, you don't really exist. They don't *know* you. Doing business by phone can be cold unless you have already built a relationship. This is not easy for an Anglo to feel in his or her gut, because no matter where we go, we carry a little circle around ourselves, and the individual remains important. But in Mexico, being part of an interacting relationship is supremely meaningful. It is not until you meet face-to-face that they recognize you, your needs, and what you have to offer in return. Until you arrive in person, *no hay negocio*—there is no business to be done.

While you are there, you will want to spend your time wisely. If you don't, you may not get a response to your later follow-up fax. When you go to lunch, you can be an ugly gringo and cross-examine your contact about why he didn't set up the meeting with the director general in the morning. You can telegraph your displeasure by glancing at your watch, knitting your brow, and punctuating your declarations with your index finger. Or, you can take your watch off and enjoy your meal and the company.

Doing business in Mexico has been likened to a mating ritual. What you want to do is chat up the relationship the way a man and a woman would in this country, rather than going for the gold on the first meeting. By using your face-to-face time effectively, learning instead of teaching, and speaking with a relaxed, softened delivery, you can increase your chances of success. Building relationships this way will guarantee that after you leave, you will not be forgotten. Your follow-up communications will be productive.

After you've been through a few experiences on the ground in Mexico, you'll be more sensitive to what's going on under the surface. You'll feel more relaxed. You've gotten a grip on your one-way gringo mentality, and you're discovering on your own that your business rituals are not necessarily better or worse than theirs.

Turning the tables

One of the false assumptions Americans have about Mexico is that foreign direct investment is a one-way street—Americans' capital flowing south of the border. In fact, there are many examples of Mexicans investing in the United States. Imagine that a Mexican company wants to set up an automotive stamping plant in Indiana. Not knowing any Americans personally, Roberto Garza, the president, contacts the Mexican trade commissioner in Chicago, who is extremely helpful and provides a telephone introduction to the director of economic development in the Indiana state government. So far, so good: Mexicans dealing with Mexicans are working with the same cultural set pieces.

But as soon as Señor Garza begins to interact on his own with the Americans, things start to go sour. When he calls the state director to confirm his appointment and invites him to lunch, the American tells him he can't make lunch but agrees to meet at 9:15 A.M. Tuesday, along with his industrial development manager, who is also on the phone. Before they have even met face-to-face, the manager asserts, "I know exactly what you need. I'll get you a manufacturer's directory, a demographic study, and a wage survey." When Señor Garza inquires politely if it would be possible to meet with the president of the drivetrain plant in Kokomo, the manager replies, "I'll work on it."

When Garza arrives at his hotel in the United States, he gets a call from the manager who informs him that he has four of the six tasks completed, but to rest assured that all will be prepared by the time of his arrival. (Could anyone doubt his efficiency?)

At the meeting in Indiana, Roberto Garza is met by the industrial development manager, who has set up appointments with the county surveyor's office, a construction company, a freight forwarder, and a real estate broker. But, for various reasons, he has substituted an antenna plant for the drivetrain plant. After a PowerPoint presentation on the economic development of Indiana, the manager tells Garza how to get to all the offices. He says that if the Mexican will give him more notice in the future, he can arrange a meeting with the director of economic development. "If you think of anything else, just give me a call." Glancing at his watch, the manager assures Bob that he has plenty of time. "Your first appointment is only three minutes away." Being adept at sales, the manager offers the next step, "We'll stay in touch by phone, and we'll have to have dinner sometime."

There will be no parties, no lunches, and no real exchange of personal interests or peripheral information—just three reports and a bill. According to U.S. conventions, the American did everything right. But statistics and reports are only so much paper. The bill was to be expected, but was abruptly presented. And the quick pace left no time for discussion.

The Mexican goes home and unburdens himself about how cold Americans are:

> Nobody takes the time to talk about the big picture. Instead, they kick me downstairs to the people who answer technical questions. They don't take the time to guide me through the maze. All Americans know is what's on paper, and they are anxious to give me a bill. Everything has a price in the U.S. Cut-and-dried. Efficient, but chilly. They even tracked me down to give me the bad news that they didn't have all my needs met. What was the reason for that, anyway?

As a Mexican with a different sense of time, Garza believes that the Americans were too quick to cut him off. They sized him up in forty-five seconds and decided how much attention to give him. His desire to meet with the director of economic development was not fulfilled because he hadn't given them enough advance notice. Though he knew it wasn't a personal slight, he was never received by anyone on his level. He felt uncomfortable when they called him Bob. What's more, because the manager looked him straight in the eye with a smile when saying goodbye, he got the feeling the American was happy to see him leave.

Staying in touch by phone sounds hollow to a Mexican. And "Let's have dinner sometime" is one of those gringo tricks he knows all about. His more experienced colleagues have told him that Americans always invite you to dinner, but they don't really mean it.

The Americans told him yes, they had just what he needed; but when he got back and read over the data, he realized that it did not include the GM plant wages that his project calculations depended on. He did not know who to call to help him with his data dilemma. Furthermore, the gringos did business with him by fax before he even got there. "These people treat me like everybody else. Do they even respect me?" He feels stymied with less than the required information, and he is reluctant to call the manager back for fear that the manager will say he should have asked for the GM wages ahead of time. When, he wonders, could he ever have had the time to explain to his hosts that a visit to the drivetrain plant was important to a metal stamping operation, whereas antennae have nothing to do with his business. To the Mexican CEO, doing business has elements of a courtship, and in this situation, the love dance is not going well. If the Americans had seemed less hurried, engaged in more discussion, positioned him with equals, and shown a bit more formality in their communications, he would have left with a positive impression—both about the Americans and himself. Instead, he feels he has met with a lack of respect. And respect is of consummate importance to the Mexican.

Mexicans come to the United States and complain that they meet with a lack of respect. We go to Mexico and complain that we meet with a lack of efficiency. Both of these reactions reflect a lack of cultural understanding. Could it be that our frustrations are a result of failing to see how underlying cultural phenomena effect our work styles?

Winners and losers

Achieving cultural fluency can determine success or failure. I once sent an associate, Kelly, to Guadalajara and Querétaro to do a wage and salary survey for a major Dutch client. Kelly was a thirty-year-old economist and a graduate of American University, who had spent five years in Spain and Portugal working for an economic research firm. She understood her mission well and was eager to know Mexico. She seemed to be a very agreeable, flexible person. I gave her some contact names and helped to set up the first few appointments.

The meetings in Guadalajara went well, but her main appointment in Querétaro fell through. Despite a bout with a stomach bug, she pressed on, making her own appointments by enlisting the assistance of people in Guadalajara with whom she had developed relationships the week before. When Kelly returned, she handed me a completed study, speaking in glowing terms about Mexico. Follow-up calls told me that she had been warmly received.

On another project, a client needed to quietly locate medium-sized metal stamping operations that could work with a French third-tier supplier for a Mercedes project. Tom—a graduate of the University of Michigan School of Engineering—was new to me but seemed well qualified since he had spent six years in Mexico working on projects for a first-tier supplier to the auto industry. At that time, he had a staff of three Mexicans who helped him. He loved Mexico and spoke Spanish fairly well.

I set him up for a breakfast meeting with the federal government agency responsible for attracting automotive investment to Mexico. Then he was going to spend a morning at the auto show. I had given him a list of metal stamping operators, with names and phone numbers, and sent him on his way.

The first inkling that something was wrong came when I received his phone call right after the breakfast. "These people don't know anything about the automotive industry," he complained. Later the same day, I got another call. "Why don't we just call Ford Motors and ask who they use?" He had made five phone calls and wasn't getting any cooperation. He had no meetings set up. Then came his final suggestion: "Why don't we just use the Internet!" My attempts to help him think through his situation, reminding him what the client wanted, were met with tense debate. Later that day, I got another call. "I quit!" he explained.

Tom liked Mexicans. He appreciated their history and their cities. But I suspect that throughout his previous assignments in Mexico, he had gotten away with acting like a gringo. He hadn't realized how much he had been relying on the Mexicans around him to interface with other Mexicans. He never came out of his protective cocoon and had not achieved an in-depth understanding of Mexicans. For six years, everybody around him had said yes. Now, representing me, he was on his own—naked and unprepared. He is one of the reasons for this book.

Language was not the critical issue for Kelly or Tom. Knowing their métier was not a problem. Managing intercultural relationships was the single biggest challenge. Both these Americans had lived and worked outside the country, and, in fact, Tom knew Mexico better than Kelly. The critical difference was that Kelly had achieved cultural fluency, Tom had not. Even after six years in Mexico, he expected the Mexicans to be like us—the "scratch under the skin and you'll find a white guy" mind-set. He failed to see how Mexicans were prepared to help him. Because he was frustrated, he fell back on the way he had always done business—in other words, on strategies that were unproductive in Mexico. I think Tom suspected he was not going to succeed. That was the good news. In my follow-up calls, nobody ever mentioned him—not once! When we misbehave, often we don't realize we've been politely snubbed until it's too late.

Most of us have to work hard at cultural fluency. Even when we try to adapt our styles to accommodate another culture, when under stress, our cultural backup behaviors kick in. We become impatient, remote, and blunt—and we know now that those traits come from our cultural sense of time, space, and use of language.

We must remind ourselves that our hosts are not trying to annoy us or destroy us. They are not necessarily corrupt. They are not inefficient, and it's not that they just "don't get it." If tuning in to another culture doesn't come naturally, if we are not intuitively multidimensional, we can at least learn to manage intercultural relationships through a disciplined, instructional approach—one that touches upon all the important steps. Knowing what is going on under the surface is the first step. The second, and the subject of Part II, involves practicing basic intercultural work skills. The patience is still up to you.

Muchas vueltas

When going to Mexico, I am always frustrated, concerned, and fretful. I am spending time and money hearing platitudes and promises, with no initial results. I must say, sometimes it takes all the discipline and tricks I can muster. *"Hay que dar muchas vueltas en Mexico,"* goes the saying—"In Mexico, you have to go around and around." But in the end, I have very rarely been disappointed. I constantly remind myself that the underlying differences in time, space, and use of language that contribute to my frustration are tightly woven into a culture that has held together for many more centuries than ours. There is much to be learned from working with the Mexicans. In visit after visit, project after project, the Mexicans have gone far beyond expectations to assure me that my needs and those of my clients are properly served. For these reasons and many more, I always come away respecting the Mexicans.

PART II

Working with Mexicans

Work is the essential economic activity of any society. Analyzing how people work and why they work the way they do is fundamental to understanding a culture and to working well together. The factory floor provides a useful microcosm.

Individual versus Group-Oriented Work Styles

Having steeped yourself in the cultural differences between Mexicans and Americans, and having acquired a few tools, you embark on your first assignment south of the border. As you touch down in Mexico City, the nuances of all you've learned—the cultural set pieces—are buzzing in your head. You know there will be hurdles, bumps in the road, but you're ready. How hard can this be?

Individuality meets solidarity at the reception desk

Throughout some minor confusion at the airport while claiming your bags, and an interminable cab ride to the heart of downtown, you've kept your cool. You can't wait to meet the management and workers at the plant the following morning. You enter the upscale hotel. There are four or five people ahead of you checking in at the reception desk. You wait your turn without so much as glancing at your watch, then confidently step up to the counter. Behind the marble divide, impeccably attired, bright-eyed, energetic employees shuffle back and forth, yet not one will give you full time and attention. Just as your blood pressure starts to rise, Marta, whose English is infinitely better than your Spanish, gives you a big smile and says, "Good evening, señor. Welcome to the hotel Buena Vista." You say, "Good evening, I have a reservation. The name is Magoo." "Yes, sir. Is that with an *M*?"

Marta goes to the computer to call up your reservation. Just then, the phone rings. "Oh, yes, Señor Alvarez, your fax came in this afternoon." Yackety-yak. Marta motions to Jaime who has just walked in, and, pointing in your direction tells him, "This gentleman would like to check in."

Jaime's English isn't as good as Marta's, but he intones a mellifluous, "Good afternoon, señor. May I help you?"

You respond, "I'm checking in."

Jaime says, "Yes, señor, and what is the name on your reservation, please?"

You tell him, "Magoo. M-A-G-O-O."

Jaime responds, "Just a minute, señor. Hello, housekeeping? Is number 433 ready? No? How about number 447? No, I'll wait." To you, smiling, "Just one moment, señor."

At this point, a not-so-little old lady with an abrasive Midwest accent rolls over your insteps with her Samsonite luggage and pushes up to the counter, interjecting, "I just have a quick question. When does the shuttle leave for the airport?"

Putting the phone to his lapel, Jaime launches into a protracted discussion with her about the schedule—how to get the shuttle, where to get it, describing in great detail the airport terminal locations and layout, the baggage requirements, etc. Then in walks his coworker, Eulalia. "Eulalia, could you please help this gentleman with his registration and his credit card?"

Eulalia says, "Good evening, señor, and what is your name?" By now you are totally burned. You've barely landed in Mexico and you're so hacked you want to spell Magoo with an *F*. You are seething. You are shaking mad. You are thinking, "Cheez, if this is what it's like checking into a hotel, how am I going to make it through two months of straightening out production on the factory floor?"

This is your first test, and you're ready to shout orders and give these misguided clerks a quick lesson in Anglo efficiency. But you don't. You know better. Anyway, they wouldn't understand. Instead, trying to keep your voice from cracking, you squeeze a mild objection through clenched teeth, "Could one of you just *please* take care of me?" Eulalia, Jaime, and Marta turn in unison. "But *señor*, we *are* taking care of you."

Okay, here's what really happened. You were just hit with a combination punch: the Mexican sense of space, with the Mexican sense of time, and the Mexican group-oriented work style. And all you had to defend yourself with was your individuality and your Anglo-Saxon sense of efficiency.

With regard to space, you were on one side of the counter, and they were on the other. On their side, they see themselves as a cohesive group—the reception clerks. They also see you as part of a group—the guests. All of you are standing in the space where guests stand in order to get help. In keeping with the Mexican sense of time, you have no special priority simply because you were there first. Remember, to them, time is a river. You are all going in the same direction and will arrive at more or less the same time. Like a river, sometimes things go fast, sometimes they go slowly. In the desk clerks' minds, all of the described events are happening at the same time, not in logical sequence. When the not-so-little old lady asks a question, they *have* to answer. Not to answer would be disrespectful. (In circular, flexible time, many things can happen at once, not in serial order.) Recognizing that good service requires it, they quickly get their coworker to intercede with you. As for the Mexican dynamics of group orientation, they see no reason that all three of them shouldn't be involved in helping all three, or six, of you. And it doesn't seem unusual to the clerks that you and the other guests are all being helped at the same time. They are a group and you are a group. *Their* group is helping *your* group.

Why is this so hard for us to get through our heads? Why are we still feeling uneasy? It's simple. We're thinking, "There should be a line. Why isn't there a line? Can't they see that it's more efficient if one person stays with a guest throughout the check-in process? Marta should help me, Jaime should handle the phone, and Eu—whatever—can take care of the old lady, who should be made to wait her turn anyhow."

As long as your assessment is based on sequence—that is having the string of clerks mesh their availability with the string of guests in accordance with the order in which the guests arrive in line—you're doomed to frustration. So, go ahead. Try to convince them. Tell them about *your* concept of time, *your* concept of space, *your* concept of customer service, and *your* concept of efficiency. It's better to blow it now and learn your lesson here than on the factory floor. Try telling them to discard all those silly notions and two-thousand-year-old habits that pose a monstrous inconvenience to Americans. Try persuading them to change their ways. Guess what? It won't happen.

From the standpoint of the Mexicans, the worst scenario would be to have one obstreperous clerk take his brass buttons too seriously, step out of the pack, and wreck group harmony. Quickly, the clerks would break into opposing groups, and the team would become dysfunctional. Their rhythm would be broken. Then your experience would be truly intolerable. You wouldn't get checked in within any reasonable time frame. Room 447 would be occupied by a clan of smelly tourists. Nobody would help the old lady, and even Señor Alvarez—that most agreeable frequent guest from Puebla— would be complaining.

The Mexican clerks know exactly what they are doing. They are going to treat the group of guests well and see that they are billeted, sent off, fed, pampered, happy, and tucked into bed in the most efficient way possible. But they are going to do it according to what works in Mexico. A self-absorbed Mexican supervisor or a gringo inflicting his own ideas on the group's work habits will only muck things up. The best approach is to pull back, watch what they do, and observe how the natural patterns unfold. For this and other situations you will encounter, it will help to absorb as many insights as you can into the dynamics of the group-oriented work style.

Group orientation

The American thinks in terms of "I," while the Mexican thinks in terms of "we." Americans are independent people. We draw boundaries around ourselves and are self-referential. We are in too much of a hurry to get our hands on the levers to show what we can do to let some abstract notion like group orientation slow us down. In contrast, Mexicans are strikingly group-oriented, working easily together as a team. They don't break out of the pack or strip any gears if it would upset the harmony of their household, their church, or their workplace. They draw lines around their group and refer inwardly to the group. They converse politely and respectfully and are willing to wait for the slowest among them so that they can all walk together deliberately toward the same goals.

> The American asks, "How am *I* doing?"
> The Mexican asks, "How are *we* doing?"

The American irony

In the United States, we put high value on personal initiative. We appreciate self-starters and reward the worker who comes up with an idea that saves the company money. Yet, we also want people to work together. Many human resource specialists in the United States don't see the irony of our own newspaper ads: "We want self-starters who will work together as a team." So we hire independent go-getters only to bombard them with slogans about teamwork. In the final analysis, we are a nation of individualists who come together to work, perhaps begrudgingly, because we must work together in order to succeed—to beat the competition. As a result, a major contradiction characterizes the typical U.S. workplace.

If you want to know what's wrong with an American company, read its slogans. Listen to the discourse that surrounds the exhortations to the workers. If you hear the word *teamwork* a lot, chances are the group is *not* working well as a team. Let's face it, Americans have to try hard to become team players. Because we're so competitive among ourselves, we're conflicted about working as a team. Our children take Suzuki violin lessons, and we think it's cute to see them playing in unison, but secretly we dream of the day when our little virtuoso will stand up alone on the stage at Carnegie Hall.

If you placed countries around the world on a scale of individual- versus group-oriented work styles, Mexicans and Americans would fall at opposite ends of the continuum. Along with the Chinese, Spanish, Italians, and others, the Mexicans belong at the group-oriented end. The Czechs fall about in the middle, with Americans close to the opposite extreme, along with the French, Australians, Israelis, and others. The French may be even more individualistic—they comment on how well we Americans work as a team. It's a matter of orientation and perspective.

As further evidence of our independent bias, we make fun of other people for behaving like robots, and we add a bit of racism as we deride the "Chinese fire drill," or a "truckload of Mexicans stomping out a fire."

Rather than speak inclusively and politely to draw closer to a coworker, we tease each other. Our teasing, you could argue, is intended to break the ice, but many foreigners see it as taunting. When we say "Good afternoon" to a coworker who showed up ten minutes late for the early shift, we do it light-heartedly. But a Mexican would be emotionally trammeled by such a throw-away remark. In fact, you don't need to exhort Mexican workers to pull together except under extraordinary circumstances. They would never hurl such barbs. That would not be polite. It would not be harmonious. Mexican workers will tell you, "We work together because that's what we do." No conflict. No hesitation. They are naturally group-oriented.

Team players

In a group-oriented work atmosphere, workers perform best when they're treated as a team. When you enter their work space, you say "Good morning" to the entire bunch. You should recognize that group activities work well and that work is in some ways a social activity. Giving workers an hour off periodically to watch an important soccer match is more important than any exhortation to work harder. Christmas parties are not simply a good idea; they are mandatory if you want to maintain group harmony. Chatting should not be discouraged unless it creates a safety hazard. Nepotism is not an issue. If the worker has a brother, hire him.

Being a member of a company team and wearing the company logo are more valued in Mexico than in the United States. Here, workers will play basketball on break but would just as soon leave the factory to do something else on their own. In Mexico, if logistics permit, the workers will be back at the factory lot playing soccer on their own time, late in the evening. In fact, all over Latin America, overhead lights shine down on vacant lots next to factories where workers return to play soccer at two or three in the morning.

Mexican factory and office workers assume that working together is the ideal. People who work better in solidarity with others, valuing loyalty to the group above individual effort, will prosper in a group-oriented work environment. They exhibit humility and are competitive only with other groups, but not within the group. They may well fall back into escapism if confronted by internecine games. Such workers don't want to call attention to themselves for outperforming a coworker and may be ashamed if rewarded for producing more pieces than a brother or sister.

In a group-oriented environment, individual effort and self-starting are met with suspicion. If you work together, you start together. Work starts at 7:00 A.M. To arrive early requires an explanation to your coworkers, or they will think you are trying to get ahead by showing off. To arrive late requires an apology not only to the boss but also to the group. For a worker to leave his workstation to talk to the supervisor or to get spare parts is disquieting to others in the group, unless the worker has mentioned his need to communicate to the supervisor beforehand.

In the States, we experiment with giving workers more authority and flatten the organization by trying production without superintendents. The effort is intended to take advantage of the individualistic nature of Americans. An individual, after all, should be independent enough not to need an immediate supervisor telling him what to do. In Mexico, the more common arrangement is for a group to have an immediate supervisor who stays with the members and becomes integral to the group. That way, the individual Mexican worker feels that the supervisor is part of the team effort and is there to keep order among the group—to keep one misbehaving employee from interrupting a smooth workflow.

Perfect harmony

The ideal in a Mexican factory is for the *jefe* to tell the workers how many pieces he needs, stay with them to make sure they are sufficiently trained and understand the methods, and then to get out of the way. If the jefe is American, this can best be achieved by appreciating the talents Mexicans have, rather than bemoaning the ways in which they are not like us. I can never erase the image of a remote glassblowing operation I once visited. The workers performed like the Bolshoi Ballet. One worker carried a molten glass-laden pipe from a red-hot furnace to the fixture table. As he lifted the pipe high into the air, another worker ducked smoothly while advancing toward a furnace on the other side of the room. A dozen or so workers glided and spun around in a dazzling display of choreography. Each knew the other's moves. Each understood all the functions of the process. This is their ideal. Of course, they did not have safety glasses, protective garments, superintendents, Occupational Safety and Health Administration (OSHA) rules, and material safety data sheets posted on the walls. So, as we work with Mexicans to improve efficiency and modernize processes, we have to find a balance with their native group-oriented work style. Modernize, but don't Americanize. The jefe is there, inspecting and counting pieces, but his real role is to make sure that group harmony is maintained.

Who's in charge?

The typical dedicated Anglo-American worker shows respect for a boss but does not show deference. The latter might be perceived as weakness, inviting competitors or management to take advantage. White-collar workers negotiate with their bosses freely, inhibited only by their individual sense of propriety. Blue-collar workers in the U.S. maintain a distance from their supervisors. For this reason, Anglo workers tend to walk tough and talk tough. To do otherwise would be to appear vulnerable. There are Anglo types who rumble into the employee parking lot in a red Ram Charger, signaling to the boss that this is one worker not to be trifled with. Typically, such workers aren't afraid to confront the supervisor about their conditions. Then they report to the group that "I told the boss a thing or two." Not surprisingly, this kind of work style invites tough management reactions. The boss is the boss. If he walks like a boss and barks like a boss, he's a boss. If an employee develops an attitude that work starts when he gets there, he meets with strict enforcement of tardiness policies. Consequently, when a new procedure is initiated, rather than working things through together (i.e., via the group), mandates are passed down without being discussed with the workers who, after all, must implement the new procedure.

As for the Mexican worker's attitude toward the boss, it is virtually never confrontational. This is true despite centuries of abuse by Mexican bosses and Aztec *caciques* (warrior chiefs) before them. In the history of the Mexican labor movement, the best a Mexican worker can hope for is a decent boss who is not abusive to him or her. Mexican workers maintain strength because they have always been free to vote with their feet. If they find themselves in a difficult work environment, they may simply leave without saying a word. The modern Mexican jefe behaves more like a wise uncle or father figure. He is paternalistic in a way that American workers would feel uncomfortable with. It is not in the Anglo-Saxon repertoire to treat workers like sons or daughters.

Look for the union label

Considering the differences in our approach to work, it isn't surprising that Mexican unions are not at all the same as in the U.S. In Mexico's group-oriented work environment, unit cohesion is the rule. There is unity of purpose, shared identity, and conformity of thought about what has to be done. The workers view unions as a line of defense to be called upon only in dire situations; otherwise, the union's purpose is to get federal benefits through legislation. Union leaders do not focus on protecting workers from their employers. Rather, they are concerned with using the size of their worker constituency to gain political power in Mexico City.

Mexican unions vary around the nation, but by and large, they are company-friendly. The term *white union* in Mexico means "company-friendly," often even established by the company. Because their orientation is toward presenting a large constituency in Mexico City, unions tend to work well with companies that will sign them up as their official union. They take up the cudgel of an individual grievance only if the company has egregiously violated the worker's rights. Otherwise, they will be more inclined to help the company get rid of a misbehaving individualist. We will discuss unions in depth in Chapter 14, "Political Culture."

Waxing ineloquent

Mexicans work in a group-oriented mode to keep track of each other. To do otherwise would only lead weak individuals to screw up, goof off, or worse. One benefit to the American manager is that when a worker does act up, it is quite apparent to his fellow workers who will give their support for corrective action. One operation I managed used wax molding. A worker hand fashioned a wax penis and chased women around the floor with it. The whole group was ready to give him the heave-ho! With some trepidation, I talked with the union president about the incident. He cut me short, offering to help write the termination letter.

Imperfect harmony

A group-oriented workforce values group harmony above all. A boss showing favoritism will upset the coworkers, thereby shattering the team spirit. Just as disruptive to the harmony of the group is any attempt on the part of a worker to seek special favors.

There is a curious dynamic at work among the group-oriented workers that a non-Mexican needs to understand. It's very natural for a Mexican to want to be the boss's favorite. The group dynamic tries to prevent this, but at times a worker can make a play for the boss's attention, causing the other workers to be jealous. A troublemaker in Mexico will go to the boss and say, with Mary Magdalene eyes, "*Jefe,* my locker is broken. May I please keep my lunchbox inside the door of your office?" If the unwary (culturally foreign) boss says okay, then the worker will sashay onto the factory floor telling his coworkers, "The jefe said that I could keep my lunch in his office." The other workers will be insanely jealous, and the plant floor will suddenly become a den of iniquity. The rest of the group thinks that the offending worker is trying to place herself between them and the jefe.

Mexicans from all classes will tell you that they can be jealous about personal relationships. This is why a non-Mexican needs to recognize nefarious ploys and squelch them at the onset. This also explains why you don't go into the meeting room and say hello just to Señor Astor and Señor Fernandez. You greet everyone. And, for their part, you will never see or hear Mexican managers or directors inject their personal opinion into a conversation if the president is there. In addition to respect for hierarchy, which we will discuss further in Chapter 10, there is the internal viscosity of the group impeding any individual from standing out. Not so in Kokomo, Indiana, where for the most part, everyone feels free to speak up.

Sense of belonging

The group that Mexicans identify with extends to the entire company. To express this bond, Mexicans delight in wearing a company logo. While on a project in Monterrey, I discovered a drawer full of brand new hats printed boldly with the U.S. company's name. When I queried the employees if they would like one, they answered emphatically, "Oh, yes! We knew they were there, but we didn't want to ask."

Group orientation also helps to explain why no individual ever came forward and asked if the employees could have hats. As I passed them out, the hats were received with a chorus of glee. Later, I personally handed one to a bareheaded gardener who had been working all day in the sun. Receiving it carefully in both hands, his face lit up. He couldn't have been more pleased. Here he is, the lowly gardener, now ascending to being a full member of the company team. Such is the identity of Mexican workers with their extended work group that they will wear company jackets rather than union jackets, which are practically nonexistent.

I owe you one, *mano*

In a group-oriented workplace, obligations are good. There is a sense of sharing of resources and knowledge between coworkers who frequently call each other "mano," which is short for *hermano*, meaning "brother." It's also fine to be obligated to the boss. Owing money to the company for a loan, receiving a weekly gift of food, and getting corporate educational grants for the kids are in some ways more meaningful than additional pay. If a worker gives you, the boss, a cigarette, don't pay him back. Let it stand, unless the worker seems to be misusing this small debt as proof to his coworkers that you are in his pocket. This little debt will be repaid to him in other ways. Paying someone back for an act of kindness is tantamount to closing accounts and severing the relationship.

When a plant manager I hired moved to Edinburg, Texas, I helped him and his family become oriented. He had never had a lawn, so I loaned him a spare lawnmower. When I left the project, I collected, by prior agreement, for the lawnmower. We both knew what this meant. He could not count on me for work anymore. He would have to build a new relationship with the new gringo coming to oversee the company. We would still see each other over the years, but only as occasional friends, not as two people dependent on each other.

Whereas it is appropriate not to pay back a cigarette or a drink at the cantina, be wary of *big* debts. If the worker asks you to be the godfather of his newborn son, find a nice way to decline the honor. Once you are his kid's godfather, you are signaling that you will stay in touch for life. If you have acquiesced to him, he may use his status with you to craft evil webs among his fellow workers. Or he may expect more of a permanent relationship than you do. When we Americans go on to another job, city, or project, we tend to drop the old relationships and form new ones.

One thing they hate about us

If there is one habit we have as gringo employers or managers that the Mexicans hate, it's telling them what to do, leaving them on their own, and coming back a week later barking, "That's not what I wanted!" This immediately drives a wedge between *them* and *us*. If you want to be a successful manager, state clearly what you want to accomplish, and stay with the team until you are satisfied that the goal and the approach are well understood. As a foreigner, you want to be seen as *part* of the team. Then you leave. When you return, the job will be done correctly.

What is an effective incentive?

American analysts often insist that Mexicans do not respond to incentives. Nonsense. Of course they do. But what constitutes an incentive? Is it merely money? In the United States, where the worker wants to be paid and left alone, money is the best incentive. But is money the best incentive in Mexico? No. If you give a worker money in a group-oriented work space, he or she will appreciate it and thank you but won't necessarily equate the gesture with working harder. You also stand a chance of diluting the group work ethic unless you give all the workers the same amount. A show of solidarity— giving workers something for all of their families—is much more motivating. Jealousy in Mexico is about relationships, not money and benefits.

Given the Mexican's sensitivity to equal treatment, what happens when a benefit or incentive, such as school tuition reimbursement, goes only to those with children? No problem. If a worker doesn't have children, he doesn't apply. Because of the group's unity of thought he feels no animosity that one is getting something others do not. In the States, a worker may squeal, "It's not fair that Charlie gets tuition reimbursement for his kids and I don't!" "Wait a minute! You don't have kids." For the Mexican, *fair* does not mean that everybody gets the same thing. It means that people get what they need and can use. If Carlos needs it and Pedro does not, no one complains that Carlos gets it and Pedro doesn't. Part of the practical nature of Mexicans is that they never get hung up on such tomfoolery. As an integral part of the group, they respond to what is best for the whole. There is no jealousy or perceived unfairness and no issue with the union.

Effective incentives have to keep pace with a modernizing Mexico. Just twenty years ago, workers wanted to be paid in cash in a clear plastic, sealed envelope so they could count their money and take it home to their wives untouched. Years ago, Mexican bosses found ways to cheat workers out of their money, so visible cash was a necessary remedy. Today, Mexican workers want direct deposits to their bank accounts and ATM machines, which are right outside the industrial park gates. Because this practice is convenient, modern, and applies to everybody, it is perceived as a benefit and serves as a viable incentive.

What we do, what we don't do

Safety in the workplace is another concern requiring an understanding of group behavior. U.S. companies generally insist on implementing the same standards in Mexico as they would here. But in the case of eye protection, for example, the Mexican workforce will not willingly wear safety glasses. Maybe it's machismo. Maybe it's lack of future orientation. But, they will ignore what they view as an arbitrary safety rule unless you present the new rule properly. What's the solution? Rather than castigate one fellow in the lathe department (where eye protection is mandatory) and point to the rule in his departmental manual, make the use of safety glasses the rule for *everyone* in the factory. Get all of the workers together from all departments and say that whenever *anyone* steps into the factory building they will wear glasses. Then it becomes a rule for everybody. It becomes a part of "what we do."

The same applies to smoking. Rather than accommodate people with smoking areas, it's better to ban smoking inside altogether. Then smoking becomes "what we *don't* do." It may be a minor inconvenience that employees have to wear glasses and can't smoke in the break room or in the bathrooms, but the "no exceptions" policy is easier to understand. No one will be tempted to say that he didn't know, or he forgot, or he didn't think it applied to him. By making the rule a matter of "what we do and don't do," it becomes a part of the group-oriented culture in their workplace.

Guide workers

Training in a group-oriented work setting can have some interesting dynamics. In Mexico, if you are trying to show a work cell how to assemble a new cartridge or how to fill out insurance forms, you may be surprised that a guide worker (*obrero guia*) will emerge from the group. Guide workers are the ones who master the tasks first and take over for you. They see the pattern, analyze what has to be done, and then willingly take on the responsibility of training the others. The light goes on, they say "Aha!" and they turn their backs on you. They proceed on their own to show the other workers how to do the task. Let them. They will continue to instruct new hires. And you don't have to pay them more or give them a title. This is an example of how a group-oriented workforce cooperates. It's what they do. *Es mi trabajo* ("It's my job") means that the worker has self-respect because he identifies with a skill he can teach others and use for self-improvement.

It bears repeating: in a group-oriented workplace, teamwork is the natural order of things, and you, as the boss, will be most effective if you recognize the way the group works and modify your approach accordingly. This will become more apparent in Chapter 11 when we address conflict resolution.

Within the collectivist culture, there will always be exceptions—a strikingly independent type who spontaneously appears with his own ideas. In the independent workplace, this person would be treated as a rising star. But in a group-oriented work environment, he will be frustrated out of his mind, because before he can try anything, he must first work out all the arrangements with the group.

All in the family

The strong tendency toward the group is rooted in the Mexican family, where it is vigorously reinforced. I recently interviewed a Mexican businessman whose family had been prominent in the region of Aguascalientes since the age of Shakespeare. Every Sunday the seven brothers and one sister met with their mother at the big house for family time and dinner. All eight sib-lings, plus the mother and respective family members, together owned eleven companies. This ambitious, entrepreneurial, independent fellow wanted to consolidate three of the family companies to make one that would work more efficiently and significantly curb expenses. He was willing to buy out his brothers so that everyone would be compensated fairly. It was a very practical plan, and the other two brothers who owned the majority of stock in the two companies to be consolidated were cooperating. On paper it made sense, but mother wouldn't allow it.

Among the siblings were two weaker sons working in the companies my friend wanted to close. "What would they do?" *Mamá* asked. The two weaker family members relied on their more aggressive brothers for jobs, direction, and status. The proposed changes would eliminate their positions. Never mind that they would be compensated. Never mind that the changes would save money. Money can never replace the need for work, self-respect, and identity. In such a group-oriented setting, an individual-style entrepreneur will be extremely frustrated with his fate.

While the need to succeed is something Americans and Mexicans share, our underlying approach to achieving prosperity is markedly different—largely because of the difference in individual versus group orientation. The group bonding process begins the minute Mexican children are brought home from the hospital and put into the *children's* room—not their own, separate little pink or blue nursery. Their families tend to congregate in one large room. They are taught to play nicely with each other. Toys are toys and are played with by all the children. They are not owned by boy number one or girl number three. The children wear uniforms at school. In Anglo culture, the more we misbehave with our siblings, the more attention we get. And for the most part, we wear what we darn well please to school. Our teenage boys put their caps on backward and wear baggy pants and designer names on their shirts to show their individuality, yet somehow they all look alike. But beyond the conflicting pressures of adolescence, we seem to emerge as indi-vidualists. We adhere to the "make way for me" approach, unlike the Mexi-cans, who believe that the more they conform, the more they will all prosper.

The Lone Ranger, or *llanero solitario*

American bosses can misread individual versus group-oriented cues. I coached a plant manager named Cliff. Cliff had promoted a maintenance worker, Chucho, over a maintenance supervisor, Victor, because the former was gregarious and struck out on his own, whereas the latter wore a tie and was quiet, even retiring. Chucho was indeed a self-starter with a happy, can-do demeanor. But the plant manager mistook a "Lone Ranger" attitude and a pleasant disposition for leadership. As for Victor, Cliff stated, "In the States, maintenance supervisors don't wear ties." The problem was that while all the workers liked Chucho, in the end he couldn't do the job. His can-do attitude was limited to what he could do. He didn't know how to direct other workers, and they viewed him as something of an odd clown. Victor, as it turned out, was quite well qualified, and the workers knew to follow his lead. He had only worn a tie in a mistaken attempt to please the boss. Victor left for another job, and maintenance suffered under Chucho's temporary tutelage.

Renegade

Enter a renegade into a group-oriented atmosphere and group harmony is threatened. The individualist may be the kind who wants to get ahead by political maneuvering, showing off, or cottoning up to the boss. Such actions will dilute the natural tendency to work as a team. Members of the workforce will become unpleasantly jealous of his new relationship with the jefe and will either form cabals or quit. The biggest mistake American managers can make is to view this person as a rare find, a true self-starter, a real go-getter (just like us), or an example of what we expect. Rewarding this attitude can drive a wedge between management and workers.

There comes a time when everybody in a department recognizes that a renegade has to be fired. Let's say you employ a man who has acquired the skills to do a job but who covers up mistakes by misbehaving—blaming others and playing up to the jefe. In Mexico your best tactic is to first identify the troublemaker, then let him know that you expect him to play ball with his teammates. Then, let him hang himself. When you finally fire him, it will be to the great relief of the group. And *who* are you firing? A true self-starter who might invent the next laborsaving device? A real go-getter just like you? Chances are you're firing a renegade. How can you be sure? Test him on job skills to see if he truly lives up to his position, or if he's covering up because he can't do the work. Give him due process. Investigate his background. But don't respond to the qualities in the same way you would respond to them in the States. Don't measure him according to Anglo culture. Evaluate him within the context of his own group-oriented culture. While he may have the technical skills to do a good job, he may be diluting the productivity of the whole group.

The same lesson applies to the incompetent employee. From time to time, you will encounter a worker who couldn't do the job if his life depended on it. Maybe he is the next Salvador Dali or has hidden talent as a Mexican Lawrence Welk, but he couldn't pour tequila out of a boot if the directions were written on the heel. If you find that you need to move or fire this person, you won't have to make any apologies. In the group-oriented workforce, his coworkers will have caught onto his weakness long before you. They will gladly acquiesce to the move because they, more than anyone, recognize that he is keeping the group from operating well together and achieving its goals.

Critical mass

Rarely does individuality in the workplace express itself in Mexico. In a sense, group identification is part of the previously discussed "mask phenomenon." The mask offers protection from hostile forces and conceals individual flaws. Within the group, inside their group space, Mexicans wear the mask of metalworkers or hospital workers. Their identity with the group is reflected in the way they carry themselves. Being part of the metalworking team is a source of self-respect—"We are metalworkers. It is what we do. We are a team. We are proud of our accomplishments." Fundamentally, the solidarity of the workplace extends to the national level, where Mexicans see themselves as part of a larger mass. The feeling of belonging to the group is palpable. It surrounds them. It's an unshakable belief that they carry in their hearts and in their minds, as we will explore in Chapter 13.

Avoiding a hard landing

Let's say you have landed in Mexico like Mr. Magoo. You have survived the initial confusion (in your mind) about the check-in process at the hotel. You've had your breakfast and now you're on the factory floor fired up for action. You've acquired additional insights into the dynamics of the individual versus group-oriented work styles, but how will you fare? Ingeniero Suarez, the assembly superintendent, greets you warmly, telling you how wonderfully everything is working. He takes you to his gringo manager who explains that production has virtually stopped in department twelve, that the morale has never been lower, and that you're losing workers.

If nothing in this book has sunk in, you will swoop down like a hurricane, take charge, and start giving orders: "*You,* stand over there." "*You,* I wanna see a report on turnover by noon." As for your general observations, you're thinking, "Where do I start? The gantries are in the wrong place. The material handling is in shambles. The workers don't seem to know what they're doing." So what do you do? You put the department supervisor on probation. After a string of one-on-one interrogations, you get things moving the way you want. Satisfied that you've flogged enough butt, the next day you go to Colombia to straighten those "boneheads" out. Having left Mexico all squared away, you are surprised to find out a few days later that not only department twelve, but now departments eleven and thirteen are in shambles.

Through the grace of God, you made it past the reception desk, but you've crash-landed on the factory floor. You've forgotten all your cultural fluency and have allowed your deep-seated, one-way gringo reactions to kick in. You've reverted to the time-as-an-arrow, single 'em out, in-your-face approach. Here's when you draw a deep breath and repeat the old Mexican adage, "*No hay que llegar primero, sino hay que saber llegar.*" (You don't have to get there first, you just have to know how to get there.) Then you remember how to get there!

Back to basics

In a group-oriented work situation, you deal with people first. Only later can you address the schedules, machine placement, and functional adjustments. With the American boss's blessing, you begin by addressing the whole group of Mexican management as if you were the wise uncle come to town to counsel your nieces and nephews. Tell them that the president of the company himself is concerned. Tell them that you know they can do the job. Tell them that nothing is more important to you than to have everybody get along and work well together. "Nothing is more important than harmony within the group," you say.

Having doffed your watch, you are not tempted to see how long it will take for your message to sink in. And you have touched all the right hot buttons. You have appealed to their natural instincts. Your exhortation to the management and departments are very broad. "Work on group harmony" is your overarching message. This broadness allows the next in command enough leeway to follow through and implement your wishes while maintaining his own position as the older, wiser cousin of the family. In the process, you have forced the members of the group to get beyond the "people thing," the jealousies, the intrigue that the group may have devolved into. Very quickly, the group will heal itself, come back to grips with reality, and begin addressing how they can all—together—come up with solutions to the material handling problems.

You go to the cafeteria to have a quiet cup of coffee with the financial staff and to discuss the budget. An hour later, you go through the three departments with your American production manager. How's it going? Better. Now, you ask (not tell) about the placement of the gantries, the material handling, etc. Having first dealt with the harmony of the workforce, you can now ask about the necessity for personnel changes. You may find out to your surprise that without venom, without raising your voice, with a few technical adjustments, you will get back on track. Now is the time to suggest, not point at, a location for a new gantry. Not only are you the wise uncle or aunt, but you are also the expert at material handling. With little or no passive resistance, you can set up a planning group and give them instructions for a preventive action study. You have dealt with people first, then dealt with things.

By the numbers

1. Group-oriented workers are focused on group harmony. You wouldn't go to a dinner party at a friend's house and speak only to your friends. You would include their other guests in your conversation. Similarly, when in a group space, you address the entire group. Say hello to everybody. If you shake hands with one, shake with all.

2. Emphasize group harmony first, then turn to the cold facts. It's not difficult. Don't give the following stream of orders: "The *schedule* is supreme." (The schedule is an inanimate object—cold.) "*You* have to make production by Friday." (In addition to Friday meaning little, as we have seen, you are barking orders to an individual and not

appealing to the group.) "Open the door and bring in a truckload of bolts." (No reference to the group and too direct.) Instead, say, "*We* need to work *together* to get the job done." (First appeal is to group harmony.) "*Let's* (as in let *us*) remember that the most important thing is the schedule." "*We* need to make our production by Friday because that's when the *customer* is visiting." (Emphasis on people.) "Now, help *each other* get the door open and the truckload of bolts unloaded." (Appeal to the group.)

3. Listen to the Mexicans. They will never tell you that you have jumped into their department with both feet and made their lives miserable with your demands and coldhearted obsession with facts and figures. When they say, "Jefe, we want you to know that we are willing to do anything you ask," read between the lines. What they are really saying is, "Jefe, we can't figure out what the hell you want." In response to their plea, reinforce the "we're in this together" feeling by giving them a dose of soft soap. Say, "I know you are willing. I have always appreciated how we work together." Now you transition to your expectations. "What I would like to see by the time I leave is that you and your team have worked out a plan to open the door and unload the truck."

4. Remember the correlation between group space and group behavior. An office staff occupying the same space may have separate, quite distinct job functions. But they are all office workers. This is one reason that Mexican companies often dress their staff in "uniforms of the day." All nonmanagement people will wear similar garb on different days of the week. In addition to being a benefit for the workers who may not otherwise be able to afford several work outfits, it promotes group cohesiveness.

5. These lessons are not limited to the factory. As you travel around Mexico, you will see aspects of their group-oriented work styles at hotels and restaurants, in homes, and at play. You wonder why they are so quiet, respectful, polite, and agreeable? One reason is their group orientation.

Future versus Present Orientation

In the United States, we're constantly looking ahead. Our belief that change is progress is so pervasive that we are surprised to learn that other societies don't necessarily share our outlook. As a future-oriented country, still young and in the mood for experimentation, we want what is bigger, faster, newer, and more efficient. Our culture encourages the kind of competitive, individual performance that leads to innovation on a fast track and a grand scale. In fact, our economy has come to depend on it.

Mexicans, on the other hand, are oriented to the present. Their view of the future is tinged with memories of past fire and blood. What lies ahead is full of unknowns and peril. And since the future seems uncertain, they depend on building relationships in the present. If something goes wrong with the economy, "We'll all be in it together." Because Mexicans want what is expedient for the present and because they want to mitigate risk, they are much less experimental than Americans. In fact they are somewhat averse to risk. But this tendency must not be dismissed as unprogressive. For them, it is practical and cautionary. They harvest what they can while the time is ripe.

Change can challenge anyone, but in present-oriented Mexico, change can be threatening. Generally, Mexicans don't respond well to new ways of doing things unless presented to them in a palatable way. Americans can resist change as well, but, in the interest of progress, we usually go along. We think of innovation as inevitable and, based on our history, generally good. When our boss explains that a new procedure will cut costs, increase productivity, or sharpen our competitive edge, we're willing to make the adjustment. Our sense of economic security resides largely in staying ahead of the curve. We charge ahead, emphasizing product development and personal advancement. We are exhorted to "dream big" and "aim high." We reward lofty goals and heady achievements.

Mexicans are also amenable to change, but they look for models to follow rather than striking out with bold new ventures. In a group-oriented culture that is concerned with how change will impact the whole group, a model allows coworkers to see how others in the organization will be affected. As Mexicans watch the U.S. economy, they can see the bad and good results of the American experiment. They want to emulate the good—the improving standard of living, the opportunities for personal growth—but, understandably, they want to avoid the bad—the pressure of time, the loss of the personal touch. As we will see in Chapter 14, Mexicans cope with political change with their usual predilection for sameness—change, yes, so long as things remain more or less the same.

Assuming that others see things the same way we do, Americans are surprised to learn that "progress," as such, is not a big motivator for the Mexicans. That concept is somewhat remote and not at all assured. To be easily accepted, changes should be explained in terms with immediate and practical appeal. When introducing new equipment into the workplace, rather than enthusing over how it will speed up production and make them the industry leader, they'd rather hear that this equipment represents new products with worldwide demand. Why? Because Mexicans want to be modern and fully integrated into the international economy. This could be viewed as appealing to their sense of nationalism, but it is really a ploy to circumvent their risk-averse fear of the future. It is an easier mental jump to want to be current than it is to get out in front as a leader.

Another way to institute change in Mexico is to appeal to Mexicans' personal values, citing new training opportunities and more jobs for their community. These are practical consequences for which no one can deny a need.

When Sylvia, a Mexican salesperson with a real estate development firm in Monterrey, was offered the position of manager of the Nuevo Laredo sales office, her American boss was surprised that she viewed the move not as a promotion, but as a kind of exile. What we regard as an advancement, a Mexican might see as undesirable or even unkind. But explaining the transfer in terms of expanding Sylvia's responsibility so she can be an integral member of the management team when she comes back in two years makes the move palatable. For Sylvia, the future, per se, may hold as much peril as profit. Future implications must be made clear and positive to her. Allowing her to picture herself back in the fold in two years mitigates the concern she may have that she will be forgotten.

Risky business

In the American workplace, we are willing to go all out for the future. We dedicate a sizeable amount of time to anticipating needs and planning for the future. We create elaborate contingency plans and endless risk analyses. We prepare for the impending winter. We focus on the consequences of planning and execution. Such practices are among the many things we do fairly well. We don't take our time the way the Japanese do, and sometimes our implementation suffers, but as a rule we recognize the value of thinking ahead.

A culturally fluent American executive told me of his experience in Puebla. He had asked his clever, but definitely not future-oriented Mexican plant manager to do a risk analysis. "There are three components to a good analysis," he told the manager. "First, you have to determine with your team what *might* go wrong. Second, you have to assign numerical value to what the impact would be if it *did* go wrong. A ten for a total disaster, a five for a temporary shutdown, and so on. Third, you have to estimate the likelihood that it *will* go wrong. Multiplying the rating of impact by likelihood, you tackle the highest scoring problem first, then the second, and so on." He further explained that this analysis was designed to mitigate any damage before the fact. "Taking action now," he cautioned, "is better than reacting to a catastrophe. As we say, an ounce of prevention is worth a pound of cure." Finally, just to drive home his point, he added, "Hey, a good fire prevention system is cheaper than rebuilding the plant."

The Mexican plant manager nodded in assent and went to work. Two days later, he produced his chart. But there were only two columns: what *could* go wrong and what the impact would be. So the executive asked, "Where's your estimate showing the likelihood that it'll happen?" The manager responded fretfully, "It won't happen!" That was his risk analysis. It won't happen. The ceiling won't fall down.

The executive could have started an argument with the plant manager, insisting that indeed the roof *might* fall down, but he didn't. He knew that this approach would not be helpful. Something else was lurking beneath the surface that the executive had to deal with in order to build a bridge of understanding. (One that wouldn't fall down!) His cultural fluency enabled him to see that the plant manager's resistance to risk analysis stemmed from a deeply ingrained present orientation, which carries with it a general unwillingness on the part of some Mexicans to deal abstractly with contingencies. The executive stressed again how he wanted the analysis done. He reminded the plant manager that part of his job was to assure the safety of those working with him—for the long term. With more light-handed coaching, the plant manager learned well and went on to teach the subject through the auspices of his local manager's association.

This strong present orientation also explains why a Mexican engineer will hang a gantry from the overhead beams without checking on the building's load capacities. After all, a quick solution is needed. It further accounts for why Mexican-run factories often appear to be a mishmash of put-togethers—the cumulative effect of lots of immediate remedies, without much thought to long-term or unintended consequences.

One of the first orders of business for many U.S. vice presidents of manufacturing who are starting a tour of duty in Mexico is to change the location of gantries and reinforcing columns. At the same time, they will institute new safety procedures, going on to change material-handling processes. These are generally good moves, but will accumulate into a series of makeshift solutions unless the VP can get his plant manager to think ahead, recognize potential safety hazards, and buy into the concept of preventive maintenance. Here, in a nutshell, is the difference between a future-oriented and a present-oriented work environment. The VP of manufacturing will be inviting frustration unless he understands that to straighten up the mess on the floor (i.e., to create a fully productive and safe work environment), he'll first have to spend some time teaching the steps patiently. If there are three steps to a risk analysis, as in the prior case, he must teach them step by step. He mustn't go on to step two until the employees have fully absorbed step one. The American assumes that it is possible to make a list of things that could go wrong. The Mexican has great difficulty projecting along these lines. Since safety, too, involves prevention—the recognition of what could go wrong—rules of personal safety must be taught in sequence, without false assumptions. It takes time to make sure the workers think through the consequences of not abiding by the rules.

I have visited a lot of Mexican operations with American VPs. More often than not, their criticisms about Mexican operations have to do with material handling. Sensing a crisis, the Americans' first instinct is to jump in and tell the workers what to do, but the quick-fix approach won't change mentality. It isn't enough to tell them to move things around. The first step is to get the manufacturing engineers off the floor and talk to them about the need to plan material handling, not only for the present but also for future operations. By getting them together, we can better instill a new mental attitude—in the group. Then, rather than appealing to the Mexicans in terms of what *we* see as the benefits of future planning, we should appeal to them on the basis of *their* cultural values. Because the workers want to please, we should tell them that when the president comes in May, he will be delighted with how well they perform this function. We must explain that in order to be modern it's important to plan for the new technology that is coming. Finally, the VP or plant manager, or the training team from headquarters, should stick with the Mexican engineers long enough to make sure they have internalized these techniques and procedures as part of "what we do."

Since present-oriented Mexican workers do not anticipate future needs naturally, VPs have to set up basic training programs designed to walk them through the process. Once they understand the rationale, they will see the value and maintain the procedure. For example, one company teaches workers specific steps to refeeding their stamping presses. The worker must put a specified sheet of paper behind every twentieth subassembly to serve as a flag. When the worker gets through the subassemblies to the paper, he gives the flag to the expediter, who will carry it to the warehouse. The paper is a standing order for twenty-five more subassemblies. Another company has the maintenance supply warehouseman hang the next-to-last fan belt on the peg backward. On the blank sleeve, he writes, "Order more of these."

Understanding that such basic training is necessary, the VP will be very pleased with the changes in the manufacturing culture. He will be setting himself up for happy surprises. But changing procedures or material flow, or adding safety glasses in certain work cells, won't make much sense without a deeper explanation to the users. To say that he is making these changes for reasons of safety, or increased productivity, won't change behavior. Later, he may discover that his program was not fully implemented, or that his sense of urgency was not shared by all.

Further, to be effective, management should relate all changes to a personal benefit, such as self-improvement: "Training will qualify you for a certificate that presents you to your coworkers as a material-handling specialist." Changes might also be related to self-respect: "Being a qualified material handler also means that you will have your picture on the wall of fame with your certifications listed." This kind of recognition within the group does not interfere with group harmony because such accolades are available to all.

There is a wall of fame in all departments. Being on the wall of fame simply means that the worker has achieved knowledge and expertise that all members of the group should aspire to. The group accepts accolades. They show that the company values its employees, and in turn confers respect on all employees. One big difference between Mexico and the United States is that these accolades, certificates, and pictures do not mean the worker expects more money. You can't equate self-respect with money in Mexico.

Too often, Americans look at Mexicans' temporary solutions and sneer that they do not know how to come up with permanent ones. On one level, Mexicans would prefer to have permanent solutions rather than constantly having to make expedient adjustments. But we see these "nonsolutions"— an electric cable patch, a wired-up muffler, a sheet of plywood over a hole in the pavement—and assume that Mexicans can't think or don't care. In fact, what appears to be confused (while improvised) is nevertheless a result of logic—a logic that says we need a solution today, and tomorrow we'll come up with tomorrow's solutions. *Si dios quiere.* (If God wills it.)

A chronic absence of contingency planning is evident throughout Mexico. Lone workers beating star drills into the cement send the message that buildings are never finished in Mexico. There is always a gate to put up, a window to add, or an air conditioning unit to be hung. Uneven road-beds, lack of signage, missing curbs, and muddy intervals in the tarmac represent more than a lack of resources. They betray a present orientation: "We can drive today, and tomorrow we'll put up a stop sign."

Quick fixes

Mexicans do not naturally do preventive maintenance, but they are exceptionally clever at fixing things when they do break. They can make a set of distributor points out of a beer can. They can use a piece of scrap metal to fix a water heater. They will double the life of a sanding belt by turning it inside out for use in the final polishing process. I have seen them do these things and more. But ask an American VP of operations in Mexico what the biggest problem is in getting the job done, and you're apt to hear "preventive maintenance!" "The fan belt isn't broken, so no problem. Why should we do preventive maintenance? We cannot predict the future. When it breaks, we'll fix it." In the U.S, we have lighting designers and engineers who can prove that relamping our offices will save us money in the long run. But, to Mexicans, this seems incredibly wasteful. They marvel at our efficiency, but don't make the connection with replacing light bulbs before they burn out. In fact, as long as they can still see, they won't replace them even after they *have* burned out.

Being clever at fixing what is broken is the direct result of *not* being focused on preparing for the future. Precisely because Mexicans are so good at fixing things and making do, they tend to look upon preventive maintenance as a waste of time.

In Mexico, hierarchy also plays a part with regard to preventive maintenance. On the education/status scale, at the high end you have sophisticated engineers who can do a fine job of risk analysis. Further down the chain of command, among the maintenance workers themselves, the attitude is more mysterious, less inclined to predicting the future, and therefore more present oriented. Most maintenance workers tend to be farm boys from the *rancho*, for whom fixing things is easy and rational. Because they are new to the industrial world and generally not skilled as machinists, or in the trades, they gravitate toward maintenance. The same is true in the States, but the learning curve is steeper in Mexico. The maintenance guy in Mexico may never own a wristwatch.

The Mexicans' greater trust in the present than in the future is also evident in their impulse to reuse everything—"It's here and now. It's what is at hand. We can make it work." Old tires become sandals. Fifty-five gallon drums become water tanks. Old '36 Ford axles become mule drays. Old buses become chicken coops. It helps assuage the feeling of waste if you or they can come up with secondary uses for items you cycle out of maintenance inventory. Let them use old fan belts to tie trees to stakes. Use Styrofoam cups from the cafeteria as casting sprues. They will find good uses for old light bulbs, sandpaper, or fabric. Let them buy these items at the employee store for next to nothing. They will take the scrap to the *tianguis* (village market) on Sunday to make a few more pesos. Conversely, a grandiose show of waste on your part will only encourage Mexican workers to think that you don't value what you have. That may encourage stealing. Gringos are great wastrels. People in other countries could make a good living out of what we throw out. You hear a lot of hype about recycling in the States. That's because we don't do it very well and have to keep reminding ourselves.

No problem

Directly tied to the Mexican's reluctance to project into the future is the "no problem" syndrome. The "no problem" response has become so widely associated with the Mexicans that it has become a cliché. When American businesspeople hear "no problem" in reply to their hard-hitting questions about government relations, unions, sourcing, transportation, permits, and taxes, they think their concerns are being brushed off. But it is a mistake to interpret the "no problem" response this way. "No problem" carries with it more than a glimmer of that ubiquitous Mexican trait—wanting to be agreeable. Because gringos seem to fret so much, Mexicans feel even more compelled to calm our fears and tell us what they think we want to hear.

More to the point, "no problem" can be linked to the Mexicans' lack of future orientation. Unlike Americans, who go looking for trouble and obsess about what could go wrong, Mexicans tend not to see a problem until it's upon them. It's all part of their total immersion in the present—and there's no periscope up. On those rare occasions when problems *are* perceived in advance, they are ratcheted one click backward on the scale of importance for the simple reason that they haven't happened yet.

An American plant manager fusses and fumes over a steam pipe that could be ruptured by a forklift. He insists that a barrier be placed in front of it. "No problem." He may or may not get that barrier installed, because the Mexican workers really don't acknowledge the impending disaster and won't take preventive action. Nobody's hit it yet, so it's not a problem. But if ever a Mexican superintendent comes into the American manager's office and says, "Jefe, we have a problem," you can bet that there are cadavers all over the factory floor.

Different time zones

There is some variation in the future versus present orientation within Mexico. This generally runs along the same lines as orientation toward linear versus circular time. In industrialized areas such as Monterrey and Chihuahua, time moves more like an arrow and orientation stretches more to the future. Engineers or accountants, regardless of culture, have the analytical tools necessary to discover that preventing fires is cheaper than putting them out and rebuilding. But it's not unusual for Mexican personnel in the Americanized workplace to leave their analytical tools behind in the locker when they go home.

In predominantly rural areas such as the southern state of Chiapas, time still flows like a river, and the present orientation, with its detachment from what is to come, remains the norm. If you ask a farmer about the upcoming corn harvest, he may be offended that you would presume to infringe on God's work. In contrast, the minister of agriculture in Mexico City will provide an answer more along the lines of what you would expect to hear in Iowa. But don't be misled. Underlying both responses is the deep-seated conviction that the future cannot and perhaps should not be predicted. No one really knows what's in store, either for oneself or for the corn crop. If Mexicans try to predict the future and are wrong—even by a little bit—they are sure to offend someone. So why stick their neck out? If the crop is good, then they can brag. The government can brag. But if the crop is bad, you won't hear a peep. After all, bad news is to be avoided. Today the Mexicans are happy to tell you that there is good news. As for tomorrow? Who knows?

Personal objectives

As part of their present mode of thinking, Mexican workers do not relate, as Americans do, to the number of years they have worked at a job or within a company. In the United States, you hear the following: "I've been a steamfitter at ACME for fifteen years," or, "I've got twenty years' experience in the stapler industry." This view of time does nothing for a Mexican. It begs the question, "Why would anyone want to have one-year's experience twenty times?" Rather than talking about length of service, Mexican workers take pride in the amount of training and the achievements they have amassed. Becoming good at something, being able to brag "Es mi trabajo!" (It's my job!), is not a function of time, rather of accumulating skills. They point to a posted, detailed matrix showing a breakdown of jobs into skills and subskills. Each increment requires training, after which the worker gets a gold star. The *escalafon,* as they call it, might be tied to incremental increases in wage and is considered a badge of honor.

Watch where you put the goalposts

Because of different attitudes toward work in a present-oriented culture, the goals of the company, as stated to the Mexicans by U.S. parent corporations, are apt to fall on deaf ears. Achieving the billion-dollar sales mark will meet with applause, but only because they know you want them to applaud. While the Mexicans are very agreeable, they don't swell with rapture the way we would at meeting this month's sales mark. Above all, people in a present-oriented culture want to work for self-improvement and family. While they won't sacrifice for the future, per se, let's be clear, they *will* sacrifice for their children's education. Mexican workers see themselves as stakeholders in the company, not shareholders. The difference is that rather than focusing on the balance sheet, they want the company to do well so that they will do well.

No time like the present

We have seen how the Mexican worker's sense of time is elastic. As the Mexican sees it, "Tomorrow begins when I wake up and start over." For Mexicans it's true that "what goes around, comes around," but it doesn't necessarily come around at regular intervals. Tomorrow stretches into the future for an indeterminate period until the cycle repeats itself. Conversely, the American worker is culturally conditioned to divide time (and the value of his work) into discrete packets. "I work nine to five. I get paid $22 an hour. I make X amount of take-home per week. I have three weeks' vacation. I've been doing it for fifteen years. I will never go back to working for $10 an hour."

The Mexicans' present orientation toward flexible time explains why one of my Mexican workers left his job at a good, above-market wage to take a ditch-digging job for less pay but with no limitation on the number of hours he could work. He reasoned that with me he could work nine hours a day and make 550 pesos a week. But if he went to work for the city, he could work twelve hours a day or more and make 600 pesos or *more*. In other words, he was willing to work one-third more hours for one-tenth more final pay! This contrasts markedly with the American attitude of working so many increments of time for such and such increments of pay.

It is reasonable to ask, if time is more elastic for the Mexican, how does this affect their work pace? It is my experience that once the Mexican worker is sure he is doing things right, he works very fast and very efficiently, respecting the balance between speed and accuracy. Being present oriented, he performs with tremendous concentration, tenacity, and alacrity. He takes regular breaks, but not to think about the future, rather to socialize with his fellow workers—to have fun today, while today is still with us.

We'll use them until they run out

As we descended into Benito Juarez Airport, the chop overwhelmed a young lady across the aisle from me. I carry a package of Handi Wipes with me on trips, and proffered *one* to her, but she took the whole package out of my hand. For the next ten minutes, the sealing flap ripped open again and again as she and her travel mate used one after another until they were gone. I was agitated. What am I going to do now? Why did she take advantage of my generosity and use all my wipes?

The answer is that in present-oriented Mexico, you use supplies until they run out. Turn the tables and ask a Mexican for a Kleenex. He will generously offer you what he has. If you protest that he has so few left and ask what he'll do tomorrow, he'll respond, "We'll just use them until they run out."

No turning back

One way to understand the difference between Mexicans and Americans is to allow that *they* are present oriented with a bridge to the past, whereas *we* are future oriented with a bridge to the present. We do today in anticipation of the future; they do today as an extension of the past.

Ties to the past can present a problem in the area of training. For example, when you try to instruct a worker in how to polish stainless steel and he has already learned how to polish brass, he will want to do it the way he was previously taught. He is tied to past learning and to his teacher, whom

---

Tips for the minute manager

Here are some practical observations about dealing with present orientation that go beyond the factory floor:

- Expect Mexicans to be somewhat vague any time you ask them about the future. They will not make statements of a factual nature about the future. There is always an element of doubt.
- If they do state certainty about an event in the future, it is probably intended to have an effect on you, rather than have real meaning.
- Many aspects of what you observe in Mexican work habits are a result of present orientation. The uneven, patched sidewalks, the different-sized manholes, the electrical access covers in the street, the sound of a jackhammer tearing up a perfectly good curb, and the hastily constructed plywood barriers on the fronts of buildings attest to the lack of advance planning.

he deeply respects and with whom he continues to feel an emotional bond. I have had workers in Mexico say, "Okay, I'll try it your way. But if I don't like it, I'll go back to my way." If you are trying to put together a polishing department, you may be better off hiring people with *no* experience. Understand that in asking a worker to change his methods, you are asking him to give up the past. And for a Mexican, that's not easy.

If the Mexicans' grip on the past is tighter than ours, it's because the past has gotten them where they are. There is comfort in the past and uncertainty in the future. Americans, on the other hand, are so confident in their ability to control what lies ahead that we tend to turn our backs on what's happened before. You would never hear a Mexican say that he "hated history," or that "history is just about dead people." While they are not past oriented, in a world of elastic time, the past is part of the present. The past is not past so long as a memory exists. One observer noted that in Mexico nobody ever really dies.

People in Control versus Nature in Control

If you think, as most Americans do, that it's possible to manipulate the future, you also believe that people can control their own destiny—that humans can conquer nature. Looking back over the past two hundred years, conquering nature has gone rather smoothly for us. On the continent of North America, natural resources were there for the taking. Land was free. Fresh water was abundant. Enterprise was free. *We* were free. Unrestricted capital investment flowed in from throughout the world, enabling us to build our factories, cities, and infrastructure. In the blink of an eye we were able to break the bonds of subsistence living. With our six-shooters and repeater rifles, we conquered the West. We had the luxury of dreaming big dreams. In just sixty-six years we went from launching a two-stroke glider off a North Carolina sand dune to landing a man on the moon.

The explosive development of American technology has fed our sense of dominance over nature. To the extent that we "believe our own magic," we sometimes fail to acknowledge the help we had along the way. Our success owes as much to the geographic cornucopia we stumbled upon as it does to our cleverness. Therefore, when we arrive in Mexico and declare that we have a solution, it's not surprising that we are viewed with some dismay. For their part, Mexicans know something we don't: namely, we couldn't have conquered the West had they not done it for us three hundred years earlier. Mexicans also know that their brethren the Apaches and other Native American people taught them how to live in harmony with the rugged West.

We could not have sustained our rush westward were there not herds of wild horses left by the Spaniards. We could not have become cowboys had the Mexican *hacendados* not developed a thriving cattle industry. Yet we came to believe in the merit of our take-charge, gunslinging ways. As we confidently anticipate further triumphs, we don't always appreciate that our view wouldn't be quite so spectacular were we not standing on the shoulders of others.

Hi tech, goodbye soul

While Mexicans acknowledge our technological edge and appreciate what we have achieved, they wonder if we haven't given up a part of our souls, relying more on *things* than on relationships. With our focus on the future and reliance on technology, Mexicans think we have forgotten the human help and the abundance of resources that got us where we are. They see Americans as unrealistic about the true forces of nature. Whereas we feel we can control our destiny, they see nature as determining the course. As a result, Mexicans are fatalistic—more willing to consign themselves to forces that they cannot control. The Mexican believes that nature will triumph in the end—even over technology.

Don't look at me

In the workplace, you may be faced with the following situation. You call in your plant manager and ask how the inventory reduction program is going. He responds that he can't complete the report because the accounting manager won't give him the inventory printout, and that the warehouse manager hasn't pulled the stock together so that it can be counted. In other words, he blames the accounting manager and the warehouse manager. Your reaction is understandable from the Anglo point of view. First, you are annoyed by his finger-pointing at others—by his defensiveness. Secondly, you wonder if the plant manager has the gumption to get out there and tell his people what to do. If you were operating in a U.S. context, your reaction would be justified. But in Mexico, your conclusion could be misleading to others. Showing irritation will only cause bigger problems.

Don't assume that what you interpret as defensiveness means weakness. What would be seen as lack of character in the United States is predictable behavior rooted in culture. Mexicans don't share our strong feeling of individual responsibility for what happens. Rather, they see themselves as fundamentally at odds with natural forces beyond their control.

Try to enter into the Mexican's mind-set with its ties to the past. Picture yourself (this isn't going to be pretty) standing naked and defenseless, at the mercy of invaders, smallpox, volcanoes, floods, and earthquakes, subject to the fickleness of natural forces and human frailties that you cannot control. You just want to make yourself invisible, untouchable, safe. Some call this escape mechanism "mysticism." Mysticism in the Mexican context goes back to the Aztec belief that humankind is as one with timeless nature. It is a dimension that transcends rational explanation. It is neither religion nor psychosis. Five hundred years of Catholic Church tutelage, including two centuries of modernity, have not erased mysticism. As much as Americans want rational explanations of everything, even human behavior, Mexico cannot be understood without comprehending this brand of mysticism.

As hard as all this is to accept, it will slow your output of liver bile to consider that the plant manager doesn't actually want to blame the other workers so much as he wants to blend into the group. He doesn't want to shift blame on others. He is merely restating what to him is an article of faith: We are all part of the same process—part of the natural scheme. What went wrong is not just *his* fault, it's everybody's fault including his. Since he manages a group-oriented workforce, he wants you to deal with the group. So he says, in effect, "It's not just me, it's all of us. If you're going to criticize, criticize the whole group, including me." Once you acknowledge the group's shortcomings, and reestablish your confidence in the manager, he will take personal responsibility. What he wants from the American *jefe* is simply assurance—assurance that we are *all* (his *grupo* and the *jefe*) in it together. Remember, the Mexican who believes that nature is in control needs to hold on to relationships. With that understanding, he will accept personal, constructive feedback.

Because you are not Mexican, the plant manager is reacting more defensively than he might with a Mexican boss. Feeling exposed, he is merely wrapping himself a little more tightly in his cultural "clothing." He is relying on a tried-and-true means of survival—one that makes him less vulnerable than standing alone. In the minds of the Mexicans, it is only natural that at times things go swimmingly and at other times they have to tread like mad to keep from drowning. They pull through by pulling together. You can fight their reaction or go with the flow.

The worst thing the non-Mexican can do in this instance is to come down hard on the plant manager for his cultural traits. Doing so drives a

Mexican into backup cultural behavior. Instead of getting the manager to act, you will see him retreat even further into a realm where nature causes him to put up defenses. He will become more mystical, falling back on the assumption that there are truths that transcend ordinary understanding. If he's incompetent, fire him; but don't slaughter the guy for behaving normally in his own context.

Becoming a two-way gringo

Consider that your own reaction is also culturally biased. Because you believe there is one correct way to handle things, and that responsibility resides in the individual rather than the group, the plant manager's defensiveness strikes you as particularly egregious. What's more, you feel that with enough willpower, the plant manager could complete the report—he could make it happen. This is the time to remind yourself that you are a one-way gringo operating in a two-way world—that balling up a fist and becoming insistent does not deal with the forces at work.

When the manager comes to you and complains that the accounting people and the warehouse guy aren't cooperating in closing out the inventory report, you should respond, "I know how you feel. It can be a challenge to *all* of us. Now, get out there and get them to work together. If you need help, I'll help. But remember, the *presidente* and the customers are arriving Friday, and it's your job to see to it that everybody works together." He'll reply, "No, no—I will take care of it." And he will. By making a small adjustment in your reaction, you will propel the plant forward, rather than create further problems.

Spiritual confluences

Mexicans definitely have a mystical side. Since nature's faceless forces cannot be fully understood, when something unusual happens they greet it with awe. If we were in church, this kind of animated response would not seem strange to us. But when it surfaces over something that happens in the workplace, we shake our heads and wonder if we're reading off the same page. We are. It's just that our cultures have handed us different lenses.

One day while I was on the job, my manager of environmental control, Jorge, charged into my office and announced that a consultant would be arriving in a few hours. The consultant had been scheduled to arrive on this very day, but for a different purpose, and that original meeting had been canceled. Jorge was breathless and his eyes were dancing. "Isn't that amazing?" he whispered emotionally. "Even though his first trip was canceled, he is coming for another reason. And on the *same day!*" So intent was Jorge on dramatizing the mysterious force at work behind this coincidence that he insisted on looking at the open page in my calendar to see if I didn't already have the consultant's name written down. I didn't. Instead, he saw where I had noted that on this day, his report on the ISO 9000 implementation was due. Gulp! He had forgotten. I merely said, "Now you have two things to do today." The message was not lost. I got my report. I didn't make fun of his mysticism, and I didn't scold him. It wasn't easy, but I have learned over time not to overreact in these situations.

American supervisors in Mexico are apt to interpret Mexican behavior from an Anglo cultural point of view. First, we expect an employee to be realistic, and not to impute mystical conjunction to what is mere coincidence. So, our first reaction to Jorge would be to tell him he was being unreasonable. Secondly, we might be agitated that he had forgotten to do the report, so we would have demanded the report. To do any less would be to tolerate lack of discipline and consequently undermine our authority—or so we think. But Jorge's reaction to our reaction will only lead to greater problems. He will think we do not respect his ability to reason. He will think we are working at cross-purposes because of the way we treated him when he was embarrassed. He will conclude that we don't like him. But, by cracking the cultural code behind Jorge's behavior, we realize that Jorge's musings are only an interesting sideshow. By accepting Jorge's temporary infatuation with the mysterious, we allow him to get over it quickly. Then, by letting him discover what he had obligated himself to do, he will remind himself of his commitment to provide the report.

Fallen angel

It is not unusual for Mexicans to regard coincidences as supernatural events. For example, one day in the break room, an older worker was marveling that on the night of an earthquake in 1957, he had a dream that an angel visited him. "That very night, I repeat, that very night, an earthquake shook the Statue of Independence, and the angel fell off its pedestal." If you are tempted to make him prove the connection, he will insist that he had the dream. (You can't prove he didn't.) He can document that the angel fell down. (It did, in fact.) But no amount of logical positivism will prove to him that there is no connection. If badgered into submission, he may ultimately admit that "it is not true, but it happened."

Only rarely, when Mexicans become breathless over a perceived supernatural conjunction, do you have to deal with such situations. But when you do, try saying "cool," or, if you want to sound more Mexican, *"Que milagro!"* (What a miracle!) Then you can get back to basics. In other instances, where they drift toward an escape from contradictions, try to focus on one reality at a time. "Yes, what was the date when the angel fell down? I'd like to know more about the earthquake." Or, "Yes, it is really unique that the consultant is coming today. What is on our agenda?" Pick up on one thread and follow it without picking a fight over what doesn't really matter. That's how a one-way gringo gets along in a two-way world.

Mystical retreat

When pressure becomes intolerable, Mexicans have a backup behavior—a way of explaining events that is not directly tied to reality. We sense this and we call it "smoke and mirrors." It's as if they've slipped into another realm— a dreamy contemplative state where they may indulge in a speculation of ideas. It seems to serve as an escape mechanism. They will fall into the "it's not true but it happened" state of mind.

While many Mexican managers fit our American template for responding appropriately to pressure, others have more difficulty. There are those who would rather not work with American management at all because we seem to tear at their cultural defenses so vigorously. Sometimes it takes a crisis to reveal what kind of person you're dealing with.

Cándido in the cactus room

Cándido served as my plant manager for two years in Reynosa, Mexico. He was an excellent production manager, but not very good at dealing with gringos. When I hired him, he moved his wife and three kids from Toluca, near Mexico City, to McAllen, Texas, just across the border from the plant. There his children could attend American schools and learn English. For a Mexican family, this was a dramatic move, one that held great promise, but one that also required their putting full faith and confidence in me, the immediate boss. Two years later, when I gave Cándido word of my transfer, he was stunned. He felt that the rug had been pulled out from under him and his family.

Within a few days, he asked if he and his wife could come to our home. As we sat in the cactus room in the late afternoon, Cándido began unloading his worries. He felt a need to explain things that I already knew about his past successes, just in case I had missed something. With his wife Marta nodding in agreement, he detailed philosophical differences between Americans and Mexicans hoping that I would explain them to management back at headquarters. When my wife encouraged Marta to share her feelings, she dissolved into tears, telling how hurt she was that my wife had not included her in a shopping excursion with the wife of the manufacturing engineer. "We Mexicans can be very jealous." My wife apologized, explaining that she had only been trying to help the wife of a new arrival.

Fueled by his wife's distress, Cándido carried on. With a burst of sunset orange illuminating his face, he issued a blistering indictment of the manufacturing engineer and the latter's wife. He felt threatened by the impending change in management, and the perceived threat penetrated his home, affecting his own wife. Rather than address what actually happened to him, he could not be discouraged from going down a path of mysticism. He rambled about unrelated events from his childhood and lost himself and his listeners in a meandering stream of disconnected and obscure thoughts. He said, in effect, that there are truths beyond current explanations that he understands, but that I did not. It was impossible to reach him with empathy or reason. He made himself untouchable by getting more remote each time we churned the issues. Any attempt to make him feel better caused him to ratchet up the rhetoric one theoretical level higher, trailing off into imaginary scenarios with vague references to his boyhood. As the room grew darker, his speculations about what might become of him and his family became more dire.

Feeling vulnerable, Cándido began to fight back at anything concrete and reasonable. "Man" had let him down. He blamed Americans for my transfer. He politely blamed my wife for hurting his wife. On some level of imagination, he seemed to be escaping to the hinterlands where he was closer to nature—one with the earth, wind, and fire. These are the things he had grown up with in the state of Durango. He knows that the forces of nature can kill him, but they never pull the tricks that men do.

Cándido was good at driving production. He was aggressive and got a lot of product out the door. But under the new American general manager, he only lasted three months. The next boss wouldn't put up with his escapism. In retrospect, Cándido was not ready for a senior management position in an American plant. He had not learned to deal with gringos.

Lifting the smoke

It often happens in Mexico that new technology is rejected in favor of tried-and-true methods. For example, an American friend of mine had set up a small stamping operation to serve the auto industry in Nuevo Leon. He was smart. He hired the entire crew of older workers from a stamping plant that had been closed down. He used the old simple hydraulic presses and small brake presses that the crew already knew how to operate. He was up and running very quickly. Then he introduced a new, fully automated press with progressive dies and automatic steel spool feeder. He taught the Mexicans how to operate it and everything was fine—for a while.

Within a short period, the workers refused to use the new press. When asked for a reason, they first said they preferred the old way. With further questioning, they said that they were afraid to touch it. "Nonsense," the owner retorted. When he badgered them some more, they explained that they were afraid the machine would cause brain damage. "The automatic press," my friend tried to persuade, "will make more parts in a day than all the other presses combined." The workers began to express concern about even staying in the plant with the new equipment. To defuse the situation, my friend put the automatic press in mothballs, and the workers continued to make parts with the old machinery.

As business grew, he hired a production manager, a young graduate of Monterrey Tech named Balderas who had several years' experience in modern stamping operations. "What's that machine doing in the corner?" Balderas inquired. "The workers won't use it. They say they're afraid of it." Balderas asked for a few days to set it up again.

Indeed, a few days later, the machine was operating and continues to operate to this day. The problem was not that the workers were afraid of the machine. They were not superstitious. They simply didn't know how to change and maintain the progressive dies and the continuous feeder, and they were afraid to ask the boss how to do it, lest he be offended. Rather than imply that the boss had inadequately explained procedures, the group made up a fantastic excuse. The more the boss pushed, the more enigmatic they became. They concocted mystical reasons to cover up the real reason for not using the machine. When "brain damage" failed to dissuade the boss, they were in a real bind. The machine operators were in a descending spiral of mysticism with no escape. Signs of mysticism are often a warning that help is needed.

In Mexico you will run into two kinds of people: those like Cándido who know how to indulge in "smoke and mirrors," and those like Balderas who know how to "*levantar el humo*," or literally "lift the smoke." That's the expression Mexicans use when they recognize that somebody is getting mystical with them. Part of cultural fluency involves being tolerant of mysticism and conversant with its expressions.

Irreconcilable differences

Implicit in the Mexicans' view that nature is in control is the related belief that many events cannot be explained—and perhaps explanation should not be attempted. The Mexican reluctance to deal with contradictions can drive Americans crazy. "Nature," a Mexican would argue, "is full of contradictions. So bountiful are contradictions that I am happy to leave them alone." When faced with a contradiction, Mexicans will simply shrug and stare thoughtfully at nothing.

One vexing incident happened to me. I had a 10 percent discount card at the chain of Fiesta Americana Hotels. When I get to the hotel in the southern city of Villahermosa, the clerk says they can't accept the card because I am already getting the discount rate. "But what's the normal rate?" Ten percent more. "Well if you're offering a 10 percent discount to everyone who walks in off the street, then of what value is my card?" I ask. They have no answer. They can't answer. They don't deal with the contradiction. It would be rude to continue asking for an explanation. Americans state, "I want an answer." Mexicans imply, "Leave it alone."

The next morning I go to breakfast. The menu says *fruta* (fruit). I ask the waiter, "What kind of *fruta* do you have?" and he says, "*Jugo*" (juice). I then ask, "What kind of juice do you have?" and he says, "*Fruta*." Again, the Mexican position: "Leave it alone."

Here's the problem. The hotel clerk can't offer an explanation because she doesn't have the answer. She's not in control of credit card policy. She can't give me a further discount, so insisting won't help. If I keep insisting, she will tell me that the manager will call me directly, just as soon as his daughter gets off the respirator. As for the waiter, he can't answer me either.

He will gladly bring me what they have, but he doesn't know what there is. Leave it alone.

For one-way gringos, it's difficult enough to adjust to cultural clashes, let alone deal with contradictions. Even when we understand the underlying difference in the people versus nature outlook, we can't help feeling frustrated. On the one hand, our "I'm in control" inquisitiveness can help us to understand. But our insistence on resolving differences works against us. Often it is the Mexican's agreeable attitude that saves the day.

What color is the bus?

If the Mexicans' ability to live with vagaries and contradictions baffles us, what baffles them? Mexicans shake their heads when we want answers to everything, stated the way we want the answers stated, and according to a chain of logic that leads inexorably to the truth—whatever that is.

If they say that a bus will pick us up at about 9:00 A.M. to take us to the conference center, we want to know the color of the bus. If we miss the first bus, will there be a second? If they say they're working on our accommodations, we want answers as to where, how much, and whether there are towels at the pool, even though the accommodations have not yet been finalized. If a sign on the ticket office says closed, but a sign on the entrance gate says the

---

Reality check

If you ever felt as though you needed help with the "smoke and mirrors" issues, here are some tips.

- Learn to love grays and maybes. At the very least, reconcile yourself to the fact that Mexicans won't engage in resolving contradictions to your satisfaction.
- In thinking that nature or God or destiny may be in charge of events, the Mexicans may not be unrealistic. At the very least, our penchant for balling up our fists and insisting that we can make things happen will be met with chagrin.
- To paraphrase Shakespeare, there are more things in heaven and earth, *gringo,* than are dreamt of in your philosophy. We need to open up our one-way mentality to a two-way world.

theater is open, we demand to know which it is, open or closed. All these whats and whys and what-ifs puzzle them. Our demand for clarity seems like a lot of smoke to them.

As part of our "people in control" approach, we want to resolve differences and amass all the information we can. It's our way of directing events. It's our way of controlling the future. The Mexicans take a much different approach: Consigning themselves to forces beyond their control, they sit back and enjoy the ride, accept contradictions, and let the details reveal themselves. When the bus arrives we'll see what color it is. Then we'll know if it really matters.

Equality versus Hierarchy

Mexicans have never known a world without hierarchy. The Spanish had kings and queens, and the Aztecs had their omnipotent *caciques* (warrior chiefs.) The Spanish language is suffused with words that imply hierarchy. I have mentioned the importance of proper titles, salutations, and dignifying honorifics, and the distinction between the formal and informal forms of *you—Usted* and *tú*. Such distinctions are not the case in English. We threw out *thee* and *thou* years ago. In contrast, formality remains a core part of the Mexicans' language, reinforcing the view that there are people in superior and inferior positions. Just as the Mexicans distinguish linguistically between man and woman, and young and old, they differentiate between boss and worker.

More than most other Latin Americans, Mexicans hold to traditional hierarchical roles based on family, education, age, and position. Because of the value placed on self-respect and its mirror image—respect for others—a hierarchical system suits them well.

Once again, we find ourselves at nearly opposite ends of the spectrum in the United States. Of all the advanced nationalities in the world, we think of ourselves as among the most egalitarian. Our identity is tied to having thrown off all vestiges of royal hierarchy in 1776. Nobody feels equality in the gut the way we do, and no other county is so driven to rub out all vestiges of class. We reject the concept of an upper class. Nobody speaks in terms of a lower class. Everyone is either in the middle class or part of a subculture. We have a compulsion to pull snobs down and admire those who pull themselves up. We don't accept that being on the bottom of the economic ladder is a permanent condition. Class distinctions are subsumed to how much money one makes.

We reject body language that suggests subservience or snobbery. We don't shuffle, and we don't kowtow. We sneer at people who act imperious or hold their head too high. We don't stand erect, heels together, clutching our clipboard to our chest with our chin up as we wait for the boss to review our work, the way Mexicans do. We don't walk into a conference room with any expectation beyond getting down to business. There are few formalities.

Close to the bone

The absence of formality is even evident in our eating habits and lack of table manners. We bite into a whole piece of bread with butter on it, leaving teeth marks. We eat a big ground slab of burnt cow in a bun instead of a fine veal cutlet on a porcelain plate. We drink beer straight out of the bottle at a reception. Our disdain for hierarchy shows itself when we tease a dinner partner for using European manners. God forbid someone should pronounce *boeuf bourguignonne* with a French accent. We retch when someone raises a pinky when drinking tea, and we call diplomats "cookie pushers." An American adult behaving like a sophisticate is shunned by his peers. A teenager acting that way may get his bottom kicked. I know.

The Mexicans' more courtly habits follow them to the dining table. They place dinnerware on their plates carefully, quietly. They never place a soiled napkin on the table. They don't slurp. If you pull up alongside a Mexican worker eating his taco, he will offer it to you. His offer is so self-contained that it escapes the uninformed American eye. Another Mexican would see his hand gesture, motioning from the taco to you, and would respond with "*buen provecho*" (or *bon appétit,* as we say in English).

As a result of our dogged egalitarianism, we may be cheating ourselves out of the ability to show respect for whole groups of people. Our disregard for formality sometimes makes international business more difficult. European, Latin American, Asian, and African competitors accustomed to hierarchy in their own cultures are more adept at bestowing respect. They understand that language conveys not only content, but style. Further, the way they stand, sit, walk, and talk transmits a shared sense of seriousness and brand of professionalism. The main difference between an egalitarian and a hierarchical workplace is the extent to which respect is conferred on people based on their position.

Down Mexico way

Mexicans are confused and often offended by our casual ways. They find our familiar banter between people of different organizational levels off-putting. In Michigan I had a casual conversation with three drill press operators about the VP of human resources. "What's with that guy?" one worker asked me. "Doesn't he put on his pants the same as we do?" I jokingly said, "I wouldn't be too sure of that." There was no harm in the conversation. The exchange was inconsequential in the United States, but such a conversation would never have happened in Mexico. A Mexican worker raising such a personal question about a superior would display profound disrespect. For me to respond as I did would have been a consummate betrayal, a show of disrespect for my co-equal. Mexican workers are offended if you disrespect a third person. "If he disrespects his own coworker, he probably disrespects me."

Johnny Ferretti was a good-natured, typical bobbing and weaving "how 'bout them Tigers" kind of guy. He had been sent to Mexico as the American general manager to show the Mexicans how to run a jointly owned office furniture company. After three months, the Mexicans were smiling a lot, even weaving and bobbing in sympathy, but business wasn't getting any better. Johnny had taken to referring to *arquitecto* Eliazer Villegas de la Peña, the major local shareholder, as Eli. Moreover, he jokingly teased the designers about their color choices. "You call it maize, we call it corn." After they got to know Johnny, the Mexicans liked him. There was really nothing to dislike: he was not rude or obnoxious and they were willing to work with him. But they were more than a little uncomfortable when he met with the Mexican customers. In the final analysis, Johnny was too informal, and business would have gone better had he reined himself in. One of the main reasons Johnny had been sent to Mexico was to correct a troublesome six-month delay in payments from two customers—the oil company (PEMEX) and electric company (CFE)—that were the largest companies in Mexico. When it came to showing respect to the VIPs of these giant enterprises, Johnny didn't have a clue. His folksy, down-home demeanor clashed with their sense of propriety. While he liked the Mexicans, his failure to show respect interfered with their desire to do business with him.

When sales continued to be flat and collections did not improve, the Americans decided to buy 100 percent of the business. It was an exercise in "when gringo attitude doesn't make it happen, we'll give them more gringo attitude." To make a long story short, Johnny was transferred, Eli left, the headquarters building was sold, and PEMEX and CFE still paid their bills according to *their* time schedules. Had Johnny understood the history and importance of hierarchy and acted in such a way as to maintain and validate people's positions within the hierarchy, he would have been much more successful. (A more realistic understanding of terms of payment and attitude toward business in Mexico back at headquarters would have been helpful. Sometimes headquarters' assumption is that things in Mexico work, or should work, the way they do in the States. Whereas Johnny was in Mexico and had a shot at understanding, often the problem is that he and his ilk have to respond to pressure from superiors who have no clue, and will never get one.)

Here's what Johnny should have done. He should have stifled his body language. At first, he would have felt a bit self-conscious standing straight, arms at his sides, composed. Johnny should have known that a smile is fine, but not an openmouthed, toothpaste ad smile—just a restrained upturn of the lips. Dignity, Johnny, not Colgate. Johnny should have set a tone that was more serious and less "let's go out in the backyard and throw the ol' pill around." Instead of saying "*Sí,*" he should have learned to say "*Sí, señor.*" If he had shown the Mexicans respect, they would have returned it.

Follow the dotted line

The Mexican separation of *jefe* and *obrero*—boss and worker—is part of a deeply embedded pattern dating back to Aztec divisions among priest, prince, and peasant, and among Spanish queen, soldier, and citizen. For equality-seeking Americans, the social implications of superior and inferior status that accompany this pattern are hard to accept. They run contrary to our culture. We recognize different levels of authority, but believe that, underneath it all, everybody is equal. Hierarchy is essential in the military, but begrudgingly accepted by many in the workplace. "Everybody pulls on his pants one leg at a time." In sharp contrast, Mexicans accept hierarchy as the natural order, with lines that are not to be crossed. Because Mexicans and Americans use the same type of organization chart, we could be deluded into thinking that our approaches to hierarchy are the same. But further analysis of how we *treat* the organization chart shows very different underlying views of connections and separations, of egalitarianism and hierarchy. Here are some of the ways in which our differences play out in the workplace.

Every American company has an organization chart with a hierarchical layout, but we perpetually get around it with "dotted-line" relationships. Since we believe that no one is truly better than anybody else, there is little cause for trepidation. There are no class-based barriers to dotted-line relationships. The vice president of sales will normally ask the vice president of finance to provide him with an analysis of fourth-quarter sales. But if he needs the report urgently and the VP of finance is out of town, he will drop in on the accounting manager and ask for it. The accounting manager will likely comply and then inform his boss of the fulfilled request. Furthermore, people are often rewarded, promoted, and viewed as effective communicators if they establish and maintain good dotted-line relationships within the organization. The lesson: In the United States the dotted line trumps the organization chart.

It won't happen that way in Mexico. If the VP of sales were to request a report of the accounting manager, he would meet with passive resistance. The manager would feel caught between a rock and a hard place unless his immediate boss had specifically told him to comply with any and all requests from this VP. Because of their hierarchical nature, employees will not necessarily cooperate across organizational lines. Similarly, visit a government office and the receptionist will not give or sell you a report or study until her boss specifically okays the transaction, even though it is clear that you're the customer and she knows explicitly what you need. The reason is that in addition to the organization chart, there is a social hierarchy that you, the receptionist, and her boss are part of.

Rather than dotted-line relationships, Mexicans hold to an informal patron/client system that operates in parallel with the organization chart. Often, the person who gets a worker into a company, and who is therefore responsible for the well-being of that worker's family, becomes his patron—as distinct from his boss. The new employee becomes the patron's client. The patron is thus an extraofficial boss within the organization—the *padrino*, the godfather. Over time, a network of patron/client relationships develops.

Let's say the warehouse manager gets a maintenance man a job in the company. The manager may be the godfather to the new employee's son. Family obligations may have existed between the two for generations. Now, the maintenance man is beholden to the warehouse manager. Never mind the organization chart. If the maintenance man should do something to offend the warehouse manager, he could lose his patron. That can be more threatening than losing his job. So if there is a conflict of interest, generally the patron relationship is most carefully guarded. The new employee might need his patron in the future for another job.

It gets labyrinthine. The maintenance man, for his part, may get another person a job in the assembly department, thus creating a subpatron/subclient relationship. The Mexicans have no problem with nepotism and rely on extended family contacts and personal networking to get jobs. In this way, the patron/client relationships within the organization are a manifestation of a larger network that reaches outside the company's walls, involves the subjects' families, and survives the company's mergers. One result of this is that whole groups of employees can quit and move to another employer for reasons the human resources manager cannot quite figure out. The uninitiated American will be left shaking his head.

The grim mower

An American president of a Halliburton subsidiary in Reynosa, Mexico, told me the following story. Three days prior, he had been sitting in his office looking out the window when he noticed that the grass hadn't been cut for more than a week. He stormed outside, flagging down a groundskeeper sweeping the parking lot, and gave him a direct order to cut the grass. A day passed and nothing happened. Second day, nothing. Then he collared the plant manager, telling him: "Every time I look out my window I see that god-damn grass getting higher by the minute. What the hell do I have to do to get somebody to follow an order around here?"

He cannot fathom how this happened in a hierarchical culture. "If respect is such a big buzzword," he challenges, "why don't the Mexicans listen to me? I'm the boss. I ask them to cut the grass and nothing happens. Can't they think?"

What the gringo failed to see was that he had put the groundskeeper in an impossible position. On a day-to-day basis, the Mexican worker took orders from his immediate supervisor, who told him to sweep the parking lot. The groundskeeper was reluctant to go to his supervisor because that might have caused a conflict. The supervisor told him one thing, but the president told him something else. So, a Mexican worker faced with such a conflict would probably go to his unofficial boss (his patron) instead. "I'm getting conflicting orders. What do I do?" Answer? "Wait—maybe the problem will take care of itself." Or he might say, "Wait—Juan will be back

Thursday, and Juan is your supervisor's godfather. He will fix everything." Or perhaps, "Maybe we can find a middle ground."

The following day, I am chatting again with the president in his office. Feet on his desk, hands laced behind his head, he looks out the window and sees that the worker is mowing the lawn. "There, I made my point!" he tells me with a sense of triumph. Right? Wrong. When I leave that day, I discover that the lawn directly in front of his window has been mowed—nothing else.

A Mexican executive would have treated the situation differently. In the first place, as president of the company, he would never, ever have gone directly to the worker. He would have kept more distance. He would have called in the person immediately under him to see that the grounds were attended to. The message would have been passed down through the chain of command, and the job would have gotten done.

The Mexican executive knows how to keep both the organization chart and the myriad patron/client relationships in context. He becomes the father figure, responsible not only for the proper management of the business, but also for the personal lives of his "family." This approach seems natural to him and his workers. The lesson here: Family hierarchy trumps the organization chart.

Dear old dad

Where the society is basically hierarchical, everybody understands dear old dad best. Some American presidents operating in the United States believe you motivate workers by showing that you are one of them, but that approach does not work in Mexico. Other American managers order their employees to jump and then berate them for coming back down. A Mexican president would not try to be buddy-buddy, nor would he be a domineering, table-pounding martinet. The successful Mexican executive sees himself as the CEO and superpatron. Ultimately, he is the person the workers depend on for their paycheck, their livelihood, and their family's well-being. Not only does the Mexican CEO occupy the top box in the organization chart, he is the top patron in a hierarchy of patron/client relationships. He is "dear old dad *el presidente*."

In the case above, a Mexican president, after giving the order, would probably have waited patiently two days for the grass to be cut, allowing time for underlings and clients to rearrange their shifting responsibilities. We assume that if our orders are not acted upon immediately, nothing is happening, whereas the Mexican boss has confidence that his subordinates "are working on it."

The female factor

Within the Mexican household, the mother ranks highest with regard to family matters. In the workplace, a businesswoman can build on this and become a leader by taking a presumptive attitude about the respect she deserves as "dear mother." Or if a woman is of roughly equal age with her staff, she may rely on the role of the respected aunt. Any disrespect to her would be tantamount to disrespect of one's own mother or aunt, which Mexicans find intolerable. While men will show respect, let's be clear, *machismo* will never completely disappear.

Capitalizing on the inviolate nature of the mother's role, the female Mexican boss doesn't try to "outmacho" the machos while carrying out her duties or asserting authority. She recognizes that *machismo* is often reflected in innocuous ways—like putting up a cheesecake calendar in the workplace—and that no disrespect is intended in such an act. An American woman trying to appeal to a Mexican workforce will do well to take her cues from the Mexican woman's cool handling of such issues. Rather than overreacting to *machismo*, the American woman should rely on the male workers' freely offered respect. Some American women might be tempted to try to win the support of the men by acting buddy-buddy with them. But this can be easily misinterpreted and ineffective.

I had lunch with an American colleague in Mexico City. She was nine months pregnant with twins. She is married to a Mexican. No shrinking violet, she has a Ph.D. in economics and is a corporate director. She told me unequivocally, "It's true what they say about Mexican men—that they are domineering and macho. But I have never felt so much *respect* in my life!"

American women can ascend to the highest ranks in Mexico just as Mexican women can succeed. But, either way, the rules are different from here. A female American attorney working for a Mexican law firm may be offended by the *Sports Illustrated* swimsuit edition on the reception room table. But her objections should not be louder than those of her female Mexican colleagues. She will find that the latter, too, recognize the inappropriateness, but they are not inclined to complain. The Mexican women's attitude is more like, "It's not important in the big scheme. What matters is not that men are oglers, rather that I get respect for my position and the work I do." *Machismo* is more overt in Mexico than in the United States, but respect is much more freely and sincerely offered in Mexico. If the offense is intolerable, then a quiet word to the boss that the magazine is disrespectful suffices to have the magazine removed. Cultural fluency means understanding what is tolerated there. Some American women may want to make adjustments.

Generally, Mexican men mean no disrespect and may be willing to make adjustments too. Often I had to take women to a construction trailer where workers had hung up *Playboy* calendars. Even though the crew didn't work for me, I would call ahead to ask if they would take their calendars down. They did, but word got back to me that they wondered why *Señor Eduardo* made the fuss. After we would leave, the pictures would go back up. When I explained that many women consider it disrespectful, the calendars came back down for good.

We are all children

Both men and women are raised the same way in Mexico in that their sense of hierarchy is more acutely developed than ours. Both sexes freely offer respect to those in authority, no matter the gender. Mexicans frequently say, "*Somos todos niños*" (We are all children). Our Anglo ears hear a derogatory reference, whereas Mexicans are actually asking for nurturing. American children are expected to be independent and grow up making their own decisions; Mexican children are not. Instead, they are expected to discuss matters within the family and then submit to the final authority of the family, which is the mother or the father. Mexican children are more nurtured. Native women suckle their children often until age three. Children in middle-class homes traditionally stay with the family until they marry. The oldest daughter may not marry so that she can be at home to take care of the parents in their dotage. When Mexicans say, "We are all children," they are submitting to authority so long as it is administered in the long-term interest of the family. In the three stages of life (i.e., child, adult, parent), American families work toward achieving an adult-to-adult relationship between mother and daughter or father and son. In Mexico, the relationship of parent to child remains in place forever.

Leaving the door open a crack

While overseeing a construction project in Mexico, I call upon the services of a talented interior designer. Employing a bit of old-world formality, I explain to the young woman that the plant is barely started, and I am working out of my home. Could she meet with me there? I quickly add that, of course, she may bring someone with her. Given the traditional and hierarchical nature of Mexican society, I know that the male/female situation could make her feel uncomfortable. The next day, Claudia arrives right on time . . . with her mother.

Mamá speaks no English. I shake hands with her, making a point of holding my hand parallel to the floor with my palm up. I stand straight but bowed ever so slightly from the waist, smiling in a cheerful way that demonstrates I am pleased to make her acquaintance. As I show Claudia and her mother in, I leave the front door open a crack, inviting them to sit down. I continue with the formalities, commenting on Claudia's beautiful English and speaking of schools and Mexico and places she has visited. I offer *mamá* a cup of tea and she declines. *Mamá* takes out her knitting and, seemingly, pays no attention to us. I continue with the polite banter for a few minutes, again offering a cup of tea—again declined—then bring the subject around to the business at hand and engage Claudia in a planning discussion. When the meeting is over, we all shake hands. In a few days, Claudia returns with her proposal and presentation charts, this time without *mamá*.

By letting Claudia know ahead of time that she might be coming into a situation that would be less than ideal for a traditional family, and by telling her it was fine to bring someone along, she was assured that my intentions were honorable. Bringing her mother was a throwback to classical Spanish social mores. There are still many places in Latin America and Spain where mother shows up with the daughter to assure her honor. *Mamá* may even go along on dates.

In leaving the front door open, I signaled that Claudia and her mother were free to escape, should I suddenly run amok. This is an archaic practice that is still observed in the more traditional, hierarchical environment of Mexico. By taking *mamá*'s hand in my open palm, I was signaling that I understood that in past times I would have kissed her hand. That would be out of place today, but women over sixty still appreciate a tacit nod to tradition. (Remember when men here used to tip a hat to a lady? Remember when men would take their hats off if a woman got on the elevator?) Incidentally, the reason *mamá* did not accept my offer of tea was that she sensed I didn't have maids, as she undoubtedly had.

By treating Claudia and her mother with the respect they deserved, I had won *mamá*'s approval. Claudia later told me that her mother had repeatedly asked her if she had finished the work for that nice Mr. Crouch. By ratcheting my behavior back a half century, I had the whole family hierarchy working for me. Fortunately, I understood these quaint cultural dynamics from having lived in Spain under Generalísimo Franco in the 1950s. My experience was unique, but anything we can do to expand our social vocabulary will improve cultural fluency.

It ain't easy, but learn to enjoy respect

As an American egalitarian in a country that is strongly hierarchical in its social and business relationships, you are in the minority. Don't be embarrassed if people show you deference. Observing the local hierarchies is in your best interest and that of your organization. Remember that relationships are driven by position, title, gender, age, class, and patronage. The hotel you stay at tells your hosts if you are a CEO, an engineer, or a sewing supervisor. Where you live tells them your status. Your title, the size of your office, and your bearing set you apart as the true leader. Do not shrink from showing the trappings of power. By the same token, don't assume by the deference shown you that you are really superior or have total power. Deference is payment of respect, it should not be repaid with disrespect.

Develop relationships with people who are in the same position or of the same class as you. A company VP in Mexico, for example, might get to know people at the Mexican Industrialists' Club and meet corporate attorneys and directors of international accounting firms, as well as other VPs. When faced with a problem, it is these people and their respective network of relationships that can help with contacts up and down the hierarchy— that is, with the governor of the state or the safety engineer who can reconfigure your fire protection system. Working with a Mexican team of laborers in the United States, and taking the time to identify and cultivate guide workers and patrons within your group, will help you solve attendance problems and find new workers.

Mexicans doing unto Mexicans

Many times, Mexican managers will take advantage of a "power distance" the way Americans would not. Don't be surprised if a Mexican supervisor assumes that he can browbeat an underling. This is quite common. One of your challenges as an American dealing with a Mexican workforce is to manage your Mexican managers. You have to find a middle ground between what is acceptable local practice and what is appropriate to your company's culture and American standards. Mexican managers can treat lower-class factory hands like dirt. Mexican personnel managers who have never worked for an American company take it for granted that they will not hire ugly ladies, the handicapped, or anyone over thirty. They can be harsh in their firing practices.

Sometimes Mexican American supervisors are more overbearing and abusive than native Mexicans. Perhaps because they have rejected much of their ancestral mythology, they may show disrespect for what they regard as the backward ways of their former compatriots. Some of these individuals carry a bigger chip on their shoulder than any gringo. An American business owner told me that he discovered that his Mexican American supervisor was taking advantage of deferential Mexican workers. Deference on the part of workers can easily lead a supervisor to think that he has more control than he has been invested with.

There are occasions in which a Mexican American who has lost his sense of, and respect for, hierarchy can come off worse with Mexican officials than an Anglo. Consider Freddy, the Mexican American foreman of a McAllen, Texas, roofing company, who wanted to know if he could use my import permit to get his crane across the Rio Grande into Mexico. The roofers were completing the propeller plant construction project and needed to raise the roofing materials topside. Using my import permit would speed things up considerably. Once they got the exception (or *ampliación*), Freddy assured me they would finish the job and re-export the crane immediately. This seemed logical enough, so I approved the action and promptly forgot about it.

Three weeks later, I got a call from the Mexican government's local Department of Commerce office. I was well acquainted there, so I was puzzled when they told me that I had to come into the office in person to discuss why my application for an *ampliación* for the crane was being denied. What? This had never happened before. I always had good relations with them. They had always been willing to make appropriate exceptions for me. I headed for their office straightaway.

When I arrived, Nancy Oropeza was visibly shaken and unusually straight-forward with me. "As you know, Señor Crouch, we do not *have* to allow you to import this crane."

"Of course, but pardon me," I responded, "can you help me understand what this is about?"

"Well, your representative, Señor Blanco, has been in here every day badgering us and giving us hell about where his permit is." (She didn't put it like that, but that's what she was saying.)

Sensing what had happened, I apologized profusely, telling her that I made a mistake. I explained that Sr. Blanco was an outside contractor; and that, in granting permission for his company to use *our* permit, I had no idea he would abuse the privilege. I empathized with her, confirming that she was right to turn the application down. I told her that it would never happen again—which it didn't. I assured her that I would speak to the roofing people the minute I got back to the office and give them holy hell—which I did. Finally, I promised that neither they nor anyone else would ever be allowed to use my permit again—which they weren't. Having made these promises, and kept them, the cooperation of the Department of Commerce was cemented for future work.

Sometimes Mexican Americans can lose their sense of place within the very hierarchical Mexican work environment. While my all-Mexican staff knew how to deal with government officials, I had failed to realize that when Mexican Americans interact with Mexicans, different dynamics are at work. Here was a guy from southern Texas who thought he was better than the people he left behind. He spoke Spanish and knew lots of derogatory words. He believed that he was a perfect blend of Yankee aggressiveness, northern efficiency, brown skin, and fluency in Spanish. In fact, this poor fellow had forgotten Mexican manners, overlearned Anglo intensity, and was determined to show his blue-eyed client that he knew how to get things done in Mexico. However, by inflating his posture in representing me and abusing people with his lack of respect, he polluted the business climate and threatened long-standing relationships.

My contacts among Mexican government officials were always more than happy to treat me as the customer or the boss, so long as I respected their authority. Although you have to be sensitive to perceive it, a Mexican's back will stiffen ever so slightly if you cross the line. While the displeasure will not be articulated, you will not make any friends or influence any colleagues by violating hierarchical standards. When things go awry in Mexico— and you can bet your burrito they will—there is no substitute for finding the appropriate words of respect to reestablish the Mexicans' position within the hierarchy.

With respect to . . .

Here are some words of respect that will help you cement good relationships with Mexicans by honoring their position in the hierarchy.

- Whenever possible, substitute *"Sí Señor/a"* for a simple *"Sí."* Our own language usage has deteriorated in the past several generations. We have gone from "Yessir" to "Yes" to "No problem, you guys." We don't mean disrespect, but that is how such comments are taken in Mexico.

- Respect for a person's position runs up and down the hierarchy. Showing respect for workers' products will pay dividends. When they say *"Es mi trabajo"* (It's my job), they mean to say that they identify personally with the work they do and want to be respected for it. Reinforcing their sense of self-respect will encourage good work. "That's a fine job." Conversely, corrective feedback to an employee should be given without a tone that could be interpreted as disrespect. "That's a good start. Try to tweak this a bit more," you say with a smile. Don't snap, "That's not what I wanted!" Coming from up the ladder, such a comment will also seem threatening.

- An American construction foreman might be able to watch his Mexican immigrant workforce interact with each other. If he can spot the *obrero guia* (guide worker) or *padrino* (patron) among them, he can solicit his help with the rest of the crew. By saying, "I need your help with the workers," the construction foreman will show respect to the unofficial leader within the group and get his cooperation.

- Before tackling an important meeting, practice what to us may be old-fashioned manners. "After you." "No, after you."

- Be a bit more formal. Play the role of a symphony patron, not the stagehand.

CHAPTER
ELEVEN

Tasks versus People: Conflict Resolution

Intercultural conflicts are, by definition, shared problems. When trouble occurs, failure to see ourselves in the way others see us gets in the way of resolution, as do our common stereotypes about the other guy. By the same token, the Mexicans do not easily recognize what we are trying to say or do. They too have stereotypes of what gringos are like. We will never settle a fender bender, an argument over a real estate contract, the transfer of ownership of a plant, or the termination of an employee until we first recognize and then deal with the intercultural issues.

The following is a short list of stumbling blocks that cause 90 percent of the conflict between Mexicans and Americans. It's difficult to deal with larger, more substantive problems until you get beyond these intercultural hang-ups.

Three things Mexicans hate about us but are too nice to bring to our attention

- First, we tell a contractor what we want, and then wave him off. Or we tell the worker what we want, and then leave the room. The contractor comes back with *his* concept of what we asked for, or the worker presents his finished product, and we react miserably. "That's not what I wanted!" We get upset. We show our displeasure.
- Second, we ask Mexicans to do something for us, and they agree to do the work. But before they can turn around, we call them asking why it hasn't happened yet. Or we ask for room service and as soon as we hang up, we call back asking angrily what's happened to our order.

- Third, we stand in line behind somebody at the customs patio and jump up and down trying to get the clerk's attention, signaling our displeasure at something—not sure what—by clenching our teeth, our fists, and looking angry. When we get to the window, the clerk says we need a copy of a permit. We have to get a copy then go back to the end of the line. We show our impatience at their ineptitude.

A common theme in American-Mexican conflict is our irritability. Mexicans really don't understand the anger factor. They take it personally. They don't realize that we treat everybody with the same impatience.

Three things we assume about the Mexicans and are only too happy to lay on them

- First, nothing ever works in Mexico, and they never get anything quite right. We are too quick to point out their shortcomings without understanding the factors operating under the surface. We forget that our airlines don't run on schedule, that our public toilets are pungent, and that we have slums, pregnant teenagers, and drug problems.
- Second, they give us promises, promises, and they don't deliver. They're lazy. After a while you just have to crack the whip and start breaking pottery to get any action. We are quick to set up a conflict over unfulfilled duties, but we are slow to ask if we can help.
- Third, there is no sense of efficiency in Mexico. They don't know how to organize according to international standards. They waste time. They are so laid-back that they don't care if you're in a hurry to get to a dinner engagement or not. We let them know we are displeased, and the matter only gets worse. That convinces us we are right. But we are too quick to judge.

So how can we be more effective and avoid the kind of purposeless stereotyping and steam letting that's only going to obscure the real problem and charge the emotional atmosphere? We can begin by stifling our impatience, intensity, and irritability, while remembering that our frustrations with the Mexicans are rooted in cultural differences, not ineptitude or character flaws on their part. Now you're ready to approach the big issues constructively.

Uno, dos, tres . . .

Step One: Deal with intercultural conflict first

This depends on learning to recognize an intercultural conflict where it exists. You get the feeling that you and the Mexicans are talking past one another, that there is no meeting of the minds. As soon as you detect an intercultural impasse, pay attention to everything you have learned regarding Mexican sense of time, sense of space, use of language, and work styles. You have to be sensitive to subtle hints—when their back stiffens, when you detect passive resistance, when they say yes but we think they may mean no—all these are signs that you had better slow down and refocus.

Step Two: Deal with backup behavior

When we Americans get irritable, we self-destruct. If a little gringo attitude doesn't get action, we give them more gringo attitude. We start breaking pottery. But this just makes everybody, including us, feel worse. Consider that the Mexican is feeling tension and is going into his backup behavior, which is to shrink from conflict and to try to set an agreeable tone. The more pressure we put on him, the more he is going to dodge us. Put him under yet more pressure and he may even misbehave. Finally, he will retreat into mysticism. This is not the road we want to go down. So get a grip and be effective, not defective. Take a deep breath and relax. Then take step three.

Step Three: Deal with the substantive conflict by focusing on people, not tasks

Forget references to schedules, matrixes, and nuts and bolts. These are inanimate and cold. By rolling up our sleeves together and tackling our conflicts on a personal basis, we will be able to handle problems with contracts, accidents, or knotty situations in the office. Rather than assume the conflict is about concepts or things, such as inefficiency, lack of urgency, incompetence, ketchup, mismatched windows, or pottery, start by considering the personal angle. "Here we are, just you and me." We must look our counterpart in the eye and ask for cooperation and understanding—appeal to the Mexican's human nature.

Because resolving conflicts in Mexico starts with people, building strong interpersonal relationships is paramount. We hear a lot of talk in the United States about how important it is to build relationships in Mexico, but little explanation as to *why*. The answer is simple: Mexicans, with their group-oriented work style, rely on relationships because they believe that someday the procedures will break down. A shipment *will* arrive a week late. Mail *will* get misdirected. Stock *will* plummet. The good silver *will* melt in the warming oven. Something will eventually go wrong. And when it does, as a Mexican explained to me, "We would rather rely on a human being to bail us out than to depend on a piece of paper. Why would we want to leave our fate up to a procedure written two years ago by a bureaucrat or a lawyer who's not around?" When trouble hits, Mexicans count on their friends and family to pull their cookies out of the oven. They want to have someone they trust like a brother come to their rescue.

People people

In the United States, efficiency and practicality are driven by task definition. We have a tradition of division of labor, of responsibility and action stemming from the early industrial revolution. Flow charts, operations management, information technology, policies and procedures, job descriptions, and organization charts dominate. If something goes wrong in an organization, we immediately review the procedures to see if they've been followed. Then, if we still have problems, we redefine and reshape the process and rewrite the job responsibilities. After all the exhaustive paperwork still hasn't solved the problem, only then would we deal with the human factor. If we continue to experience difficulty, we conclude that Bill or Betty couldn't do the job if their life depended on it, and they are removed or replaced.

In people-oriented work cultures like Mexico, it's just the opposite. First you must sit down with the employees, reemphasizing the need to maintain group harmony and rededicating people to their human relationships, all the while relying on the team to work out the hiccup. If the team does not solve the problem within a reasonable time period, only then would you turn to procedures. Stated another way, after the human element has redressed itself, *then* you can go department by department making adjustments in schedules, graphs, budget figures, and task lists. In Mexico, if by the time you have gone through this process it remains apparent that Juanita or Paco can't do the job, you can rest assured that you have the entire group's cooperation if the employees must be released or relocated. You end up at the same place and at the same time, but you got there by a different route.

We could say that Americans solve problems with procedures, while

Mexicans solve problems with people. One approach is not inherently better than the other. But in a people-oriented culture, reliance on policies and procedures first, rather than on people, is viewed as improper and wrong-headed.

Case in point

The following case study illustrates the consequences of failing to deal with intercultural conflicts appropriately. It also demonstrates that positive results can be achieved by taking the three-stepped approach.

Tackling intercultural conflict—Step One

Six years after leaving a plant that I had set up for an American company in Mexico, I got a call from the president. "We've sold the product line and are selling the plant. Can you help us manage the transition to the new owners?" This was a unique opportunity to evaluate how a fledgling American management team had dealt with Mexican intercultural issues.

My primary duty was to close down the original operation and to manage the staff, keeping them and the core of trained workers on board while the new owner took over. Having set up the company, I knew where all the important levers were. With the competent accounting and engineering staff then in place, I expected that it would be relatively easy to get the job done. Nevertheless, there would be some interesting challenges. With any change, there can be conflicts. People are on edge wondering what will become of their jobs. But in this case, as I soon learned, there had been a breakdown in intercultural understanding between the American managers and the Mexican staff.

Homer—who was serving as interim manager—invited me to attend a general staff meeting. In the three months since he replaced the previous American manager, he had hit a few walls. He was clearly frustrated. Nevertheless, he tried his best to be friendly with the Mexican staff. "*Que hay?*" ("What's new?") asked Homer as they assembled. "*Que hubo*," came the familiar jargon reply from Eliud, the enthusiastic engineering manager. "Huh?" replied Homer, scowling. This was my first clue that Homer's intercultural receptors were out for tacos.

In a show of efficiency and without further personal exchange, Homer unfurled his manufacturing schedule, his administrative checklists, and a memo from his boss, along with individual task lists. Then, he began telling everybody what to do.

"Okay," Homer said, getting right to the point, "let's go around the room and see exactly where we are on the task list." All the while, he was knitting his brow, doubling his fists, and questioning everything anybody told him. He constantly referred to charts, schemes, schedules, and job descriptions—in other words, the cold approach. "I don't get it. Why do you have to do that?" he kept asking. The staff was smiling and alert, but they offered little. They waited for the next question and tried to answer it respectfully, but I sensed the passive resistance.

On one occasion, Macarena, the experienced human resources manager, told Homer that she had to go to the Department of Labor with eleven workers to sign a declaration that workers were renouncing the union contract. This was met with an untrusting, "Why? What for?" Having explained politely that such an action was required to absolve the new owners of any preexisting obligation to the union, Macarena was clearly taken aback by such a contentious reaction. Ignoring Macarena and further diminishing her position of respect within the organization, Homer turned to me and asked, "Ned, do you know why she has to leave the plant with *eleven workers?*" I responded, "Yes. In fact, let's get out of her way and let her do her job." With that, the staff laughed and relaxed. There was no disrespect to Homer, just a shift in intercultural messages.

Homer, like many American managers who need help in penetrating the cultural differences, still expected things to work in Mexico the same way they do in the United States. When they didn't, he couldn't hide his impatience, intensity, and irritability. Maybe he was worried that word would leak out, and he'd have to explain to his boss why so many workers had left the plant that day. In addition to Macarena's task, there were many other similar, complicated steps, and time was a-wastin'. Clearly, we all had a lot of work to do. But it was the broader intercultural issues that were the first real stumbling blocks—failing to deal with people before tasks, and failing to foster personal relationships with the employees.

Given the nonroutine nature of transferring operations to new ownership, and the complexity of the tasks at hand, we could not risk alienating the Mexican staff. Moreover, we had to do things right vis-à-vis the Mexican government. Unfortunately, the greatest impediment to progress was the one-way gringo mentality. The way Homer handled the situation was actually creating conflict—he was forcing the staff to explain things in a way that was acceptable to him. He was behaving normally for an American. He tried to lead, but he had the *chart* before the *burro*. As Homer became more agitated, the staff members, while appearing alert and cooperative, quietly shrank behind their pleasant masks. Clearly, Homer was making matters worse and the mission was in jeopardy.

Lack of cultural awareness was preventing Homer from reaching his target. The staff was reacting to his gringo frustrations—his backup behaviors caused their own backup behaviors to kick in. They resisted and hid. Further, in the absence of proper direction, the manufacturing operation was devolving into a disorganized soccer match in which over a hundred people chased the same ball, but nobody remembered where the goal was. Cooperation had broken down. Everybody was off in his or her own world.

Dealing with backup behaviors—Step Two

The first move in dealing with backup behaviors involved my suggesting in the meeting that we get out of Macarena's way and let her do her job. This demonstrated to the staff that management was willing to trust them and recognize that they knew how to do their jobs. Macarena then had the sense that she was in control of her own work and that management would support her. If she hadn't been put on the defensive, she could have explained that she had to go to the government office with eleven employees because of Mexico's history of labor abuses. Federal labor law states that if there are five workers, and two of them want to have a union, they can vote in a union. Conversely, in order to cancel a union contract, you need 40 percent of the workforce—in this case eleven—to go personally to the Labor Commission to foreswear the contract. But Macarena knew that this was too much to explain to an impatient gringo. Indulging in her own backup behavior, she shrank away from an explanation, hiding behind "It's the law," which caused Homer to dig his heels in deeper.

The next positive signal to the staff came when Homer left the Mexican operation as per the prearranged plan. But there were other eruptions of backup behaviors to deal with. As I conducted the next meeting, Elmer—a production superintendent—repeatedly interrupted. "I know how to set up a new company," he insisted. And then, "I used to be president of a company. I can help the new owners." These interjections were slowing down the meeting, disrupting the flow, and not well received by the rest of the staff. It turned out Elmer was Colombian, not Mexican. Feeling somewhat threatened by all the changes, Elmer was trying to build himself up in the eyes of others. He had even moved some of his stuff into an unoccupied office in the executive area, which upset other managers. The rest of the staff also objected to Elmer trying to stand out in the crowd, so dealing with him was important to restoring a sense of group cohesiveness.

Faced with yet another intercultural challenge, I resisted the temptation to say, "Shut up, Elmer. *I* was hired to do that. Your job is to manage the machining department." Instead, I took him aside. "Tell me Elmer, about your experience in the past." "Oh, well twenty years ago. . . ." He went on for ten minutes. I let him spin out his whole story. "Well, that's very interesting. As you go about your daily activities in the machining department, rest assured that I will let the new owners know about your past experience." This indirect way of saying, "Your job is managing the machining department," was not lost on him. Beyond that, he felt that I understood his potential, and perhaps he figured that he would be better off letting *me* carry his cudgel rather than sticking his own neck out. Then I got a bit more direct. "In the meantime, don't talk so much in the meetings," I said. "Oh, okay," he smiled. I wouldn't have been so direct with a Mexican, but with a Colombian it worked.

The lesson here is that when devising solutions for resolving intercultural conflicts in Mexico, it can be a mistake to assume that "one size fits all." In this case, we were dealing with a behavioral pattern that was out of character with the two dominant cultures in the meeting. In Mexico, as in the United States, you might find yourself dealing with a multicultural workforce. While the steps outlined here still apply, the specific approach may have to be tailored to the individual situation.

Handling conflicts by relying on people—Step Three

On the third day of my assignment, the accounting manager, Gloria, came to me. "Señor Ned, I can't get the books closed. I can't get the people to do the inventory. If I can't get the inventory done, I can't make a final reconciliation with the customs people, and we seem to have about a million-dollar disparity between our customs declarations and what my inventory sheets show." She looked like she hadn't slept for days and was close to tears.

"Furthermore," she continued, "instead of helping, Marcos is out there computing the tonnage capacity of the Wheelabrator, Eliud is trying to position himself for a promotion with the new owner, and Manuel is not giving me the raw materials inventory. They are all trying to set themselves up for the new owners." She went on and on, until I too was convinced that the wheels were coming off the wagon. There was only one thing to do—call a meeting. But how I conducted the meeting would result in success or failure.

I began by emphasizing to the assembled staff that the most important thing was transferring the company to the new owners. I had no papers; my hands were laced on the conference table. I reminded myself to sit straight and yet try to relax. No huff and puff. "Gloria needs our help. Without the inventory, we can't close the books. Unless we close the books, we can't close the deal. And furthermore," in my best avuncular lilt, "remember . . . above all, we must maintain group harmony. We want the new owners to know how well we work together." With this, I shut up. There was an extended hush. I had to force myself not to add anything else.

Marcos was the first to open up, offering that he could stop doing his calculations and continue with the inventory sheets. Eliud joined in, not to be outdone. And so the dominoes tumbled, neatly completing the circle around the table, with each staff member in turn volunteering support to Gloria and the team in solving the problem. But they didn't do it because of charts or job descriptions. Nor did they line themselves up just because I told them to. They did it because their "uncle" had reminded them nicely that we were a family, and we all had a job to do. The next day, Gloria was holding meetings without my help, and the inventory was reconciled. The "people approach" had worked.

VP, don't phone home!

Sometimes dealing with intercultural issues first involves finessing the management back at corporate headquarters. One of the biggest problems faced by on-site American managers in Mexico is managing the boss back home. By the same token, there is often a communications breakdown in the United States between a well-versed Anglo supervisor of a multicultural workforce and his bosses upstairs. Those gringos who need a fixed explanation according to their standards of logic will take up all your time with their questions. It's too complicated for them to understand. They won't get it. All this intercultural crap is overrated anyway, or so they think.

Most Anglo management has little patience for complicated explanations. How would Homer in the example above ever explain why Macarena had to take eleven workers out of the plant on a perfectly good workday?

Would Homer's boss have been delighted with a history lesson? Try telling the home office that Mexican unions are there for the protection of the workers against a long history of slavery, and they'll jump to conclusions, asking if slavery is still allowed. Try telling them that Mexican *caciques* used to grab wandering peasants with hooks, kidnapping them for work in the copper mines of Cananea, and they'll leap to the conclusion that all Mexicans are thugs. Try explaining that Mexican federal labor laws state that Mexican workers must elect a representative and send him by bus to Mexico City to register the contract renunciation, and the employer is expected to pay for his bus ticket. See what I mean? It's too complicated to explain. Instead of force-feeding gringo management back home, excuse yourself by telling them you'll be back in touch just as soon as your mother is off the respirator.

My experience is that working with the Mexicans to resolve conflicts, rather than involving upper management back home, ultimately serves the best interest of the corporation. Faced with the dilemma of whether to reach out to the Mexicans for help in solving a problem, or whether to cover one's tail feathers with the people back home, nine times out of ten, the U.S. on-site manager will choose the latter. Naturally, the boss back home overreacts and starts issuing orders that may be completely off the mark, but the local American is now obligated to carry them out. Then, as things go from bad to worse—and this happens a lot—the U.S. boss hops a plane and shows up with guns blazing to let the Mexicans know who's really in charge.

If you absolutely *have* to explain certain situations to your boss in Ohio, you could make something up—but do it Mexican style. Say that eleven workers had to go to the Labor Department to be tested for impetigo. Or tell the personnel director back home that Macarena wasn't there because she broke her other coccyx—Mexicans have two you know. It is so much easier to tell your U.S. purchasing manager that everything arrived on time, on budget, and without quality problems, and then to let your Mexican staff handle the hassles of cross-border paperwork. Tell them the truth and you'll only aggravate the Americans. Instead, immerse yourself in the Mexican context, trust your staff, work through conflicts by relying on the Mexicans to get things done, and tell the people back home how brilliantly you handled problems after the fact.

Of course, the best approach is to carefully knit together relationships among homologues in both countries, that is, among purchasing people, human resource people, and accountants in Mexico and at the corporate headquarters in the United States. Once the doors are open on the lower levels, American managers can find their own ways of appealing to the boss for a desired response. This is also the best way to open the eyes of people back home who have thrown themselves into "organization for globaliz-ation," but have never understood that the rest of the world doesn't give a damn how things are organized on paper—that what matters is how things work on the ground. The gurus in Atlanta, Georgia, need to appreciate that your local Mexican contacts care only about *you*—the lonely, outposted foot soldier—and what you bring to the table. So don't forget to manage the people back home. Doing so effectively will prevent a hiccup from becoming an autoimmune deficit.

By the same token, when working with a mostly Mexican workforce in the States, anything a supervisor can do to foster more personal contact between the workers and management—at coffee breaks or by joint meet-ings—will promote understanding and set the stage for more effective con-flict resolution.

Crash course

What should you do if you have a conflict with a Mexican and there is no opportunity to build relationships? Say you're a visitor, and you have a fender bender in Pachuca. The other guy gets out of his car and starts right away claiming that you were going too fast. It doesn't make sense to you, because he hit you from behind. Is he trying to sting you? In the States, you'd argue with him and call the cops. Not so in Mexico. First of all, if you get into an argument and the cops are called, the police may well take their compa-triot's side—he is better able to argue his point of view than you are.

Here's how to win: 1. You have to see the Mexican as another kind of being. He doesn't think the way you think. 2. Sit on your will to fight. Take a deep breath. 3. Proceed by persuading him person to person. Rather than starting with road rules, stop signs, and damage estimates, remind him that it was an accident, and that these things happen between people of good faith. Then, "I can't explain to myself how, if *I* was going so fast, you hit me from the rear." He responds, "Well, I didn't see you, so that means you had to be going really, really fast." "No-o-o," you smile. "Tell me again. Why was it that you didn't see me?" You are not only lobbing soft questions logically, but you've boiled the conflict down to a "you and me" level. If you are arrogant and argumentative, he can be the same, and there is no end to it. But handled *mano a mano* (brother to brother), he has no recourse but to relent. He can sting an ornery gringo he's never met before, but he can't take advantage of you now, because you've become a real person. He will look down, sway side to side, and search for an out. You tell him it's okay, everything will work out. Now, having recognized and addressed the intercultural matters and defused the backup behaviors, you can deal with the problem of the fenders on a friendly, human basis.

When no means no

What should you do when you have to say no to a Mexican, leaving no doubt about your meaning, and giving no wiggle room for further argument? This intercultural challenge can lead to unintended consequences if not played out appropriately.

In the United States, an American worker comes up to you and asks for a raise. You tell him you'll check with human resources to see where he is within his matrix of job descriptions and time with the company. A week later, he spots you and asks again. "Well, I checked, and *no*, we can't give you a raise. You're right where you should be with everybody else." That should end it. It would be rare for a worker in the U.S. to come to you the following week and ask for a raise yet again. If he did, you would be justified in telling him to pipe down and get back to work. You would feel justified at looking somewhat cross and even raising your voice.

But put an uninitiated Anglo supervisor in the same situation in a Mexican workforce and the following is what is likely to happen. The worker asks for a raise. You say that you'll check it out. A week later he asks about a raise, and you say, "*No*, we can't give you a raise," and you explain the reason. But the third week he asks again. And he *will*. This time you have two courses of action. Either you deal with the intercultural aspect first or you don't. If you don't, you'll stitch up your eyebrows, ball up your fist, and say, "I told you last week the answer was *no*, and the answer is *no!* Now get back to work." The fourth week the worker won't show up for work. You've lost ground. The three months you put into training are lost forever. Because of the way you have told him no, you have also inadvertently told him, *I don't like you.* He will report home, and he and his wife will conclude that he had better look for another job.

Here's how you should have handled the situation. One, recognize that the Mexican worker considers asking for a raise a part of his role, part of what he does. Since he is not as dollar focused as Anglos are, he will weigh the raise against how much he likes the work. Recognize too that he wants to know that you are in the swim with him. Two, deal with backup behaviors. Stifle your irritation and realize that he is merely asking. There is no reason in his mind for anyone to get upset. Three, when you tell him no, do it in a way that doesn't make him feel slammed. Smile, look him in the face, and say "no-o." He will accept the answer and skulk back to his buffing jack. He then recognizes that you still love him, and that you see your interchange as part of the game of life.

A sword, a horse, a shield

The signal that you're dealing with an intercultural conflict—that sinking, persistent feeling that *they* don't understand—can surface on any level in an organization. It can happen when working with lawyers.

Having known Americans long enough to overcome the Mexican reluctance to bring up an issue, Gloria, the accounting manager from the previous tale, brought her latest problem to me. "The lawyers in Detroit insist that they want the sale to close in the U.S. for tax purposes. The lawyers in Monterrey say that according to Mexican law, they have to close in Mexico. The lawyers in the U.S. are saying that the Mexican lawyers are unresponsive and resisting the client's needs. The Americans are threatening to replace them. But I think the Mexican attorneys are just trying to do their job according to Mexican law." Gloria understood that if the matter could not be resolved, if we had to change lawyers, it would delay the transfer of the plant another month—or more. "I can't blame the Mexican lawyers," she said, "and I don't think changing firms will affect anything. The next lawyers will tell them the same thing. What should we do?"

In this case the underlying cultural issue involved a major difference in how Mexican lawyers and American lawyers perceive their respective roles. In Mexico, it is the attorney's duty to assure his client's compliance with government regulations. His role is that of friend of the court—someone to help clients look good in the eyes of the authorities.

In the U.S., lawyers are our knights in waiting. (That's what *esquire* means.) Our lawyers' first duty is to take up our mission, battling against defiant bureaucrats. Second, they build a defense in case we get sued. Third, they keep us from shooting ourselves in the foot by taking a wrong course. We take the role of lawyers as shield-bearers seriously. To us, it's about combat. To Mexicans, it's about propriety.

Gloria had never seen it quite like that, but she understood the pugilistic references. She had seen the fighting spirit in Yankees before, so she knew how to interpret the explanation. She also noted that the Mexican attorneys preferred to deal with her because the American attorneys seemed too combative. "So what now?" she asked. Our approach had to take the intercultural conflict into account. Neither group of lawyers had dealt with the other on a personal basis. This intensified the need to satisfy intercultural communications on both sides.

As to the substantive issue of where to close down the corporations, Gloria and I devised a plan for closing the Mexican corporation in Mexico and the U.S. corporation in the U.S. Ninety percent of the assets were held by the U.S. entity—and that should have satisfied the Americans' tax concerns. The exception to the assets was the real estate, which is and would continue to stay in Mexico. So the real estate sale would have had to close in Mexico anyway. The substance of the case was fairly easy. It was the intercultural matter that required our time and effort.

The first step forward was to bring the attorneys on both sides along on our intercultural exercise. Gloria called the Mexican attorneys to *tell* them what it was we would like to do. Then she *asked* them if they could make it legal. The answer came back: "Yes, we can do that."

We then called the U.S. attorneys to siphon off some of their angst. We let them know that Gloria and the Mexican attorneys had arrived at a possible solution, which we detailed for them. Would that be acceptable? Delighted, the U.S. attorneys dropped their shields. "We were wrong. Those Mexican attorneys really are on our side! Actually, a great bunch of guys."

Heads up

Whether it's xenophobia or one-way gringo attitude, sometimes our inability to relate to Mexicans takes us from a bad situation to a catastrophe. The surest way to avoid conflict and to accomplish our mission in Mexico is to be accepted early on by a group of serious peers—lawyers, accountants, construction companies, government officials, teachers, church groups, retiree groups, whatever is appropriate to the endeavor. Such groups will have a network of relationships already in place and will be able to put us in touch with the personal contacts we will need. They will keep us out of trouble in the first place. Think of the enterprise in Mexico as if it were a big card game. We are welcome to sit down and play, but we must be respectful of local manners. If conflict arises, our peers are there to lend advice and to serve as valued intermediaries.

Of course, there will always be some Americans who prefer to pick their way through the maze of doing business in Mexico without bothering to make alliances along the way. They go here and there, to this person and that, culling what information they think they will need, then running it through their own matrix to try to figure out what to do. This fits with our reliance on procedures and the superiority of our logic. But at the end of the day, they have nothing of value in Mexico. They have bits and pieces of information, but they have no cohesive picture, no workable game plan, and no established relationships. When these go-it-alone types strike out on their own, they always stumble, create conflict, and wind up blaming their failures on the Mexicans. Meanwhile, savvy Americans put themselves in the hands of serious, helpful Mexicans who can guide them through the local context.

Detachment versus Contextuality: Building Relationships

Mexicans feel connected to what is around them. They see themselves as part of a larger whole. The distinct features of the Mexican character we have discussed—their agreeable manner, group orientation, sense of group space, living for the present, consignment to fate, and adherence to hierarchy—are consistent with a highly contextual, or interconnected, outlook. Contextuality also underlies the Mexican approach to doing business. Depending on people requires trust, and Mexicans trust one another according to how well they know one another's families, backgrounds, and neighborhoods, as well as how others are likely to react if the roof falls in. When the going gets tough, they tend to rely on people with whom they have ties—with whom they have developed context.

It is easy to see how the American experience, with its independence, future orientation, self-reliance, and egalitarianism, has taken us down a different cultural path—toward detachment. While detachment has served us effectively in the United States, in Mexico it's a dead end.

When two Mexican business associates greet each other for the first time on a given day, they begin by developing context—exchanging protracted greetings, asking about each other's families and how their day is going, waiting for appropriate responses. With extended rituals proffered, they settle softly down to business. Rather than open a meeting with a clear declaration of need, a "Who called this meeting?", or launching immediately into business particulars, they start by building business context. Mexicans begin with diffuse comments and gradually work down a spiral of information until they get to their target subject. They start with the general and later get to the specific.

Detaché case

Unlike Mexicans, Americans separate family from business, flights of verbal fancy from business, and core business issues from the surrounding discussion of detail. Our detachment is a function of all of our cultural set pieces and work styles. We are direct, independent, we work toward a target with as few impediments as possible, and we seize control. We begin a meeting by saying, "Hi, how are you? I'm John Smith (or Jane Doe)." While perfectly polite in our context, it strikes Mexicans as odd that we ask "How are you?" but never wait for an answer. Inadvertently, this signals to Mexicans that we don't really care how they are. In our mind, "How are you?" is simply a ritual we use when shaking hands or greeting others. We are detached.

In the United States, we show up at a client's office with our attaché case full of brochures and imply through our direct language that "This is what I have to sell, and here's why you should buy it." We are the salesperson; the other person is the potential buyer. No further explanation is required. Americans believe that our product or service, even our own presence, stands on its own and does not depend on other (to us irrelevant) factors.

Whichever way you slice it

When we're buying, we can be just as detached as when we're selling. We go into a Chevy dealership in the United States and we think, "I'm a potential customer. This is a dealership. Here comes a salesman. Hold onto the wallet." That's all the context we need. I'm here. You're there. You want my money. I don't want to give it to you. Then, we begin negotiating with the salesman. We want a car, so we work toward an agreeable price and we buy it. We're completely detached. No building relationships here. All that matters are the numbers. Later, we can't wait to tell our friends, "Hey, you need a Chevy? Go to Brown's and see my buddy Tim. He'll set you up. He's a great guy." Suddenly, when it isn't our money that's on the line, we're all context.

A Mexican goes into a dealership and he's thinking, "I am entering the dealership space where people sell cars. I expect a person to come up to me to greet me with the respect I deserve as a customer. If I determine that this person and the company can provide me with a car at a decent price, and with good follow-up service, I will buy a car from them." Then there follows a ritual dance of building context. Who do you know? Who have you sold cars to? How long have you been here and will you be here for the long haul?

When I come back with a blown gasket will you help me, or will you pretend you don't know me? After taking some time to establish that there is a future in the relationship, the Mexican begins negotiating seriously for the price.

Detachment and contextuality also account for differences in the way Americans and Mexicans negotiate. To visualize the difference in the approaches, picture a sausage on a plate between two hungry business-people. The American starts nibbling on his end, expecting the other American to start carving a bit off the opposite end. The two continue to negotiate, gradually coming closer and closer toward the middle. This would be a good style of negotiating by American standards. The Mexican approach is different. Mexicans need to establish up front that there is a middle ground. They want to know that there might be a meeting of the minds. They want to be assured that both parties have the potential to arrive at a mutually beneficial relationship. Symbolically speaking, the Mexican places the knife delicately at a place around the middle of the sausage and looks at the person on the other end for signs of approval—a smile, a nod, a "We can work something out." At this point, the Mexican is thinking, "Yes? Okay. Now we can begin negotiating."

We Americans often misinterpret the Mexicans' signals and come away from a business meeting thinking an agreement has been reached. We fail to see that the Mexican has only indicated a *willingness* to embark on the path of doing business with us. When the Mexican puts the knife delicately in the middle of the sausage, we're thinking, "Gee, that was easy," and we say, "Yeah, that looks good. We've got a deal." Then we ask if we can put our under-standing into a letter of agreement. "Yes," the Mexican answers agreeably. But the truth is, we aren't even close to a deal. The letter of agreement means nothing to him, except that you—the gringo—want it and he wants to be agreeable. The Mexican doesn't feel he has even begun to negotiate.

Later, as discussions ensue, we get upset when it appears that the Mexican is eating our half of the sausage. Negotiations break down. We have not understood their context, which is, "Letter or no, we have to know a whole lot more about each other to be certain that we want to do business with you."

Long-term interest

Why does a potential business partner, customer, or service provider in Mexico want to know as much about us as possible? They want to establish that we are serious about making a purchase. If we are representing a company, they want to be assured that we will be there for the long term. They want to know the history of our company and to visit with the highest possible member of our firm, because that will signal that we are committed to them for the future. In addition to judging clients or vendors based on the amount of time that they are willing to spend up front, Mexicans put a premium on talking about issues that might seem unrelated to the matter at hand. In some of the most successful business meetings, business is never discussed!

Because we are so accustomed to remaining detached, we assiduously avoid content when we make idle chatter. Lack of content has its place in our rituals, but we can sound foolish to the foreigner. Mexicans are too polite to say anything, but Europeans feel free to make fun of an American fellow traveler who looks out the airplane window and says, "Gee that sure is a lotta water down there." We are engaging in small talk; they see it as a ponderous statement of the obvious. "Have a nice day" proffered by a cashier rings hollow. Does the cashier really care what kind of day we have? "Let's have dinner sometime" is particularly hurtful to Mexicans when they learn that we don't intend to have dinner with them. "I hope it doesn't rain on your parade" leaves foreigners shaking their heads as to the meaning. When driving foreigners around the suburbs of our hometown, don't expect them to bubble with enthusiasm if we observe wondrously, "All this used to be country."

In our minds, these are nonthreatening statements intended to fill the air with harmless banter. We consider time spent in preliminary babble to be "breaking the ice." By contrast, among many Asians, Arabs, Europeans, and Latin Americans, including Mexicans, preliminary chitchat is designed to reveal something of each other's context. So to contextual types, our detached, content-free statements come off as totally vacuous.

When, however, the matter at hand is business, we go *straight* for content. Our detachment versus their contextuality can leave a gulf in the relationship, causing our listeners to think we are all business and don't care about them as people. We start with a simple statement that is intended to "net out" everything there is to know about a subject. Then, upon further need for detail, we fill in the blanks. We go from the specific to the general.

Whereas detachment suits the style of the "time as an arrow" crowd, contextuality by its very nature is more drawn out. Mexicans appreciate it if we show willingness to explore a variety of topics to determine if we have something in common. If we share some interest in travel, then that's a starting point. If the Mexican likes American football, that's where we begin. If we like the ruins outside Mexico City, we should talk about that. Topic by topic, stick by stick, we are building a little raft of mutual understanding that will carry us along together in the circular flow of time.

We Americans often find it difficult to abandon our islands of detachment and paddle out to deeper waters. Generally, we are not inclined to mix business with personal matters, and we normally don't get into conversations about family, politics, society, or religion in a business meeting. We value being detached from the larger context. After all, the workplace is supposed to be nonpolitical, nonsectarian, and nonpreferential with regard to race, creed, ethnicity, gender, or sexual orientation. We brag that we "never bring our problems to the office," although we certainly do. We present our job description. Mexicans, on the other hand—while they wouldn't brag about it—freely admit to bringing their problems to work. They see nothing wrong with this.

Gee, it sure is quiet in here

One of the biggest problems American managers of Mexican workforces have is failure to appreciate context—a failure that can leave Americans in the dark. "One day the workers just didn't show up. We have a lot of turnover, and we don't know why." According to the Mexican's context, work is for the family. A worker's reasons for leaving a job may have nothing to do with the factory or office, and the owner or boss may never hear his reasons for leaving. For example, a woman may leave the sewing department when her husband gets a job because this is their traditional pattern. She would rather leave without a word than submit to interrogation by the superintendent. A young fellow may leave because he promised his wife to go see her family in San Cristóbal, and he is afraid to ask for time off because he'll just be told no. Sensitivity toward the family can help reduce turnover.

For Mexican factory, office, hotel, and meat market workers, as well as doctors and lawyers and chief executive officers, context includes everything in their environment—past, present, and ongoing trends. Context extends from the innermost circle of family to the expanding circles of one's social, economic, political, and intellectual universe. The Mexicans' context follows them like a shadow—it sticks to their shoes. When they come to work, they bring values, politics, family problems, and triumphs. They prefer that their work environment take these traits into consideration. To do less is to show disrespect for them as complete people. They will freely share their context, and hope to learn yours.

Everything that touches Mexicans is such a huge part of their identity that not acknowledging their context makes them feel incomplete. They come to the workplace with all the components of a whole person, including gender, race, religion, and politics. It seems natural to have these interests, and they feel that to leave them at home is artificial. Because they are unobtrusive by nature, they will not impose their beliefs on others. But those aspects of their person are still present, waiting anxiously to be drawn out. There are certain topics they won't bring up because they don't want to appear disrespectful. But if the subject comes up, they will discuss race, religion, and class with natural frankness. When American management objects to a little shrine in the workplace, or to the picture of the brown virgin over a drawing board, Mexican workers are bewildered.

For a Mexican worker in a factory, it is only natural to put up a shrine to the Virgin of Guadalupe. It is part of the context. Having such a shrine is not seen as proselytizing. A Muslim or a Jew can also have a shrine, and the workers would respect it. "I may not believe what he believes, but I respect his right to believe it," sums up the Mexican's feelings. We Americans retreat to political correctness. Could this be our effort to further separate people from their context in our workplace? After all, we believe it is better to have no gender, no race, and no ethnicity when it comes to the office, so we reject words that incorporate such references. We call a post *man* and a post *woman* a post *person*. And we think that shrines should be taken down because they might offend someone. When we try to explain how we want the workplace to be nonpolitical, nongender, nonwhatever, we are met with a blank stare. The problem is that the Mexicans *just don't get it*.

Different weaves

There are things about the Mexican style of building context that Americans don't get. Let's say you're in a business meeting in Mexico City. Your Mexican hosts want to start building context. They begin by asking how your trip was, but then, rather than getting down to business, they want to know how you feel, what hotel you're staying at, and if you have everything you need. To a detached American, these questions are beginning to seem a bit too personal. If you are meeting for the second time, don't be surprised if they ask,

"How did you wake up?" *¿Como amaneciste?* (Note the indirect approach. They don't ask how we slept because that's too intrusive.) Then quite commonly they will ask where your Mexican salesman lives, or whether you intend to employ a Mexican engineer. The purpose of this line of questioning goes beyond idle information gathering. The Mexican hosts want to know what kind of person you are, what class you and your associates come from—anything to form a bridge of partnership.

If your hosts know that you live in Mexico City, they may ask *where* in Mexico City. They are putting together a picture of you and inferring how you might do business together. If you live in Lomas, Ciudad Satelite, or San Angel, then you are upper middle or upper class and should have gone to Universidad Panamericana or Northwestern. If you live in Colonia del Valle in Monterrey, you enjoy an upscale neighborhood where other Americans live. If you're staying at the Nikko, you're taking the safe route of the foreign investor. The Camino Real Hotel tells the prospect that you know your stuff. The Casa Gonzalez bed-and-breakfast tells the host that you know Mexico rather intimately and are there on the cheap. Such conversations usually continue over lunch or dinner because they require lots of time. We wonder when we'll get around to business.

Building intercultural relationships

What should you talk about with Mexicans? You can start by reading the "dos-and-taboos" lists that are out there. But if you want to understand *why* one man shouldn't tell another man how beautiful his wife is, here is the guiding principle. You don't want to invade the privacy of the Mexican's home. Direct reference to a man's wife on any level is threatening. Don't ask a mother or father if their twelve-year-old misbehaves. Don't ask what they're having for dinner. Consider that the home is his final refuge and any invasion, even on a conversational level, is impolite. But do feel free to ask about family on an abstract level. You will find that they are proud to tell you that their son is in the second year at Northwestern, or that their daughter is a lawyer for Grupo Saltillo. Family is a value shared between Americans and Mexicans. Whereas we would not normally talk about our families in the preliminary run-up to a sales presentation, they would.

Do we talk about the weather? Sure, but the weather won't get us far. The Mexican is talking to build a common bond, to find a mutual interest.

Logically, talk of the weather could lead to an exchange of favorite vacation places. Both of us like to visit Miami because the weather and the water are always great. That may lead to fishing, or golf, or Hemingway, or politics.

It's okay to talk politics in Mexico, but keep it lighthearted. Referring to party politics, an acquaintance uses this line: "Well, some of my friends like the PRI (*Partido Revolucionario Institucional*) and some of my friends like the PAN (*Partido de Acción Nacional.*) Me? I always go along with my friends!" Let the Mexicans be critical of their own politics without using the opportunity to jump on their heads about how a democracy is supposed to work. They love to have us acknowledge that Mexico has to find its own solutions. This is a refreshing approach because so many Americans can't wait to straighten the Mexicans out. Mexicans also love to be thought of as modern. That doesn't mean, however, that they want to be the first on Mars.

Fixed values

One measure of the difference between our detachment and the Mexicans' contextuality is the degree to which we are in touch with our respective values. Compared to the Mexicans, we are not in touch with our values at all. "Values?" the American questions. "Hell, I don't know. I like basketball, golf, fishin'. I dunno. Whaddayamean?" Some more astute Americans may also have trouble articulating their values, because today *values* has become a war cry about issues that separate us rather than a commitment to what binds us together. Ask a Mexican to cite his values, and whether it's a man or woman, grandmother or college student, banker or street sweeper, you'll consistently hear the following: self-respect, self-improvement, family, God, and country.

Because the Mexican's values are clear and unchanging, it is always safe and effective to begin a relationship by building context around these ideals. In a country where context is everything and where family is all-important, you'll never go wrong in talking about family, education, how wonderful Mexico is, and what a nice staff the host has. Beyond being polite, it is actually important to ask a potential business partner if he has a family, where the children go to school, what they are studying. As your relationship develops, you may be in a position to help them get into college in the States. Sending your lunch partner a book for his kids is a winning idea. With respect to self-improvement, everyone understands that this is a common goal within the family. Generally, talking about the education of young people, shared experiences studying abroad, and the need for training will strike a chord.

Who's on first?

In the U.S., we use sports as a common topic for opening a discussion between men in particular, but to some extent in mixed gender groups. We use the noncontent of sports (having nothing to do with business) to prove to each other that we have no other subversive or ulterior motives, so that we can trust each other when it comes to doing business. In the States, you could boil your idle chatter down to an exchange of agreement about last night's game. Then we go straight to business. That is our detached approach.

Sports is *not* an automatic door opener in Mexico, and not a way of reducing tension. Mexicans engage in light chatter too; but theirs is a search for content. They explore possible areas of mutual interest in order to build relationships. Sports is only one of many topics that may be of mutual interest, and since we are neither soccer players nor horsemen, we probably have little in common with them on this level. As we begin to develop a bond with a potential Mexican business partner, we may discover that we are either avid tennis players or skiers. But it is also profitable to talk about current events, books, or travel. In Mexico, the conversation could go on well into the night and continue the next day. Like a fond exchange between husband and wife, the talk never ends.

A funny thing happened on the way to the pyramid

Humor, in general, can be one of the trickiest areas to broach. It is only after you have established a considerable level of cultural fluency that you are in a position to judge how the other person will react. Once you've reached that point, you have a rich repertoire of things to talk about. There are many American jokes that translate well and that Mexicans have never heard. Some American humor is universal, such as that of Mark Twain: "Reckon it'll stop rainin'?" "Always has!" Down-home humor from the southern United States is basic and colorful. "It isn't the size of the dog in the fight; it's the size of the fight in the dog." Humor with an ironic or improbable twist is great fodder. Yogi Berra said, "When you get to a fork in the road, take it!"

Bathroom or bedroom humor, on the other hand, is dead on arrival, and telling dirty jokes is even less appealing than teeth marks in the butter.

Curiously, the Mexicans are much more proper than many other Latin Americans are. The Cubans and Puerto Ricans love a good dirty joke. The Mexicans would only tell one after they know you very well. Use humor judiciously, because a dinner partner wants to know that we have a serious side—we're not all gags and rim shots.

With Mexicans, you definitely want to talk about our respective cultures—politics, economics, society, books, and food—anything under the sun. You search for things you agree on. You can venture opinions about our own literature, history, art, or science, but while presenting our culture positively, we should be neutral with regard to comparisons with Mexico. It's okay to talk about their politics, but without all the oppressively hollow, stereotypical malapropisms that insinuate, "Now that you have a president with an Anglo name, maybe you'll get democracy right." How you talk about a subject is important. Rather than blurt out an observation about Mexican politics, even a valid or positive one, you may ask for a critique of a point of view you heard from someone else. Rather than, "I think Mexico City is unsafe," you might ask if the taxi driver was right when he said it.

Ask questions rather than make declarations. Ask general questions rather than going for the direct answers. Use open questions rather than those that call for specific conclusions. Be interested in what your dinner partner has to say. Be genuine even if you have to fake it. If you have the sense that you're not getting anywhere, you're not. Start over and try another subject. Back off. Relax. Try again to establish a common bond and build on it.

Because Mexicans' identity is so closely tied to country, whatever you say about Mexico may be taken as a reflection on them. Add this to Americans' penchant for critical observations, comparisons, and straight talk, and you've got a prescription for trouble. So when you speak about Mexico, be sure you say something positive.

An American company sent one of its own to Mexico City to show the Mexican subsidiary how to run its business. The gringo had that all-American bounce. I'll call him Bob Weaver because so many Americans bob and weave. On the first day, the local manager, a Mexican with a master's degree in computer science from the State University of New York (SUNY), picked Bob Weaver up at the hotel. Leaving the hotel, Bob looked around and said, "Gee, there sure is a lot of activity around here for a Third-World country." The American clearly had never bothered to find out that, at more than twenty million people, Mexico City is the world's largest metropolis.

Nor did he know that the city is a thousand years old, that the Aztecs called it Tenochtitlán, or that "place near prickly pear cactus" was the Aztecs' land of plenty, which they found after centuries of wandering. Even in 1520 when the Spanish first arrived, it was the biggest city in the world. Bob knew nothing of the Mexican's context, and he had made no effort to find out. As it turns out, the Mexican local manager had gone sailing on Lake Michigan and knew all about Bob's hometown, Muskegon, which is Chippewa for "swamp." Nothing against Muskegon or swamps, but the relationship never amounted to anything. Bob never realized that his attitude was off-putting, and he never quite figured out why he couldn't get local cooperation. When he got home, his faxes were ignored.

On an initial approach to a business partner or Mexican government official, the culturally fluent American will rein in his enthusiasm and hope to accomplish just one thing—to leave the Mexican thinking, "Now there's a gringo I can do business with." The Mexican will then be interested in further developing mutual context and later getting down to brass tacks. Follow this pattern and doors will open.

The midnight ride of Paul Revere

Because the Mexican businessperson is generally steeped in Mexican history and culture, he or she will enjoy filling you in on the details. This kind of conversation plays to the Mexicans' strong sense of context and is considered to be deeply respectful. The more you know about their history, literature, art, etc., the more effective you will be in building relationships. You are not expected to be an expert, but it is appreciated if you engage in conversation that shows admiration for the country's rich cultural legacy. Above all, show interest. Often, the way you field a question can make a big difference. "No, I haven't read Octavio Paz. Which of his books would you suggest I start with?" If you don't know Mexican history, ask questions. "That is a beautiful (interesting) monument outside your window. Can you tell me its history?" Or, " I saw the statue of an Indian chief in the street. Can you tell me about him?" You are showing respect for the Mexican's culture and opening a dialogue.

Talking about history and statues may seem superficial or off the subject to you. If the tables were turned, and a Mexican calling on a lender at Citibank in Boston steered the conversation toward the Midnight Ride of Paul Revere, the American wouldn't be flattered in the least. In fact, he'd be turned off. "What's this guy trying to prove? He's wasting my time. What's Paul Revere got to do with the price of rocks?" With Mexicans, on the other hand, since they don't expect Americans to know much about their history, any show of knowledge or interest goes over well. To the extent that you know a subject you are not expected to have mastered, you're hitting a home run.

Eggs, Mexican style

We have all had career-making coups. Mine was delivered on a visit to the director of foreign investment for the Mexican government. I arrived just a few weeks after the horrendous earthquake of 1985 had taken down the entire Commerce Department building—the director's office included. He showed me into his suite with the aplomb of an entitled bureaucrat. I presented myself and my company properly in the Mexican context, avoiding superlatives and declarations. He listened with increasing interest and complimented my Spanish. I thanked him. He then asked if I knew Mexico. "Yes, somewhat," I replied. He inquired if I knew the National University. "Yes," I told him. "Of course I've been to the campus numerous times." Pressing further, he asked if I knew the Netzahualcóyotl Theater. It wasn't clear where he was going with this line of questioning, but recognizing that I had been given the opportunity to lay a golden egg, I responded, "Yes, it is a beautiful, modern theater in the round, constructed in about 1978, and named after the third Aztec *cacique* whose name means 'Hungry Coyote'." With this, my Mexican host laughed and dropped about a dozen masks. He knew he had been had, and he loved it. Now he was ready to cut the b.s. and get down to business.

While I was the one being questioned, I learned a great deal about him in the process. First, he wouldn't have asked about the National University (UNAM) had he not gone there. Having gone there, he was probably considerably left of center in his political philosophy. He was testing me to see how I might do in future political or business dealings with his department. Being leftist, he was probably not as favorably disposed to foreign investment as a business-oriented colleague might have been. I knew to avoid hyperbole about how important my capitalist company was, and to talk about training workers and offering above-minimum-wage jobs and health benefits. His world had just been shaken, and his building destroyed. I sensed that he didn't need an American to tell him what was good for Mexico. Not only was my meeting with him a success, but I have been received by every director of foreign investment since.

It's true that building context takes effort, but it's also fun. Not everyone has been on archaeological digs in Mexico or has a degree in Mexican history. That's not required. The point is to ask heartfelt and educated questions about their history, thereby inviting them to open up and brag a little. Questions about their city or museums show interest in the culture and by extension, respect. You don't have to be an expert.

Typically, the further up the hierarchy you climb in Mexico, the more direct and less contextual the people may appear to be. Executives with international business experience have learned that Americans like to get right down to business. Generally, they know more about you than you do about them. But make no mistake. Before the deal is done, you will still be required to back up and build context.

Mexicans will ask informed questions about your culture. In response, it's fine to venture opinions about American literature, history, art, or science, and to reveal something about your personal interests: "I'm a Civil War buff." "My wife and I square dance." "We enjoyed taking the family to Philadelphia to see the new home of the Liberty Bell." While their line of questioning may feed your self-assurance, remember that you are more effective at building relationships when you turn the subject to the things that are important to *them*. The mere show of willingness to slow down long enough to learn something will leave a favorable impression on your Mexican host.

You know you've scored a success when you and the person you're meeting with connect on something and carry it forward. When you agree to continue the conversation over lunch, you are on your way to establishing a good relationship. But it all starts with building context.

PART III

Building Context

Ultimately, achieving cultural fluency depends on building context. We begin by scanning the broad spectrum of the Mexican experience. Looking through the lens of culture, a clearer, more cohesive picture emerges. The process advances with each conversation and every encounter. It never ends.

CHAPTER Thirteen

Archaeology of the Mexican Mind

Mexicans have three unshakable ideas they carry around in their heads: "We are part of a procession; we are all imperfect; there are many versions of reality." These fundamental notions set the stage for all thinking, for evaluating oneself and for judging others. These ideas are the alpha and omega of Mexico's intellectual identity and resonate with all its people.

There is no need for explicit communication or conscious inculcation of these ideas. They are intuitive, emerging from the totality of the cultural experience. Facts, times, and circumstances do not change these intellectual traits. They are shared by wise guys and sycophants, by the weak and the strong, by CEOs and floor sweeps, forming an ethos that goes with them wherever they go. No matter which side of the border—whether in Mexico City, New York City, Monterrey, or Minneapolis—one Mexican knows how another Mexican will react, because they hold to the same sense of self and the same view of the cosmos.

It is no exaggeration to say that understanding these unshakable ideas is just as important to doing business with Mexicans as a knowledge of local marketing, accounting, or logistics. What's more, exposing the central intellectual themes is as essential to building context as familiarity with political, economic, or social patterns.

In exploring the archaeology of the Mexican mind, nearly every inexplicable reaction, misunderstood feint, and puzzling backup behavior fits in one way or another with the unshakable ideas. While these concepts serve as a useful starting point, building understanding and context is an endless process. Indeed, part of the pleasure of doing business in Mexico is getting to know the people, asking questions, and piecing together your own finds to form a more complete picture. Every meeting, every conversation, every exchange with a taxi driver, a waiter, or a shopkeeper offers an opportunity to dust off your trowel and screen.

We are part of a procession

A Mexican's sense of self is inextricably tied to family, work groups, and region. These associations form psychic layers of identity, contributing to the feeling that one is part of a larger whole. The procession idea is unshakable because it is embedded into the notion of mission. Whatever else intervenes, a Mexican cannot separate his fate from that of his associations. When you are part of a procession, you share a need to keep marching. You are carried along together. You are part of something larger than self.

Nowhere are the ties that unite individuals more nurtured and maintained than in the family. Bonding is meticulous and relies on use of the father's *and* the mother's last names. Following Hispanic tradition, important decisions involve approval by both sides of the family. Moreover, such matters as marriage, dating, or moving out of town are always thoroughly vetted by the extended family, with aunts, uncles, cousins, and grandparents weighing in.

A look at how our different cultures treat a simple invitation is illuminating. In the United States, if a girl invites a boy over to her parents' house for dinner, he'll say yes, because no red-blooded American boy ever turns down a free meal. In Mexico, the boy will say, "Let me call you in the evening." This means, "I will give you my decision once my family tells me what it is."

While only the immediate family may be consulted in some personal matters, the Mexican family's extended network is always there when needed. It is inconceivable that a third cousin would move to a city without local family members knowing about it ahead of time. Nor would the nephew of your sister's brother-in-law be left out of the loop if a young woman plans to go into the same business. The family reinforces the sense of mission that extends well beyond the life of an individual, and the family must proceed.

Beyond extended family, work group, and company affiliation, regional identity is part of belonging to the mass. The Mexicans define themselves as "from Oaxaca," or as "Tapatíos" (from Guadalajara). They are more homogeneous and more emotional in this conviction than we are. Generations after leaving a region, they continue to consider themselves natives because they still have family there. Their feelings are a bit like those of U.S. southerners who are closely tied to their roots. A northerner or midwesterner may go to South Carolina for the first time and be surprised that southerners have such a strong regional attitude. Many stick to their old flag and talk about North and South issues in a way that never occurred to the visitor. Mexicans from each region hold to their traditions and histories in the same way.

The Mexicans' regional identity is more profound than ours because their roots go deeper. Typically, their people have inhabited the same region for centuries, whereas the average American changes houses every seven years and changes regions almost as often. We tend to say, "I'm from Michigan, but not really." We may list the places where we've lived. The Mexican identity is so strong that several generations after living in the States, Mexican Americans still know where their kin came from within Mexico. The fact that they are in Idaho or Massachusetts does not alter their sense that they are part of a movement—*Veracruzanos* in search of a better life.

Whereas Mexicans identify with their home regions, they also have a tradition of mass migration. The Olmecs moved from the Veracruz coast inland to the west of what is today Mexico City and explored the center of the country en masse four thousand years ago. The Aztecs migrated from Aztlán in the north to Tenochtitlán. The Toltecs moved from Teotihuacán outside Mexico City to Tula in the state of Hidalgo. Throughout their prehistory, Mexican cultures migrated in organized fashion in search of better settlement conditions. Mexican migration to the United States today is part of the same phenomenon.

While Mexico has great diversity, there is no myth of the melting pot. Regional affiliations are maintained and respected without driving national divisions. In a culture that downplays the individual and elevates the group, identity lies not with oneself, but with the group and its mission. Thus, the tendency is to identify themselves as *Potosinos* (from San Luis), *Chilangos* (from Mexico City), *Jarochos* (from Veracruz), or as workers, ranchers, or government officials. Or, they identify themselves precisely as the Gonzalez *Gutierrezes* as opposed to the Gonzalez *Garcias,* referring to their particular clan by both father's and mother's lineage. Such a practice has little to do with social manners and everything to do with how highly cohesive people see themselves in the larger procession of life. Not only are they bonded to those who march beside them, they are part of an unbroken file—a physical extension of the past.

In view of their cohesiveness, it is not surprising that migrants from one region will stick together. The state of San Luis Potosí has about 1.5 million inhabitants, with 1.1 million living in the capital city of the same name. But migrants from San Luis Potosí have come to the U.S., with 30,000 settling in Chicago. It would be inconceivable to Potosinos that they should split up once across the border, going in different directions.

Because Americans are so doggedly individualistic, we simply don't respond to the "marching song of the masses" in the way that Mexicans do. At the same time, as we promote team playing and bonding with the group, we single out the *best* team player without recognizing the inherent contradiction. We hope in our hearts to stand out from the crowd as the Most Valuable Player (MVP) or Miss Congeniality. The individual matters to us. We can't wait to stand out from the crowd. Have you noticed how celebrities singing the national anthem before a baseball game have to put their personal stamp on "The Star-Spangled Banner"?

In corporate life, we walk a fine line. We encourage the notion that one person can make a difference, while insisting that we must all pull together. We like a conformist on the job who is an individualist off the job. He likes to skydive. She's got a black belt in karate. But he's a team player and she has lots of friends at work. We wear an article of clothing to set us apart. We drive a red Toyota convertible with graphics to announce "Here I come." Not until the Mexican businessman has gray hair, deep character lines, and the title of *Presidente Emerito* does he become venerated as an individual. By then, Don Pedro is out of the day-to-day decision-making process. Rather, he is carried aloft at the head of the parade.

The Mexican tendency to hide among the masses, with all its manifestations, is baffling to most Americans. We can't get a definite answer to a simple question. We think they're jerking us around, but they're just being part of the mass on the march. Rather than make a mistake, the worker, insurance agent, or businessperson holds off on answering our question until the matter can be talked over with family, the work group, friends, or regional or national allies. We can insist on a simple yes or no, but we'll rarely get it. "Why stick your neck out when you rely on the collective wisdom of the group?" they seem to be saying.

Putting pressure on a businessperson for a yes answer will get us a yes answer. But as we now know, we can't believe it. With a less direct approach, we get positive feedback and a deferral. Typically, the Mexican executive wants to think things through and discuss matters within his various groups. As we leave the meeting, he will thank us for coming, but look away as we leave. This can be disconcerting. We wanted a yes, a determined look in the eyes, and a firm handshake. We don't get it. One explanation is that he does not want to appear happy to see us go, but he is also slipping out of the person-to-person context. Like the metalworker who was reluctant to make eye contact when approaching us for instructions, the corporate executive is blending back into his position in the rank and file.

With the explosion of Foreign Direct Investment (FDI) in Mexico between 1965 and 2000, many *maquiladora* plant managers were astonished at how quickly their labor forces turned over. When discussing the difficulty of employee retention with plant managers from other industrial centers of northern Mexico, they were surprised to learn that in certain cities or regions, there was virtually *no* turnover. Analysis revealed that high turnover plants had located on top of migration routes, while low turnover plants had lucked into regions where people made the best of their lot while staying home. The situation is much more stable today, for reasons we will explore later, but Tijuana and Nuevo Laredo were major migration routes to *El Norte* (literally "The North," figuratively the "promised land"). Today, Tijuana is a magnet for young workers who are trained in some aspect of electronics, mitigating the flow of migrants who would otherwise look for an opportunity to jump the fence.

We are all imperfect

The Mexican believes human beings are imperfect and prone to misbehaving. Here's how it works. God made both the good person and the bad person. God created nature and natural responses. Misbehaving is natural. Fellow workers are not necessarily to be trusted—they are only human. Politicians misbehave, but then, I would misbehave too. The workaday Mexican plays the system for a fool: "I will secretly climb out on my roof at midnight to tap into the corner light post and siphon electricity off the line without paying for it so that I can run my new TV. I will drive my car up to the border and get border state tags by paying a bribe to the official. That way I can cross into the United States with my car, but I will continue to live in Veracruz and let people think I have a house in Matamoros."

Playing the system in Mexico stems from two convictions. First, that people are imperfect. Second, that imperfect people have created a flawed political system. Spanish kings managed their Latin American colonies by layering bureaucracy upon bureaucracy, as *conquistadores*, governors, *corregidores*, viceroys, and other political and religious authorities were sent to the New World to manage rich but remote possessions, and to keep an eye on one another. This led to a system of dispersed responsibilities, but with no real authority vested in bureaucrats. The result is that even today, citizens fill out five different forms in quadruplicate, visit five ministries, and still don't get a straight answer. So what is the average citizen to do? Cheat a little, lie a little, offer a *mordida* (bribe), and misbehave. Imperfect people do what they must do in order to cope with a labyrinthine government. Sometimes it's the only way out. In the end, God will judge the citizen and the bureaucrat.

In Mexico there is a wrinkle in misbehaving that has nothing to do with bureaucracy and everything to do with natural instincts. Given a chance, a boy and girl left alone together will do what comes naturally. "We will let our daughter go out with this boy only because we know his family and they are good people, and he is headed for a good life, but we would never allow them to go out in a car together. We will take them to the movies and pick them up." Seeing themselves as part of a group, Mexicans believe it is up to the group, not the imperfect individual, to maintain discipline.

Shortly after we were married, my wife Elizabeth, a violinist, and I were living with a Mexican family in Mexico City. One evening, a German cellist came to drive Elizabeth to quartet practice. I waved goodbye at the door and turned back toward the foyer to see one of my Mexican housemates with his mouth agape. "*Eduardo,* you permit that?!" To him, letting my wife take a ride with a man was tantamount to permitting her to commit sinful acts. In his eyes, I was condoning it and telling them to have a good time.

This extreme caution with women is part of the *malinche* phenomenon. Malinche was an Indian maid of considerable local status captured by the Maya just before the *conquistador* Hernán Cortés arrived in 1519. Since she had lived as a privileged slave among several tribes, she spoke three native languages. She served Cortés as a translator, and in so doing, also helped him conquer Mexico. She bore him a child who was given a Spanish surname. The pattern continued throughout Mexican history—Spanish men mating with Indian women to bear mixed-blood children with Spanish surnames—leaving an indelible impression on the Mexican psyche. Since virtually all Mexicans have Spanish surnames, and, as previously noted, 95 percent of Mexicans claim to have Indian blood, then by extension, virtually all Mexican men have had incidents of betrayal by women in their past. All women have the capacity to be *malinchistas* who would betray their partner for another. This helps us understand Mexican machismo.

Today, *malinchista* applies to any Mexican who gives in to the temptations of dealing with foreigners at the expense of their fellow Mexicans. In order to do business with Americans, but not be branded *malinchistas,* Mexicans will play games. They are usually harmless, but nevertheless real. Wanting to operate as I do in the States, I asked a Banamex bank branch manager if I could get a credit card. He took me into his confidence by telling me a banker's joke. With a glint in his eye, he said, "You know what we call people who have credit cards here?" he asked. "No, what?" "We call them *cobrones,*" he replied. (*Cabrón* is the vulgar term for a male goat, and when used for a man means that he is cuckolded. *Cobrón* refers to the verb *cobrar,* meaning to bill or dun someone.) He was saying that people who have credit cards are deadbeats. But his playful approach gave me insight into the Mexicans' mischievous nature. By the way, his convivial detour was about telling me no. No, I couldn't have a credit card.

Seeing themselves as prone to following natural instincts, Mexicans feel secure working in a group-oriented manner. Any other approach would lead weak individuals to mess up and misbehave. When misbehaving detracts from the group's mission, it will not be tolerated long by the well-behaved members of the group. One benefit to the American manager is that when someone does act up (you remember the worker chasing women with the wax penis), it is quite apparent to his fellow workers, and management will get their support for corrective action.

Mexicans will tell you that they need a strong central government and religious dogma because otherwise the masses will disintegrate into an unruly mob. The political system, religious beliefs, respect for hierarchy, formality, group orientation, family, and—yes—agreeableness can all be understood as internal and external controls over a misbehaving populace.

Contrast this with how we Americans see ourselves and relate to other cultures. Among all the peoples of the world, only Americans are so convinced of our basic goodness—the world should see how good we are and therefore agree with everything we do or say. We are also big, and big is good.

When we are on our mother's knee, she tells us how *big* we are, and that makes us feel good. If we misbehave, mom tells us to be good. Truth, justice, and the American way are good. When President Jimmy Carter based foreign policy on human rights, that was good. Don't people understand? We're the good guys.

Once again, we find ourselves at opposite ends of the spectrum from the Mexicans. We see ourselves as good, they see themselves as imperfect. But at least we're on the same scale, unlike the French who don't relate to good and bad behavior at all. The French tell their toddlers to be *raisonnable*— reasonable. That's how they grow up. And with enough rationality, you can justify anything! The British tell their kids to speak clearly, and they do. They may be good or bad, but they enunciate it beautifully. The British joke that they can misbehave so long as they don't scare the horses. Mexicans are taught to get along—meaning, don't do anything bad to people within your group. The family, the work group, and the village remind them of what is proper and provide cultural controls to keep them in check.

A practicing nurse brought the following conundrum to me. She is a modern, liberated American and had a Mexican woman houseguest staying with her. "She keeps coming to me and asking if she can go out with a particular young man," the nurse complained. "I don't want to tell her what to do." I suggested that she invite her guest into the kitchen for a cup of coffee. "Sit down with her and talk to her as if you were her older sister. Lay down some rules—you may go out with that boy, but be back by eleven o'clock, don't go to bars and get drunk, and don't do anything naughty." The nurse responded, "Ew! I can't do that!" I went on, "Your friend is going to do what your friend is going to do. What she really misses is the internal control that comes from family members. You are her surrogate family. With the right tone of voice from you, she can make her own good decisions. But she will be most grateful to you for acting like a big sister. And remember that for her, such ideas as women's lib and independence are way out of context. With her, it's about family."

Mexicans accept external controls like religion and strong central government. One reason is that when left to their own devices, Mexicans can have some trouble organizing themselves. While attending college in Mexico, I was asked to join the Democratic Club—an exercise in democracy preparing young people to govern themselves in anticipation of the eventual end of the seventy-four-year-long domination of the *Partido Revolucionario*

Institucional (PRI). I was the only American, and they wanted me to help them organize. The first meeting started with a party—a band, tequila, and dancing. Then came the business meeting. "Who wants to be president?" yelled the drummer. In sequence, various people stood up on chairs and yelled that if the group elected them, they would do thus and such. Everyone rallied around that prospect until someone else stood up on a chair and yelled out another instant program, whereupon the crowd migrated to that person. Finally, I took the leader, Doctor Luis, aside and coached him on setting up a constitutional committee that would agree not to run for office at least for one term. Then the club would adopt a constitution, and then they would have elections.

Doctor Luis stood up on a chair and offered my proposal as his own. The crowd gathered around and screamed enthusiastically, until someone else stood up across the room. So it went. I gave up. But several months later, I was asked to come back so they could show me how well they had organized. Doctor Luis met me at the top of the stairs, beaming. He couldn't wait to give me all the details. As the music played in the background, he concluded his presentation by asking if I remembered how the club wanted to acknowledge that men and women are equals in a democracy. I responded, "Yes." "Well," he announced proudly, "we have *two* presidents!" In this rare form of total democracy (populism?), where there were no extant groups, parties, constitutions, or rules, the individual mentality took over and chaos ensued.

There are many versions of reality

Within the elusive perimeters of their worldview, Mexicans achieve a unique and often baffling mental agility. Believing that everyone is imperfect, they can avert confrontation through childlike tricks. And when doom is at hand or all seems lost, they can slip into another version of reality. As we have discussed, when under pressure, the Mexican who believes he is part of a procession finds strength within the rank and file of the parade. Each of these intellectual domains provides a zone of comfort, invulnerability, and security.

The simplest example of the Mexican's shifting realities was referred to in Part I of this book. His world and his reason tells him that it hasn't rained in Chihuahua for forty days, and it's not likely to rain today. But if the gringo is sure that it will rain today, the Mexican will likely agree. Truth is in the mind of the believer.

Mexicans have a unique view of their own predominant Catholic faith. Priests preach the *Truth,* but "We poor peasants have to grow the corn. So, we will practice our faith, but we will also put ceramic corn gods in the field." The Mexicans seem to be saying, "God made me, but *I* make the tortillas." They live in two worlds.

There is no real parallel in the American experience. Rather than live with conflicting versions of reality, we tend to polarize over our separate views. To draw an admittedly imperfect analogy, in the United States, conservatives criticize liberals for "living in their own world." Liberals blame conservatives for "being incapable of understanding the *Truth.*" Arguably, there are two worldviews existing within the same culture. With Mexicans, it is as though two worldviews exist within the same psyche—one that meets the day, and the other that shrinks from the night.

Particularly for "yes or no" Americans, the shifting panorama and escape hatches of the Mexican mentality can be maddening. Frequently you hear, "It's hard to pin the Mexicans down." Just when you think you understand them, they perplex you with artful dodges that they don't fully understand themselves. Whatever the individual temperament—shy or outgoing, cautious or daring—Mexicans consistently avoid committing to a definite opinion or position. You're having a discussion about government, literature, religion, or sports. You're sure you've got them backed into a corner, but they surprise you by taking one more jump. It may be unclear where they have landed intellectually, but this much is certain: In the Mexican mind, there is always a place to hide.

To the Mexican, truth and reality are relative, conditional, uncertain, and complex. It is true that two plus two equals four. It is true that the dog I had as a kid is dead. It is true that man has walked on the moon. The balance sheet balances. But thinking that this explains the world is too simplistic. Aphorisms, slogans, mathematical formulas, budgets, generalizations—all are true to a point, but they don't approach the epistemological definition of reality. The Mexican perspective is much closer to Shakespeare's: "There are more things in heaven and earth . . . than are dreamt of in your philosophy." Reality cannot be known. It is relative to one's context. There is room enough in this philosophy for reality to be whatever you want it to be. That is the Mexican view.

This is far different from cheating on your expense report or lying about whether you did your homework. Where concrete answers are demanded and determinable, reality is what it is. But when raised to an intellectual level, a Mexican will get very relativistic. In this view of the world, the future is undeterminable. Only the past and present are real. Since the past is open to reinterpretation, and the present is infected with imperfect people, it is acceptable to fall back on myth and mysticism.

It should surprise no one that Mexicans embrace at least two views of reality, considering that they embody two distinct bloodlines—each with a deep civilization, prehistory, and history. Both the Spanish and the Aztec strains continue to animate the Mexican mind.

The Aztecs thought they were alone in the universe. In their minds, there were men, and there were gods from the netherworld. There was no heaven or hell. The world was not divided into good and evil; rather, there were the people and the gods. When they died, they went to the netherworld. Man traversed easily back and forth between the here and now and the other place.

Whereas the Aztecs were self-referential fatalists, the Spanish were worldly optimists. The old-world explorers saw themselves as riding atop brave steeds, standing up in their stirrups to look over the horizon. They were heady adventurers, anticipating treasures just out of reach. When the natives first discovered the Europeans, they thought that these six-legged creatures (men on horses)—part flesh, part metal—who floated to shore on "clouds" must be gods. They must be gods because they are real but they are not one of us.

The optimism versus fatalism dichotomy still exists and informs us of the Mexicans' beliefs in multiple realities. The Spanish may have overpowered the Aztecs militarily, but they did not extinguish the Aztecs' view of themselves or of the world. Make no mistake. The preponderance of Spanish surnames and technology does not mean that the Spanish culture dominated. As noted earlier, we tend to think of the Mexicans as being Spanish, and we refer to the whole area as *Hispanic* or *Latin American*. But Mexico, which is distinct from every other Latin American country with the possible exception of Peru, had a highly developed indigenous population much larger than the Spanish. While its empire fell, the Aztec culture survived the Spanish onslaught. It could be said that the Aztecs found a way of enveloping the Spanish in their culture. As a result, a new syncretic Mexican intellect developed. (*Syncretic* is a term used by anthropologists to describe a culture or religion that has assimilated aspects of another culture or religion, but whose components can still be distinguished as having come from one or the other.) An analogy to the Aztec and Spanish cultural melding exists in metallurgy. If you place an ingot of gold on top of an ingot of lead, the two will grow together. Yet, upon microscopic inspection, the gold atoms can be distinguished from the lead atoms.

During the five-hundred-year colonial and national periods, the separate cultures and bloodlines merged into one ethos—a combination of fatalism and optimism that is distinctly Mexican. It was not until Moctezuma and the Virgin Mary fused intellectually that we had the emergence of the true Mexican worldview. Five centuries of colonial rule and two centuries of modernity have not been enough to erase the Aztec's culture, whose mystical world coexists with the Spaniard's.

Each view—the Aztec and the Spanish—is useful in its own way. Further, muses the Mexican, if there can be *two* different realities, then why not more?

The meaning of yes

As you experience Mexico firsthand, you can put yourself in the Mexicans' frame of mind, and begin to view the world through the template of their "unshakable ideas." Repeat their mantra as if it were your own, "We are all imperfect. We are part of a procession. There are many versions of reality."

Let's say you're an American businessperson getting established in Mexico, and you are looking for a reputable bank. A Mexican consultant will gladly say yes to your choice of banks, conforming to your version of reality. But the consultant will also agree with the next guy who makes a very different selection. Actually, the consultant thinks that the choice of banks will have little effect on achieving the purpose for which you are all there—to follow the procession of people establishing you in Mexico. Furthermore, the Mexican assumes that if the bank fails, it will not be because it was not a good bank, rather because some fallible human made mistakes. Who can predict that? "There are many versions of reality. We are all imperfect."

Understanding that Mexicans accept many versions of reality, you should view the first yes as just a test of your reality. The follow-up discussion will reveal the true business measures that you should take. Namely, you should ask a number of your Mexican peers where they would bank if they were you. (Notice the indirect approach, rather than asking a Mexican,

"Where do you bank?") Even after analyzing services, strengths, and assets of a potential bank, don't be surprised if Mexicans ultimately select a bank where they have friends. "We are imperfect. But, as a group, we will look out for each other."

Similarly, the Mexicans' flare for shenanigans should not be taken too seriously. It will help when you remember that they see all humans as imperfect—even full of mischief. You also understand that their antics represent a taunting of reality, not rank dishonesty, impenetrable venality, or incorrigible immaturity. When addressing individual or group misbehavior, keep it light at first. You will let them find comfort within their sphere of protection and give them time to straighten out their own behavior.

One useful word that may help you tolerate the differences in cultures is *pretending*. Mexicans may be pretending to adopt your reality, pretending to be childlike, and pretending to hide, but they are easily understood and dealt with.

Mexican businesses produce handsome brochures, but sometimes they are only pretending. I saw a promotional piece depicting office panel systems with typical graphs that you would publish as a result of sound-attenuation studies. When panels are added, you diminish the sound of human speech and machine noise in the office. As nice as the graphics were, I wondered if the manufacturer had actually done any tests on their furniture. No, they hadn't. Putting such graphs on a brochure was appropriate because that's what other manufacturers in the rest of the world do. This company was simply pretending to be a modern office furniture manufacturer. From their point of view, the brochure was not dishonest. Clearly, if you put panels between yourself and your coworker, the sound will be attenuated. The graphs were not inspired by a desire to consciously misrepresent, rather by a desire to play the role and look the part. They were just delivering a version of reality.

Along these same lines, I have witnessed some curious behavior at basketball games in Mexico. Some years ago, I watched my friend John and his American team compete against a Mexican school. The Americans were big and good. The Mexicans were short and bad. In basketball, big and good are preferable. The gringos were tromping the Mexicans, that is, until the last quarter. Suddenly the clock and the scoreboard started to go haywire, almost as if someone had their hands on the switches. Every time the Americans had the ball, the clock would stop. When the Americans ran down the court and slam-dunked the ball, the score never changed. But every time the Mexicans got the ball and took a shot, four points would ring up, whether they got near the rim or not.

The mystery was not that the Mexicans were "cheating." I had seen that plenty in Spain. But Spain was different. In Barcelona, the Spanish team had to beat the Sixth Fleet team because, if they didn't win, the Spanish referees would get their butts kicked by the locals. What was surprising in Mexico was that the people in the stands got excited that they were coming from behind. But it was hocus-pocus. It was all pretense. It was bogus. The amazing thing was that the people were caught up in it. To them, it wasn't cheating; it was real. They were coming from behind, and they ultimately won! They screamed. They chanted their only pep cheer—again and again. *Alabio-Ala-bao-Ala-sis-bum-ba*. They started waves. Mass rapture swept the bleachers. A few took side-glances at me in the stands, and I nodded my approval at how well they were doing. "Yes, you are now winning, and everybody in the world recognizes that you are winning, and we approve." I saw no use in popping their bubble.

What was really going on was this: Having gone to a basketball game, the Mexicans were now participants in a modern event, and they were behaving the way they saw people act on TV. That's what the procession was about. That's what people do in the basketball arena. Similarly, salespeople pretend to be good salespeople. Bookkeepers pretend to be studious. Manufacturers pretend to be efficient. They may in fact be good, but pretense carries them through those times when circumstance prevents them from fulfilling their functions competitively. They may escape to a world they have seen on TV.

Nowhere are the liberating inventions of the Mexican imagination more fully engaged than in twentieth-century Latin American literature. *One Hundred Years of Solitude* by Gabriel García Márquez—a Colombian who lived and worked much of his adult life in Mexico—is one of the most widely read novels in Mexico. The story traces the lives of a family over three generations. While the characters exist in a realistic context, the true meaning of their lives is revealed through the hyperbolic and the impossible. Magical realism, as this style is called, is perfectly suited to the Mexican psyche. On the one hand, Mexicans are realists—there is no escaping the past, and who can say what will happen in the future. But in the present— that fleeting moment where the individual has some control—there is always the power of magic, with its ability to transform experience and create a different and more palatable version of reality.

The Mexicans don't consider it a problem that the terms *magic* and *realism* are contradictory. Life is filled with contradictions. Magic is innate. They can easily imagine that theirs are the most beautiful women, that their national anthem is the most glorious. Their magic mixes readily with environmental metaphors such as raining flowers, blood that races through the streets, and fire that does not burn. Flowers are real, blood is real, fire is real. Flowers and blood are familiar themes to Aztecs. But in literature as in the psyche, these can have extraordinary properties.

In discussing his book, García Márquez observed that the world we live in is full of underappreciated and underacknowledged magic. García Márquez said that if he wrote about the miraculous in everyday life, many would not believe such a book, yet it would be more concrete. This view resonates with the Mexican experience in which miracles happen every day—eight babies survive an earthquake when the hospital collapses and kills everyone else. There are those who deny miracles, saying that such things just happen for no reason, but García Márquez offers up a metaphorical version of the collective reality that the masses are willing to believe.

In magical realism the places are real—or could be real. There is no fantasy. There are no devilish lords or singing swords or Merlins. There are no fantastic beasts like the Celtic dragons, no Nordic Valküre on flying horses, no Minotaurs or mermaids. There are real people, perhaps enlightened by "real" folklore, culture, and history, that form a consensus reality of the masses. There is no delusion or insanity, only a paradox that says there is magic in reality and reality in magic.

In her popular novel *Like Water for Chocolate*, Mexican author Laura Esquivel enters the magic realm as well—amplifying the moment, animating the inanimate. Foods are invested with libidinous properties. To make hot chocolate, you bring water to a seethe, not a boil. Like water for chocolate, the lovers' love is seething just beneath the surface, out of sight. To reveal their passion is prohibited by social mores. In the final chapter, the lovers are lifted through a veil of light, with the fire of candles that do not burn them. They enter a sphere where their passion is fulfilled, where there is no dichotomy between good and evil—just murky morality.

Mexico's enthusiasm for magical realism lies in its ability to capture what ordinary people feel but cannot articulate. Mexicans know that anything can happen, but they don't accept that if *anything* can happen, *nothing* is important. On one level, Mexicans take the attitude that tomorrow we may have an earthquake, so why worry about the arrangement of objects on the shelf. But throwing up one's hands over a life that is fragmented, chaotic, disorderly, and obscure isn't what Mexicans are about. They prefer to carry on, inventing their own escapes. And they delight in the book that presents a compelling version of reality—one that gives meaning and coherence to the human experience. Who better than the writer to assure that the real world will reemerge, bathed in the clarity of a new sun?

Like the writer, the taxi driver spends long hours at his window on the world. Some days, he is the common man, the provider, the realist. At other times, when the choke of the street is overwhelming, he is a philosopher, treating impertinent questions from the American in the backseat as a call to lofty discourse. He seems to be saying:

Where would you have us go to escape? We are stuck with our past. Anything can and probably will happen to us in the future. But would you have us dwell on the fire and blood, live in perpetual defeat, be realists who have no place to go but to hell? That is a cruel and negative view. No good would ever come of it.

We live in a world we did not create. But in this world, we can live on our own terms, in our own locale. It is real, but reality is complicated by contradictions that neither science nor religion can explain. Yet, in this we find nothing unusual. What's more, there will always be another day.

Political Culture

Mexicans love to talk politics. Ask a dinner partner in Aguascalientes about business, and the subject turns to regulatory reform. Mention unions to an autoworker in Matamoros, and the conversation skips immediately to the next presidential election. Politics influences everything in Mexico. While unquestionably democratic, the government there is more intrusive in the lives of its citizens than government in the United States, exerting *undue influence* (from our perspective) on economic factors and daily matters. As such, politics permeates the Mexican context, and engaging in political discussion is an essential part of building relationships.

Mexico's political system reflects a number the broad cultural themes we have discussed. Chief among these are hierarchy, group orientation, and present orientation. By examining Mexican politics through the lens of culture, we can more accurately interpret how and why the system works as it does. We can also avoid the stereotypes that betray a lack of appreciation for the Mexican experience. Here are just a few of the misconceptions Americans all too often impute to Mexico's political culture: The whole system is corrupt; it isn't a true democracy—it's more like a dictatorship—and Mexico isn't really that different from other Latin American countries. The Mexican knows, and will politely explain, that Mexico has *not* been a dictatorship in living memory; that Mexico is *not* like other Latin American countries and, in fact, has led the way toward the political opening and democratization in the region. Corruption runs against the Mexican culture, but not against its history. Your dinner host may be too polite to point out that American demand is a significant factor in Mexico's drug trafficking problem and its concomitant corruption, or that Mexico is ahead of the U.S. in addressing election finance reform and voter fraud.

To appreciate how government works in Mexico, it is necessary to understand the machinations of the PRI (Party of the Institutionalized Revolution) period, 1927–2000. It is also essential to understand how the Mexican political system matches the cultural expectations of its free and democratic-minded citizens.

Politics and hierarchy

When we first visit Mexico, our guidebooks or hosts may tell us that certain things are much the same as in the United States. For example, Mexico has three branches of government—legislative, executive, and judicial. When Mexico adopted its constitution, it used the U.S. Constitution as one of its models. Being dogged egalitarians, we visualize the branches in three boxes on the organization chart, occupying the same level. We understand the checks and balances inherent in our own structure. But the system works differently in Mexico. While its organization chart may look like ours, a better way to visualize Mexico's three branches of government is as three boxes stacked one on top of another. In other words, Mexico has turned the egalitarian architecture into a hierarchical structure. At the top, the executive branch dominates the other two. The second box—the legislative branch— has, as a practical matter, more power than the judicial. The *poder ejecutivo* (executive power) is what Mexicans understand best. Since the days of the Aztec emperors in Tenochtitlán, and the Castilian kings and queens, the only political systems Mexicans have ever known have been hierarchical. Because hierarchy is so culturally entrenched, it isn't surprising that it has carried forward to today.

Hierarchy marks one important way in which the Mexican political system is strikingly different from ours. In the States, we lobby Congress to have our needs expressed in legislation. In Mexico, citizens go straight to the top and lobby the executive branch. Why is this necessary? Because the Mexican executive branch has much stronger regulatory power than ours. Whether a law is promulgated by the Mexican Congress or by the executive branch, executive orders can turn a law on its head. The executive branch publishes new laws, proposed regulations, and regulatory changes in its *Diario Oficial* (Official Daily). Regulations might affect labor, peasants, business, or any other major sector in Mexico. People then have ninety days after publication to react—to plead their case with the executive branch in order to have regulations modified to suit their needs.

Like the United States, Mexico has a Congress. Its Chamber of Deputies promulgates laws and represents the people. But Mexicans would rather go to *mi tio el cacique* (my uncle the warrior chief) for redress of any problems or for actions that will favorably improve their lot. Lobbying, then, is more effective when done through a family-type hierarchy than through a complicated congressional apparatus. The Congress passes laws, sets the budget, and has other duties that are growing in importance as the PRI system in Mexico recedes into its past. But the *poder ejecutivo* persists because the Mexican need for hierarchy persists.

While Mexicans feel comfortable with this hierarchical approach to law making and implementation, it can be anathema to Americans. Nevertheless, American business has learned firsthand how the system works and how it can be advantageous to U.S. interests. In 1993, the Mexican Congress issued a law saying that all foreigners working in Mexico should pay income taxes. That seemed fair. The executive branch then issued regulations in its *Diario Oficial*, proposing how what became known as the "gringo tax" would be implemented. But back home in Indiana, financial managers were stunned to learn about the new tax. It amounted to double taxation since the U.S. federal government also required companies to tax wages.

An American CFO told me the following story. He hurried to Monterrey to meet with his local accounting manager and the Mexican tax accountants. He asked if the new law indeed required that he pay Mexican income tax. After a twenty-minute conversation among the accountants in Spanish, which he did not understand, his financial representative responded yes. Frustrated, he asked if that meant he would have to pay both U.S. *and* Mexican income taxes. Again after twenty minutes in Spanish, the answer was yes. "What do we do?" he asked in desperation. Finally the answer came back, "Don't pay it." What Americans don't realize is that just because a regulation is published doesn't make it so.

During the ninety days after publication of the "gringo tax" regulations, emissaries of the foreign investment community lobbied the Mexican administration with the following results. (1) Only nonproduction employees in Mexico (2) working for more than six months of the year would be taxed, and then (3) only on amounts above $40,000 per year, until (4) a bilateral tax treaty could be worked out (which it soon was). The new regulation, once reissued, took the foreign investment community's needs into consideration. The amount of double tax actually paid by American investors in this case amounted to *cacahuates* (peanuts). The culture shock experienced by the American CFO in this case could be tied directly to looking at the regulation, but seeing something quite different from what the Mexicans saw. Namely, in hierarchical Mexico, the executive branch could and did turn the law upside down.

The fact is that the *poder ejecutivo* is practical. Unlike the United States, which has never been seriously threatened by foreign domination, Mexico has had to maintain a strong central authority with the will to act quickly in the country's interests. Whether for self-defense, or to walk the fine line between attracting foreign investment or protecting against foreign domination, Mexico's hierarchical governmental structure has worked well.

The executive branch recently used its unilateral regulatory power to open up Mexico's natural resources to foreign exploitation. The Mexican Constitution says that only a Mexican can be *the first seller* of its oil. The intent was to protect Mexico's natural resources from the kind of predation that characterized its colonial and early national periods. In practice, during most of the period in which the PRI dominated that meant that the state controlled all petroleum, petroleum derivative production, and sales. The state owned all mineral rights, exploration and drilling operations, fertilizer plants, and petroleum-based chemical operations—all the way downstream to the gas stations. But with the recent political "opening," the executive branch changed the long-standing definition of the term *first sale*. Now, for all practical purposes, *first sale* means at the well head. All other aspects of the petroleum business have been opened up to foreign investment and private ownership. Once again, the central government, and the PRI, turned the Constitution upside down. They did it authoritatively, yet with the consensus of the people as manifest in the party apparatus.

Opening their oil trust was no easy task for the Mexican people, who had authorized President Lázaro Cárdenas to confiscate foreign oil assets in the 1930s. Native women had gone around the country collecting *centavos* (pennies) to pay off the foreigners. Oil was close to Mexican citizens' hearts. But in recent years, Mexicans realized that its PEMEX (Petroleos Mexicanos) bureaucracy had become hopelessly corrupt and inefficient. So they invited foreigners back in. The man in the street agreed. "We couldn't screw it up any worse. We should invite the foreigners to come back in to save us from ourselves," was a common refrain heard by the PRI.

Another aspect of hierarchical expression in Mexico's politics that surprises Americans is the Mexicans' acquiescence to strong central rule. Mexicans recognized the need for central control, admitting to being unruly and mischievous. They willingly consigned their fates to their political leader class—so long as the leaders were legitimate heirs of the revolution. Checks and balances in Mexican politics came from a complex structure within the PRI and its relationship with the government of Mexico. But to simplify for the moment, the PRI was allowed to rule only as long as it maintained legitimacy in implementing revolutionary reforms—that means looking after the well-being of Mexican citizens.

After the revolution, lest the central power forget the populace, the revolutionary Emiliano Zapata gave them a reminder. Francisco I. Madero became president in 1914 only to realize that in order to establish peace and maintain control, he had to start acting like Porfirio Diaz, the dictator he replaced. He delayed land distribution in order to pay off foreign debt, whereupon Zapata rode his horse right into the president's office. With silver spurs jangling, he dismounted and grabbed the diminutive Madero's watch fob. "Look here, if you don't give us our land, I'm going to take your watch!" Madero was suitably impressed, and proceeded apace with land reform. No, Mexico is not a dictatorship.

Emiliano Zapata never died. He is very much alive in the Mexican psyche. Zapata dressed in fancy black and silver, but he was a man of the people. He was one of the revolutionaries who sat in the president's chair for photos after Mexico City was taken from Diaz's forces. But he did not want to be on top. After the photo session, he went back to his village and raised horses. Maybe it is this image that the Maya had in mind when they revolted in Chiapas in the mid-1980s. The Maya did not want to tell the central government how to run the country; they just wanted to be able to use their land freely. They call themselves *zapatistas*. The zapatista revolt was a major embarrassment to the PRI. Had the leaders forgotten their obligations to the revolution?

The persistence of hierarchy reflects a deep strain in the Mexican culture—one that we have talked about before. In business we saw how Mexicans tend to rely on people not paper (i.e., organization charts and job descriptions). The same is true in government, where Mexicans would rather put their trust in an individual, such as Zapata, than in the system. The Mexican need for hierarchy will survive the passing of the PRI period.

In 2000, Vicente Fox was elected president. For the first time in living memory, another party—the *Partido de Acción Nacional* (Party of National Action or PAN, a conservative business-oriented entity) controlled the executive branch. Many Americans see the emergence of a true multiparty political system as a move toward more open and transparent democracy. Mexicans see that too, but because hierarchy is so much a part of the culture, it is apt to survive and continue to be a major factor.

Politics and group orientation

The autoworker in Matamoros will tell you how he's faring in today's changing economic conditions by giving you an earful about politics. To the worker, economic conditions depend as much on the political hierarchy in Mexico City as upon his employers. He was willing to put a large portion of his faith in the hands of the PRI, and now looks to President Vicente Fox and his successors to fill his needs. How did the PRI maintain legitimacy for so many years? How will Fox and his successors fulfill the worker's expectations? The quick answer is that Mexico is and has been a democracy. Democracy, one pundit noted, operated 364 days a year in Mexico. The exception was election day. But Mexicans knew what that game was. They were tolerant of such shenanigans as missing ballots and stuffed boxes so long as their voices were heard and their needs addressed. Today elections are fair, but the name of the game is still backdoor politics.

How were the autoworker and the business leaders' voices heard in the PRI period? Democracy worked the other 364 days a year through the PRI's "corporate" party organization. The PRI was inclusive. It included leftists, rightists, intellectuals, and the indigenous people. The executive committee of the PRI "corporation" worked with a board of directors made up of representatives of all the major political and economic sectors including state governors, the military, and one ultimate union boss, Fidel Velazquez. They also had a board of advisors consisting of teachers, business leaders, and peasants. The PRI listened to all of these factions, which the government had organized into unions, peasant collectives, and business chambers. Such organizations encompassed every identifiable group in the country.

For Mexicans and their group orientation, being organized into labor groups and party cells worked well. The PRI and its handmaiden, the government of Mexico, created congresses of workers, regional unions, and professional unions, such as electrical workers. The Mexicans' need to belong to a group is so strong that the major unions will continue to be party affiliates despite the PRI's loss of the presidency. This type of organization explains from yet another point of view why unions are different in Mexico than in the United States. Union members in Mexico do not look to their employers for benefits; they look to *mi tio el cacique* (my uncle the warrior chief) in Mexico City. Mexicans have little stomach for making demands of the people who pay them—they are not confrontational by nature with their political leadership. The cultural trait that drives their negotiations is group orientation. To become strident and demanding is to admit that they can no longer work as a group.

Mexicans looked within their own group for influence in the executive branch in Mexico City, rather than relying on Congress. It was the union's integration into the PRI "corporation" that assured federally mandated benefits. Mexican workers will tell you that the PRI, the executive branch of the government, and their union boss chain of command were responsible for creating the social security hospital system, or *Instituto Mexicano del Seguro Social* (IMSS). Workers and their families, that is, anyone who has held a fixed job and who is therefore a registered beneficiary, enjoy the social security health delivery system. "When we go to the U.S., we lose that. We take jobs with no benefits. Here, we often have to wait a long time for an eye operation, but when we eventually get it, it's almost free." This and other benefits were suggested by organized labor and instituted in the 1930s at the behest of the PRI during a swing to the left under President Cárdenas.

Another aspect of how group behavior affects Mexico's political culture is evident in conflict resolution. In contrast to the U.S., conflict is rarely public in Mexico. Conflicts are resolved within the group, so that a territorial dispute between two unions will be settled behind closed doors. Conflict may be kicked upstairs to the next group in the hierarchy, such as the regional party headquarters. But conflict is rarely broadcast. In the past, this has enabled citizens to be heard and conflicting needs to be negotiated before the elections took place. Elections then conferred legitimacy upon the ruling class. TV sets glowed with stunning support.

In fact, mostly good news is broadcast in Mexico. The conflict that inevitably arises when people with vying interests interact is handled *inside* party walls. Then a big show is made of the resolution of a concern that was "nipped in the bud." It's not that TV isn't free to report anything it wants; rather, group behavior dictates that the differing factions get along with each other. TV in Mexico is and has been free, though the PRI controlled the supply of electricity. The press is and was free, though the PRI controlled the supply of paper.

Politics and present orientation

The very name of the dominant PRI political party shows the present orientation of Mexicans. The Party of the Institutionalized Revolution walked a fine line between *revolution*—change and future promise—and *institution*—hold on to what you have, because the future looks scary. A gringo wonders, "Isn't that contradictory? What's going on, a revolution with sweeping changes, or an institution with its internal resistance to change?" Not only were Mexican citizens not concerned with the contradiction of a party being revolutionary and institutional at the same time, somehow the self-negating party name fit with their sense of risk aversion. Change had brought disaster in the past—smallpox from Spain, a War of Independence, a controlling dictator who oppressed the peasants, and a disastrous revolution. With the name PRI, Mexicans could conceive of a balance between revolutionary change and control.

The genius of the PRI structure was that it met the expectations of Mexicans' present-oriented citizenry. "Today we will be conservative, tomorrow we may be liberal, but we will swing harmoniously to the left, to the right by consensus of the people, and with as little risk as possible."

The PRI machine was also self-sustaining. Party leaders would listen to economists and sociologists within the extended party family and decide if the next president should be leftist or rightist, and just how extreme the next swing should be. The current president would then select the next presidential candidate—the only viable candidate. Businesspeople in Mexico had great fun before the elections trying to figure out which political figure would win the current president's approval. As various political figures gave speeches—each appealingly grandiloquent—everyone watched how the president reacted. A double *abrazo* plus a pat on the forearm for one speaker, a triple *abrazo* to the next: Which was the stronger signal as to who was the favorite? The favorite would be the next candidate for president. Next week they would look for the same types of signal. "Who is favored this week?" They would cheer on their own favorite, but know that the choice of candidate was out of their hands. Democratic? Not from our point of view, but there was little open strife. During the PRI period, there were no assassinations, no coups, and no military dictatorships, as was often the case in the rest of Latin America. Once installed, the new president would sweep out the old policies and institute his own reforms over the following six years of his term. Inevitably what followed were the economic crises that resulted from the left to right swings. Mexican businesspeople knew the pattern. In the fifth year of a president's term, they would dig a hole, figuratively speaking, and pull the dirt in on top of themselves to hide from the winds of change.

The recent past has provided its share of windstorms. Carlos Salinas was elected president in 1988 at a time when Mexico's economy was suffering one of its more serious six-year slumps. Mexicans were downcast about their fate. "If we do not change, we will perish in twenty years," was the common refrain articulated in the streets. Salinas came in simultaneously with the collapse of the Soviet Union, so the leftist model offered no viable alternative plan.

Salinas put forward a bold, forward-looking vision. Mexico would march in lockstep toward an industrial future, with full democracy and free enterprise. Whereas the PRI had managed the economy in the past, now there would be a political and economic *apertura* (opening). Manufacturing, industrial development, and foreign direct investment (FDI) in production for export would supplant oil as Mexico's main source of foreign cash reserves. With world automakers already investing in new factories, first-, second-, and third-tier suppliers flooded into Mexico offering employment, new technology, and training programs. Other non-Mexican companies invested in Mexico to follow their customers, to use Mexico as a platform for further Latin American business, and to benefit from low labor rates. The American business community was, of course, delighted. Salinas' plan was working splendidly. Until six years later.

The election of Ernesto Zedillo in 1994 promised a steadier, less bold approach. Mexicans were ready for six years of calm after six years of dramatic political change. Mexicans had witnessed their first political assassinations. Zedillo was the kind of technocrat who promised no bold new initiatives. Zedillo did what all other PRI presidents before him had done—devalue the currency. But in keeping with Mexico's new politico-economic opening, the Zedillo administration decided to let the peso float. Problem: It didn't float. It sank like a rock. Purchasing power plummeted. The domestic auto industry dropped by 70 percent. It was the worst economic crisis of the entire PRI period. Mexicans did not blame Zedillo, rather they vented their anger on Salinas. Salinas' family was accused of corruption. There was nothing new in that. Most (not all) Mexican presidents had been accused of corruption, but never in the history of the PRI period had so much promise ended in such abject disaster. Salinas was likened to the *chupacabras* (literally goat sucker), or bloodsucking vampire of Mexican folklore, and had to leave the country.

These events reinforced the already embedded Mexican belief that the future brings as much peril as promise. And while the political and economic opening continues, the man in the street remains skeptical. Mexicans wait patiently for real progress. Americans see free, open, and transparent elections; a call for reforms; the new balance attained in a multiparty system; and we say, "This is good." Mexicans look at the same changes and say, "This is scary."

The politics of corruption

Corruption goes against the grain in both the United States and Mexico. Nothing in the Mexican cultural core justifies corruption. There are, however, two reasons for it. The first involves the historic *imposition* of hierarchy that was perceived as illegitimate. The Spanish kings layered bureaucracies over colonies, such as Mexico, in order to control their empire from a great distance. The crown did not grant authority to correspond with the responsibilities it foisted on bureaucrats. Lack of authority at the local level thus led to a need to "grease the skids."

Bribery also stems from the historical way that the Spanish rulers compensated their bureaucrats who governed Mexico. Rather than pay wages to the layers of bureaucracy, the crown granted concessions. The *corregidor* for example, who was sent to the New World to "correct" priests' abuses of peasants, was given the right to levy export duties on sugar to pay for his time and trouble. Governors were sent to correct the *corregidores,* and viceroys were sent to stifle the excesses of governors. Each was, in turn, granted a right to collect revenues from one source or another. This was his *encomienda,* or concession—his license or his patent. For the bureaucrat, an *encomienda* could be a bonanza. For the crown it was free.

The complexity of relationships between competing responsibilities versus lack of local authority to make decisions often meant that the only way through a morass was to pay a bribe. Today, people have to go to five ministries and fill out ten forms in quadruplicate just to get one nonanswer. This phenomenon is historically tied to the hierarchy set up by the Spanish crown. It could be argued that Mexicans' group orientation inhibited their taking initiative to change the situation, even after they won independence from Spain. And their present orientation led them to make expedient adjustments rather than reorganize for the future. *Mas cambia, mas queda igual:* The more things change, the more they stay the same.

Institutionalized corruption

Some aspects of the old days persist in Mexico. The cop on the corner still pays for his own car, uniform, and gun. The city gives him an *encomienda*, or a concession to maintain order on a certain corner. If he helps you find an address, you tip him. If you run a stop sign, he will chastise you, then say, "I wish there were something I could do." Coming from a straightforward American cop, that would probably mean, "I can't do anything about it." Coming from the agreeable Mexican policeman who deals with things more indirectly, it means, "Let's open up a discussion about what we can do." Then, it's either pay the policeman or pay the judge and the policeman, and by then the fine is doubled. Either way, you made a mistake and you pay. Corruption becomes institutionalized when the government knows that this situation exists and acquiesces, saying in effect, "It's okay for us to pay the officer less because he's making money on the side." This scheme is not unlike the way we settled the Wild West. U.S. marshals often had to catch a crook and collect the reward in order to get paid.

But, Mexico is not systemically corrupt. In almost four decades of doing business with Mexicans, I have never been asked for a bribe by any representative of the Mexican federal government or from any state or local government. I have worked with the Mexican department of commerce (SECOFI), their environmental protection department (SEMARNAT), treasury (Hacienda) and others. I repeat, never. The only bribes I have been asked to make were to local cops.

On my way to work one day I got pulled over by a cop in an ill-fitting uniform driving a beat-up brown '78 Olds. He said I was driving too fast in a school zone. Okay. There were no signs, but there was, in fact, a school nearby. I was determined not to pay a bribe, but this Mexican was a better negotiator than I was. Everything I tried to explain was met with a counter-argument. The threat was that if I ran, he would call the guys with guns, and then my fine would at least triple. So I played along. He eased the way for me by saying, "I wish there were something I could do-oo. . . ." Rather than say, "How's about twenty-five pesos," I asked him if he had any kids. "Yes," he said, straightening up proudly and indicating the three boys' heights with the palm of his hand. "Just a minute." I went to the trunk and took out a toy truck stamped with my company's logo. "When they get this big," I said, indicating his height with my hand, "have them come to us and ask for a job." That was good enough for him. I was off to work. Bribe or recruiting opportunity?

That level of bribery will go on in Mexico until each state or municipality can afford a clean, professional police force. I hasten to add that there are honest police forces. One example is the city of Querétaro, whose police force is thoroughly professional. Other policemen have distinguished themselves for their bravery in times of disaster. There are instances of policemen dying to save schoolchildren from floods and protecting citizens from assault. For every case of a bad policeman, there are many cases of good ones.

No one has been more affected by corruption than the Mexican. It was endemic government corruption that allowed building contractors to get by with substandard materials and construction, resulting in the disproportionate failure of modern buildings to survive the gigantic earthquake of 1985. As a consequence, an estimated 17,000 people died, and many more thousands were rendered homeless. It is realizations such as this that cause Mexican citizens to protest and ultimately change their city government. One of the checks on government officials is that a Mexican with nerve can always take a bureaucrat's watch away.

Corruption also infects some of the highest positions in the land. Recently the general appointed as drug czar was jailed for taking bribes from the drug lords. Drugs are the big wildcard in Mexico. In a country still trying to develop much needed resources, drug trafficking represents easy money.

Mexicans know how to relieve corruption. As resources permit, they raise salaries and cut regulations. Even the most venal customs officer, *gobernación* clerk, or cop uses some regulation to hold up a citizen. When the government is capable of raising salaries to a decent level, they also cut regulations, making the agent's job more perfunctory and thus discouraging venality. Mexico's federal prosecutor's office has extraordinary powers to jail white-collar people for malfeasance. Mexico also went through a thorough vetting process in bringing its voting regulations into the modern world. No longer are polling places located in PRI, or any party, headquarters. Today's elections are transparent and legitimate.

Seeing Mexico with corrected vision

When trying to define Mexico's political system, we tend to use outside measures for comparison. When discussing the Mexican government and the PRI with political analysts, I have been struck by how often they draw parallels with the former Soviet Union. The PRI operated behind the scenes of government much like the Bolshevik party and the Politburo operated in the Soviet Union—as a shadow government. Both modern Mexico and the former Soviet Union were forged in the crucible of revolution. In both cases, the original revolutionaries and their conservative enemies perished, and the country was inherited by the street rabble. In the case of the Soviet Union, it was the Bolsheviks who took over; in Mexico it was the *mestizo* lower- and middle-class city dwellers.

The heirs of the Mexican Revolution did indeed witness the Russian Revolution and tried to learn from it, just as they had used the American model to inform them. But the differences between the Soviet Union and Mexico tell us much about the Mexican psyche. Mexican culture took Mexicans down a much different road.

Mexicans avoided ideological myopia by allowing leftist intellectuals and right-wing dinosaurs to participate on a relatively equal playing field within the same group. Rather than hold up a theoretical ideal or ideology to measure themselves against, the PRI negotiated the contradictory challenge of stability versus change, of permanence versus evolution, of institution versus revolution. Theirs was a very practical approach. The swings to the left and to the right accommodated change and permitted progress. The periodic swings were institutionalized by the PRI and codified in the constitutional restriction against a president's succeeding himself. Historically, in Latin America as elsewhere, when a dictator's regime begins to fail, his response is more dictatorship. When a socialist scheme fails, the socialists first assume that the solution is more socialism. But in Mexico, there were clear shifts in course every six years to cope with existing realities. Power was passed peacefully from the left to the right to accommodate the citizens' need for change.

In his book *Insurgent Mexico,* written in 1914, American author John Reed assumed that the Mexican Revolution was an intellectual parallel of the Russian Revolution. There were similarities, to be sure. They were roughly contemporary events. Revolutionary Venustiano Carranza wore fatigues and a beard and mustache, reminiscent of Russian revolutionaries. There were also clear class distinctions and abuses, but Reed was ultimately wrong. He saw the world through pink glasses. There was one factor that kept Mexico from going communist—the practical nature of Mexican politcal culture. Communism never took hold because Mexican workers, teachers, farmers, and even politicians saw the ideology as too complicated. The Mexicans really wanted land and jobs. They also wanted the ability to freely decide how to pursue their own ideals.

Ask a peasant vendor, laborer, or farmer and they will tell you (politely and after prodding) that they are tired of being patronized by foreigners. Mexicans are also tired of being stereotyped as politically backward. Most will tell you they want change and accountability. They need judicial reform because they don't yet trust the courts or the police. They expect better opportunities that will come with political and economic opening. But, they are long suffering, fatalistic, and will work exhaustive hours to make up for the deficits their country has brought upon itself.

CHAPTER
FIFTEEN

Economic Culture

The boy approached with a piece of broken mirror in his hand. Would I like him to show me the tree? I can see that the *ahuehuete* is enormous. What could he possibly add? "How big around at the trunk?" I asked, recalling that somewhere I had read about the two-thousand-year-old wonder located just outside Oaxaca City in the town of Santa Maria del Tule. "Fifty meters," (164 feet) came the reply. Then throwing his arms wide, he added, "It would take at least twenty-six *americanos* to reach around it today."

Beckoning me under the canopy, the young Mexican raced from point to point with his little reflector, knowing just where to catch the sun in order to wash the features of the gnarled trunk with light. For him, the tree is a living object, rich in symbolism. "Look, there's a crucifix," he exclaimed, illuminating a natural configuration of a branch crossing the fluted trunk. Then, moving from hanging limb to limb, he showed me an elephant, a saddle, a face of Jesus, and other images I could barely make out. I wished he would slow down, but he rushed through his story of the tree. After earning my peso, he had to quickly earn another. As I paid him (they never complain that it's too little), I asked if he went to school. "Yes, when I can," he replied.

Forget the *ahuehuete* tree! Here's a kid with nothing more than a piece of broken mirror, and he's making a buck. His roots go back to *Huitzili-pochtli,* the Aztec god of smoke and mirrors. His future is uncertain and depends on what training and education he can acquire, and ultimately on the kinds of jobs available. Chances are great that his search for a job will take him far away from Oaxaca.

Mexicans joke that the biggest problem with Mexico is Mexicans. But, in fact, the people are its greatest resource. The amount of capital needed by an individual to become a modern professional is relatively small. Today, a PC in Mexico costs the same as in the United States. There are affordable government, private, and parochial schools, generally considered to be of good quality. With the value placed on self-improvement, Mexicans have achieved a world-class 96 percent literacy rate, compared to 23 percent immediately after the revolution. Those who also learn English are paid twice as much as their monolingual schoolmates. For the lucky ones who have acquired both education and experience, earning power increases sharply. Intellectual capital bears fruit in the hands of talented people.

Epifanio

Not everyone in Mexico has difficulty finding a job. When, in addition to having education, training, and experience, you are exceptionally talented, the jobs chase you. I once interviewed a fellow named Epifanio for a position of superintendent of investment casting. Having started as a common laborer in a plant in his native state of Mexico, Epifanio had worked his way up to supervisor of the Investment Casting Department at a company that made golf club heads. There, he had earned enough to buy three workers' houses in addition to his own middle-class home, qualifying each time for the favorable mortgage rates. My plant manager had worked with Epifanio in the past: "He really sticks his nose into the process. He knows more than anybody in his company." "Does he speak English?" I asked. "I don't know," he replied.

We met with Epifanio in Mexico City. A full-blooded Otomí, his skin was so dark it seemed ashy blue. He was short, round-headed, barrel-chested, and full of confidence. His story reminded me of Benito Juarez's life drama—leaving the fields in the mid-nineteenth century, going to school and becoming president of Mexico. Epifanio had had the advantage of attending the German school in Mexico City, where they encouraged him to be inquisitive and to pay attention to detail. As part of my interview, I asked if he spoke English. He laughed and recited some Shakespeare. Not only did he speak Spanish and English, but also German and his native Nahuatl language. As much as I wanted to hire him, I couldn't afford him.

I initially offered Epifanio $35,000 a year, then upon recognizing his potential value to our operations, I increased our offer to $45,000. Meanwhile, back at the ranch, a vice president named Tex (though not a Texan) put his opinion to me delicately: "Why the f*** do you want to hire a Mexican for that position? If it were up to me, hell, I'd hire an American."

Being a canny fellow, Epifanio mentioned our offer to his current employer who countered with a winning $60,000 salary plus a car! His story illustrates that in Mexico today, if you are bright and luck is on your side, there are opportunities for the taking. There are jobs to be filled within foreign companies, yet there are too few people with appropriate training or experience. Epifanio started with minimal resources but managed to accumulate plenty. Lucky? Not many villagers end up in the German school. But there are many instances in which resources are available, and the mechanism for economic ascendancy is at hand.

On the bleak side, many still can't afford computers. And many more lack the time to go to school. When a child of twelve has to hit the streets to put beans on the table, his education is curtailed. In Mexican culture, the child's obligation to help the family comes before his self-improvement. Self-improvement has meaning only within the context of the family's well-being. When a talented, dedicated people discover that they cannot improve their economic condition in their current locality, they get together with their family or their village groups and come up with a strategy. Frequently this means moving.

The snake and the eagle

A recent archaeological exhibition that circulated through major cities in Mexico and the United States, entitled "Fifty Centuries of Mexican Civilization," documented how the Olmecs, the Maya, the later Toltecs, and finally the Aztecs migrated for five thousand years around Mesoamerica—between northern Mexico and Guatemala. Why did these Mesoamerican people migrate? To find resources for a better life. Amassing as a family, a group, and finally as a regional drove, they became a procession of people with a mission. Three centuries of colonialism and nearly two centuries of modernity have not erased the Aztec mission to wander in search of the land of ample resources. The Aztecs began their migration in Aztlán in the north, and, according to legend, settled in today's Mexico City Valley, where they saw an eagle perched on a cactus holding a rattlesnake in its beak. That image signified to the Aztecs that they had reached the land of plenty and today adorns the Mexican flag.

Even in the twentieth century when the central government exercised considerable control, Mexican citizens were free to wander. No one ever told citizens where to go or what to do when they got there. This is what has saved Mexicans from their fate of natural calamities and famine. Feeling that "we are part of a procession" is a cultural theme tied directly to economic survival.

Here's one way of seeing how the cultural elements we have studied come together to form a consistent thread that runs through the economic life of Mexicans. An individual's drive for self-improvement rolls up into the family's commitment to work as a group in search of resources; this, in turn, can morph into mass migration—a procession on a mission. What follows is by no means a complete survey of Mexico's economic development; rather, it is a cultural perspective on the many ways that Mexicans search for work.

Toehold in the city—a family on the move

By the 1960s, black and white images of a new economic age were flickering in the eyes of *campesinos* (peasants) across Mexico. In quest of a better life for their children, the women established a pattern of moving to the nearest large city to secure jobs as maids. Once they acquired a toehold, sisters, husbands, and children would come to live with them. Soon, largely illiterate masses joined the movement.

Margarita and her husband, Gerardo, came from the little pueblo of Jojutla to a house in Mexico City. They arrived in traditional sandals and native dress, he with his straw hat and she with her *rebozo* (shawl). The owner of the house was *Tia Tita* (diminutive address for Aunt Marta), the dowager aunt of the well-heeled Peña family. Margarita and Gerardo knew the well-to-do Peña family from their country estate and had come to town to serve *Tia Tita* in her city home so that their children would learn to read and write and acquire modern skills. Margarita did the cooking, and Gerardo oversaw the garage. Gerardo was older. His first wife had died, so he married Margarita and fathered a new brood of children. Cuca, the oldest daughter of the first marriage, became the Peñas' maid. Together, the family was squeezed into one room with the younger children—Germán, Alberto, Silvia, Laurita, and Pablito, aged ten to two. The entire family bunked together.

As everyone had predicted, Cuca fell in love with Braulio, a quiet, hardworking young man who apprenticed in the shop attached to the house where

Señor Carlos Peña ran a printing business. The Peña family had founded one of Mexico's most prestigious publishing houses. Because of their position and resources, the Peñas represented an opportunity to Margarita's family in Mexico City. They could offer work, a room, and food. Later I show the importance of any one of these elements on a decision to change cities.

Soon Braulio and Cuca married, and in spite of inflation and the precipitous slides of the peso, eventually they saved enough money to buy a small worker house on the outskirts of Mexico City. Margarita's plan was working. The family was moving up. The children tended the chickens on the roof, fetched firewood, ran errands, and went to school. The young ones prospered. Germán eventually became an accountant, Alberto an architectural draftsman, and Pablito a purchasing agent. Silvia received her master's degree in psychology and began teaching school. Laurita, the flirtatious one with long eyelashes, shacked up with a German. But it wasn't until Braulio and Cuca's eldest son José Luis graduated from the National University (UNAM) in 1989 with a degree in mechanical engineering that the family felt the true measure of their accomplishments.

Because of Margarita's bold move to the city and the family procession that followed, her children were able to achieve the dream of self-improvement. Having diligently prepared themselves for the future, all the younger generation needed was jobs.

From zapatista to brain surgeon in three generations

An American friend, John, married Amalia (nicknamed Yaya), whose family is also representative of the economic progress in recent decades. Yaya's father had fought alongside Zapata during the revolution. Subsequently, he became a fine cabinetmaker and fashioned a comfortable middle-class existence, subsidized by renting out rooms in his house to American students. He had accumulated enough resources for his family to take the next leap forward. Having had two wives and living long enough to father two generations of children, this former zapatista saw one of his offspring become an engineer with Xerox in Aguascalientes, another an attorney with United Airlines in the United States, and the youngest, a brain surgeon.

These spectacular advancements are representative of Mexicans who have accumulated modest resources. In Mexico, progress is measured in family terms. The transition in three generations of Margarita's family from country illiterates to professionals, from servants to teachers, from ten-in-a-bed to a home-of-one's-own is a familiar one throughout Mexico. The story of Yaya's little half brother—the youngest son of a revolutionary who went on to become a brain surgeon—is just one of thousands of examples driving the rapid expansion of Mexico's middle class. And with middle-class status, options open up. For instance, a good engineer or bilingual attorney can work in either the United States or in Mexico. A medical doctor, grandson of a zapatista, who speaks English can move to the States and set up a profitable practice. Today's Mexican middle class is the largest per capita, as well as in number, of any middle class in Latin America.

Margarita's and Yaya's families are united in spirit by their shared sense that the family group is on a mission. Self-improvement is defined in the context of how the family is doing generation after generation. While everyone works hard, in keeping with the Mexican notion of time, there is no sense of urgency that "if I don't make vice president by age thirty-four, I'm a failure." On the contrary, each generation does the best it can, then consigns itself to its fate in favor of improving the lot for the next generation of children.

Jobs, jobs, jobs—Mexico looks to the outside world

Once prepared for work, where do people turn for jobs? Whereas the resources required for one individual to become a professional are relatively small, the amount of capital needed to create well-paying jobs for many people is extraordinarily high. Mexico needs to create one million jobs per year to keep up with population growth and movement toward industrialization. However, Mexican resources create only about 600,000 jobs in a good year. The amount of capital required for this purpose is daunting. By 1985, moving to the nearest town to work as a maid was not good enough. By then there were many people with a minimum sixth-grade education, and some with technical training who were looking for real wages. The migration pattern in Mexico changed. Young people began to move to any city in the country to get the kind of jobs they wanted.

As early as 1965, Mexico had looked to the U.S. and other countries for resources. In that year, the *Maquiladora* Program was born. (*Maquiladora* means "milling operation," like a flour mill where the miller turns wheat into flour for a fee. A modern *maquiladora* is a place where a businessperson takes his or her raw materials to be processed.) By 1985, European, Asian, and U.S. capital had built plants throughout Mexico that offer 150,000 new jobs each year. Though not enough, these jobs go a long way toward providing a first step up on the economic ladder—a step that many Mexicans have been eager to take.

Economic change has accelerated in recent years. In the 1960s and 1970s, there were a number of regional technical schools whose graduates could find jobs as welders, lathe operators, electricians, and the like. But such schools were not set up to teach students how to operate modern machine tools. The government had neither the capital nor the expertise to keep up with the training of quickly changing higher technology. In response, the federal and state governments set up training facilities in conjunction with private enterprise. The government provided facilities and teachers, the foreign companies provided training for the teachers and new equipment. Workers could then be taken off-line for instruction specific to the company's needs. But it was not enough. The influx of foreign investment after 1985 that accelerated throughout the 1990s was such that domestic resources could not keep pace. Further, the maquiladora industry evolved. When first conceived in 1965, the maquiladora was intended to provide minimum wage jobs for untrained workers in sewing, assembly, and finishing. As the industry matured, and as the automotive industry expanded in Mexico, operations became less labor intensive. More recent investment has been in capital-intensive operations requiring highly skilled labor. The resulting gap in technical preparation is reflected in countless newspaper ads begging for qualified specialists.

For those with professional education but no experience, foreign and American companies offer employment opportunities in the form of internships. It's a two-way street: both recent graduates and the company benefit. Internships fit with a tradition of public service in Mexico. Those who do not go into the military may choose instead to attend a university and serve an internship. They may spend a year on learn-and-earn programs with foreign-owned companies. Or, if the opportunity presents itself, they often prefer to work for American companies because it may lead to an assignment in the U.S. This represents a further opportunity for their children to go to school in the States and learn English. When young professionals return to Mexico, their earning power is enhanced.

Even medical school graduates can fulfill their public service requirements with work at maquiladoras. If a company has more than 100 employees, federal law requires that a doctor be on staff. Engineers exiting school will likewise do an internship at a maquiladora for $12,000 per year. Generally, they are well prepared and may speak English, but they have no experience. The second year, their salary jumps, because now they are qualified, bilingual, *and* experienced. Their earning power increases whether they stay with foreign-owned maquiladoras or go with Mexican companies. The ramp-up in salaries is much quicker than in the U.S. American businesspeople are often shocked to learn that a qualified and experienced plant manager in Mexico makes the same as a U.S. counterpart. It's true as well of the chief financial officer and other upper management personnel. If these professionals become fully integrated into the U.S. management team, they may benefit from assignments to the United States or other foreign countries, and thus be positioned for further advancement and further educational experiences for their children.

Clarifying views of the maquiladora industry

Mexicans consider the maquiladora industry a boon to their economy, but their cultural perspectives are at odds with ours. Mexicans wonder why we have such opposing viewpoints. Americans seem to be of two minds. On one hand, some say that U.S. companies are only doing the smart thing, and that there are three important reasons for moving to Mexico. In order of priority, these are: 1. To follow customers, 2. To create a manufacturing platform for business in the rest of the world, and 3. To take advantage of cheaper labor rates. What could be more rational than that? On the other hand, many Americans argue that corporations are exploiting Mexican workers, causing slums, and contributing to pollution. Being one-way gringos in a two-way world, both sides dig their heels in and engage in acrimonious shouting. The debate in America about maquiladoras tells us more about our own cultural values than the Mexicans', and it clouds our ability to see the program from the Mexican point of view.

From the Mexican cultural perspective, the maquiladora program offers much needed jobs at market rates, training for jobs that increase the average workers' wages, and technology, including pollution controls that Mexico sorely lacks. For practical Mexicans, foreign companies offer a ladder to self-improvement, self-respect, and wages. Foreign companies provide a way for Mexico to modernize.

When recently outlining these factors to a room of college seniors, my remarks were met with some interest and some lingering skepticism. There were those students and faculty members who want to do the good thing and protect Mexicans from exploitation. There were others insisting that we are just good businesspeople, doing what has to be done to remain competitive. But after the conference, a young man came up and introduced himself. "I'm Omar. I'm from Mexico. Thank you for giving the Mexican side that you never hear in the States." Then he asked, "Why is there so much *hate* here?" With one question Omar hit me over the head with a completely different perspective. While our debate is about Mexicans, we have totally missed the Mexican point of view. Omar needs to understand that we aren't angry with the Mexicans, our argument is with ourselves. Like the Mexican who thinks we are prejudiced because we get up and move away from him at the beach, in this case the Mexican student assumes that some Americans just don't want him to have a job and training. We think we are good, he sees hate. The difference in views is a function of the cultural drag we bring to our separate perspectives.

Afta NAFTA

The NAFTA debate in the United States also stunned Mexicans. Whereas Mexicans debate quietly behind closed doors within their various groups, Americans tend to duke it out in public. Some Americans think NAFTA is great, others see it as a threat to American workers. The Mexicans wonder why we are throwing brickbats at each other. For years, we implored Mexico to open up its borders to trade, accusing them of hiding behind protectionist devices (e.g., 100 percent import duties and import bans). Then in 1988, President Salinas joined the Geneva Agreement for Trade and Tariffs (GATT). This meant that Mexico would drop import tariffs from 100 percent to world rates of less than 10 percent. The deed was done. Americans were free to sell, invest, come, and go.

Then we debated NAFTA. One side shouted, "It's *good* for business!" Opponents yelled, "You're going to kill us and pollute Mexico, and that's not *good!*" Some readers will recall Ross Perot's chant that "jobs will go south with a giant 'sucking sound'." That last one really irked the Mexicans. A Mexican friend told me, "You Americans always wanted to come into Mexico to do business. Now we are welcoming you, and you greet us with all this debate. Why?" From the Mexican perspective, *they* were taking all the risk. It was they who opened their borders to possible foreign domination. It was the normally risk-averse Mexicans who suddenly threw their arms open to join in a march with the rest of North America toward an industrial future. And now it was we Americans who talked of pollution, abuse, and sucking sounds.

Putting the migration patterns in proper focus

The first wave in Mexico's economic modernization involved women like Margarita leaving their villages to get a toehold in the nearest large city. The second wave—beginning in 1985 and continuing to the present—has consisted of young people moving to other cities in search of specific kinds of employment. Some move to find professional or skilled trade jobs. Unlike the earlier traffic of traditional women in sandals seeking domestic work, today's rush teems with modern people in blue jeans and Nikes going after real jobs for hourly wages. They are eager to put their skills to work in order to move up the economic ladder. Many middle-class professionals are moving into positions of responsibility all over the world.

A graduate of a rural technical school strong in electronics may move to Tijuana. A young girl with training in quality control and metrology may get a job in a European plant in Saltillo. Baccalaureate candidates from throughout the country apply to universities in progressive Nuevo León, where they get a degree, a job, and settle in. There are still untrained young people, of course, and they move to Reynosa or Nuevo Laredo for assembly jobs.

Magali

Young people with technical training have even been leaving their native Guadalajara. Mexico's third largest metropolis, Guadalajara received much investment in assembly operations in the 1970s and 1980s but fell behind the modernization curve. "My mother and older sisters had assembly jobs. That's mostly what is available in Guadalajara, but I want something better," said Magali as she applied for the human resources job with Delphi in Torreón. Twenty years earlier, it would have been unthinkable that a whole generation of young people would pull up stakes and move to Torreón, Monterrey, or Querétaro for the sake of better employment. But since 1985, internal migration patterns have changed. As a result, Guadalajara's population has actually declined. Once again, Mexicans have hit the road to find economic opportunity. As Magali's case testifies, a woman is now amenable to moving from one city to another for self-improvement. The pattern of internal migration has continued to be defined by young women who move and are then followed by their boyfriends or spouses.

Lucas

Today young people know where the jobs are and what they have to do to get them, but not everyone is willing to take the risk. While on vacation in Veracruz in 2000, I asked a rather lethargic young waiter named Lucas what it would take for him to relocate to another city for a job in a factory. Where would he be willing to go? Immediately, he responded that for $60 a week he would go to Reynosa, so long as he had a place to live. Three things were clear. First, he had already thought it through. Second, he knew where to go to get a nonskilled job. And third, he wasn't going to live on the street. He knows that Mexico has a serious housing shortage. For the moment, that lack of resource is the only thing holding him back. Correction, there are also his ex-girlfriend and their baby son—that family thing again.

For people with little or no training, pay is low, but even these workers have more benefits than some American workers do. A Mexican who has one year's experience operating a simple drill press makes about $55 (U.S.) per week. His federally mandated benefits plus company benefits usually add up to another $55 (or 100 percent of his wages). This amount has not changed in dollar terms over the years. While Mexican workers get frequent raises in pesos, increases are tied to inflation. When devalued to dollars, the wages actually remain constant. What drives up real wages is training and experience. A well-trained, experienced computer numeric control (CNC) operator in Monterrey can make $7 per hour. That is a solidly middle-class wage in Mexico.

The considerable number who still cannot find work, or who are underemployed, either continue to eke out a subsistence on their *rancho*, move to the outskirts of Mexico City where they live in tarpaper shacks, or head to the border. Mexico City is no longer the land of plenty. The eagle has flown. Once near the United States, they may live in a railroad car or corrugated tin shelter, get a job in a maquiladora, or hop the fence. In other cases, whole villages devise a plan to provide for their citizens. They might send a representative to McAllen, Texas, to buy used clothing they then sell at the markets. After all, it's far better to sport a used DKNY sweatshirt than to stay in the white "pajamas" the Spanish made them wear.

Illegal immigration

With too few jobs, Mexicans are not likely to rebel against their own government. They know that the government cannot simply create jobs out of thin air. They are reluctant to violate the trust they have put in their political hierarchy so long as they still have confidence in their leaders. In bad times with no improvement in sight, increasing numbers of the untrained unemployed head to the North—*el norte,* still seen by many as the land of unlimited resources. But the reality is that they arrive in the U.S. only to face a different set of problems. In Mexico, the worker has family, friends, a hometown, a piece of land, roots, habits, social security hospitals, a cultural safety net, and subsistence. He could always leave a job and still subsist. In the States, he is more dependent on his job because outside the plant, service company, or lamp shop, he does not have subsistence networks. In the U.S., he becomes more dependent on money. He has fewer options. If it's true that the streets are paved with gold, as many believe, it is also true that the Mexican immigrant needs his own car, his own insurance, and he must pay for everything out of his wages. These factors tend to keep first generation immigrants in a cycle of poverty, dependent on their children.

Mexicans have a mixed view of illegal immigration. Middle- and upper-class Mexicans openly lament that Americans have a negative opinion of Mexicans because all we see in the States are lower-class, undereducated people who can't get jobs in Mexico and who live in poverty in Los Angeles or Grand Rapids. They regret that our impression is so limited. "It is part of the reason that many Americans stereotype Mexicans as maids and gardeners," an industrialist told me. "Of course there is nothing wrong with that, but we would want you to know that we also have fine lawyers, doctors, and a thriving middle class." In fact, once a Mexican has achieved middle class, he travels to and from the States easily. Mexicans vacation in Vale and own businesses in the U.S. They send their children to graduate school in Massachusetts and Washington.

El Norte

Emigration to the United States is a safety valve for Mexico. Because of the opportunity gap there, the government sees emigration as a necessary evil. Further, Mexico has its own illegal immigration problem. For decades, Guatemalan, Honduran, and Salvadoran refugees from poverty and political persecution have been sneaking across Mexico's southern border seeking relative improvement in living conditions. These illegal Central American immigrants add to the already heavy pressure on job availability and, as a consequence, to Mexican migration to *el norte*.

Once legal or illegal immigrants arrive in the States, they congregate in low-rent neighborhoods and pull together. People from the same region tend to move to the same cities. There is safety in the group.

Migrating to California

Depending on where they land, immigrants are met with differing attitudes. Texans tend to accept the Mexicans, while many Californians are resentful. One reason is that historically the Tijuana (TJ) area was sparsely populated, whereas both sides of the Rio Grande in Texas were occupied by families of Mexicans for centuries. When a Mexican crosses the border into California, he has fewer historical ties. True, Mexicans were there for centuries, but they were widely dispersed. New immigrants have few roots. Many of the so-called Mexicans crossing into California are in fact Salvadorans and Nicaraguans. Some take advantage of the system. It happens that pregnant women from TJ will drive across to San Diego to have their babies for free in the emergency room. Then, the baby is eligible for U.S. citizenship. The citizens of California have to pay for it, and they get no help from Uncle Sam.

Aside from such opportunism, the Mexicans are not troublemakers. The sheriff's department in Riverside, California, regards the Mexican community as exceptionally law-abiding, the only problem being domestic disturbances. Chancellor Bob Bersi of Cal State, Long Beach, says that Mexican women are the superstars of his campus, so there is good news with the bad for Mexicans. The bad being proposed legislation to stop paying for illegal immigrants' medical care, schooling, and other benefits, a measure that affects legal and illegal immigrants from all over the world—Mexico, Central American, and Vietnam. ("Good news with the bad" is a recurrent theme in the Mexicans' cultural context.)

Migrating to Texas

In contrast to California, Texas has a tradition of greater interdependence with Mexico. The U.S.–Mexican border has been occupied by the same families for centuries. They know each other. A nurse in the Edinburg Hospital in Texas might say, "Silvia, you'd better get back to Matamoros now, your contractions are getting too close." Further, Mexicans contribute strongly to the U.S. economy in the region. Southern Texas is full of hospitals that cater to a wealthy Mexican clientele. If Señora Navarro wants a nose job, she heads to McAllen Memorial Hospital. If the señor needs a heart transplant, he goes to see a world-class surgeon in Houston. Mexicans spend $4 billion each year in shopping malls around McAllen, Texas, alone. They also buoy up the real estate market of South Padre Island. During the U.S. banking crisis of the late 1980s and early 1990s, border banks such as Texas Commerce Bank did a land office business. Mexicans' patronage is duly appreciated.

A tale of two cultures

Many people living near the Mexico–Texas border have dual citizenship and family on both sides. Of these, some choose to work in Mexico and go to the hospitals there because they are free. Others use private hospitals and doctors in Tamaulipas because they are good and cost a quarter of what care costs in the United States. With relatively high wages in the maquiladora industry, they are better off living an entirely Mexican lifestyle in Reynosa, Nuevo Laredo, or Matamoros, Mexico. They are better off than their Mexican American cousins who live and work in Mission, Elsa, or Zapata, Texas.

Some binational locals enjoy the benefits of both lifestyles. It is relatively easy to get permits to go shopping in Texas where prices for middle-class items are more competitive than back home. When asked why they shop for food in the U.S., I have been told, "Everything is better in the States. In Mexico, if you buy sour cream, in one week it turns green. Sour cream from the States stays white for over three months. Hot dogs stay the same color."

Pulling the countries together

Señor Saenz puts all his weight into pulling the rope that connects the United States and Mexico. With three helpers, he draws the flat-bottom ferry across the Rio Grande from Los Ebanos, Texas, toward a weathered post on the opposite bank. "We make the crossing about twelve times each day," he says. "We are usually full, with three cars and about thirty people." Rubbing his callused hands, he continues, "My family has been doing this since the 1570s." He pays little attention to the Mexican and American border patrols that check papers on both sides of the river as they would at any port of entry. After all, they have been there only since 1848. Señor Saenz's experience is much larger.

"They don't even see the border," said a University of Texas professor. He's right. Mexican natives treat the border between Texas and the northern Mexican state of Tamaulipas as a figment of bureaucrats' imagination. Locals have been dealing with the minor inconveniences of border crossing for generations.

The book according to Isaya

Isaya was taking a break by the swimming pool at a housing development where he works on the U.S. side of the border. His perpetual smile belies the fact that he is in Edinburg illegally. Aware that I might be treading on sensitive ground, I ask, "How do you get into the States to work?" "I have a day card that allows me to come over to shop," he says. "But they don't keep track, so I work." Then he adds, "Once, I forgot my card, so I tied a bunch of empty milk jugs to my belt and swam across the river." He laughs in benign glee at having beat the system.

The illegal immigrant's mission in the U.S.

In the United States as in Mexico, unskilled Mexican workers are following the jobs. A worker can make $9 an hour working at Burger King in Dallas. Texas has a special program where Mexicans won't be chased down by state authorities, as long as the immigrant agrees not to make more than that amount of money. Mexican workers are also in the mountains of North Carolina cutting timber. They are in the big cities getting any manufacturing, service, or other job they can find. They are driving nails in Minnesota and scraping and painting in Michigan. In the past, Mexican migrants wound up in border states. Today, they are spread out all over the continent. Wherever they go, they are uniformly seen as having an excellent work ethic and as having good attitudes.

Many North Americans see their presence as a relief, because companies can't find labor. Others see it as an invasion that must be stopped. Mexicans don't really understand the debate among angry *americanos*. A Mexican immigrant knows perfectly well whether he's in the States legally or illegally. He would much rather be legal. At the same time he knows that there are plenty of jobs in *el norte* and not enough people to do the work. He wants a guest worker status, but some Americans scream that if we let one Mexican in, we will have to let them all in. And once we let them in, they will just stay. The Mexican is less sure. He won't say this, but why would he want to stay in a cold place where he is not welcome? He wants to work. He wants to help his family back home. He will sacrifice. As for how long he will stay, who can predict the future? You can drive from Chicago to Monterrey on a weekend. There is no work on the weekend. The trip will cost you $140 in gasoline. Let's see, divided by five . . .

The three-generation family pattern

Immigrants from Mexico probably do not speak English. Their ability to earn is limited. Their children go to school and within three months of arriving in the United States are able to translate for their parents at the grocery store or hospital. By the next generation, some Mexican Americans have become fully acculturated in the workplace, though they may still live with parents and grandparents under the same roof. In this case, they speak English on the job and Spanish in the home—they are bilingual and bicultural. Others want their *own* car, their *own* house, their *own* life. The economic advantage of speaking English may eventually cause them to lose their Spanish. As we detailed in Chapter 5, the features of an individual language are formative to culture, so when people lose their language, they also lose their culture.

You can go home again

There are many cases of Mexicans returning to the village they call home when their mission is accomplished, and there are signs that Mexican workers intend to return. The most recent migration to the United States— that is, after 1994—may be temporary. Many are sent by their villages to earn money to send back to the group.

As of 2004, Mexicans migrating legally and illegally to the U.S. for jobs were sending $17 billion a year back to their families in Mexico. This expatriation of dollars now represents the second largest source of foreign currency reserves for Mexico—behind oil exports and surpassing tourism and the maquiladora industry.

Why would a worker send money back to his village if he did not intend to return? Back home in the village, families are using the money to fix up their houses. Other immigrants are sending money back to build small sewing operations so that the village can have permanent jobs. With such a high demand for minimum wage labor even in the U.S. recession of 2001–2003, there was plenty of work to be done in the States. However, if jobs dry up, if more jobs become available in Mexico, or if recent immigrants tire of the confrontational attitudes of Anglo straw bosses, they could leave.

It's not just about money

Our Anglo mentality tells us that we live in the land of plenty, that we are the promised land. There is no assurance that Mexicans see that as a permanent condition. They look at the United States and marvel at our technology and our accomplishments, but to the Mexican self-improvement is not only about money.

Especially for recent immigrants, the cultural set pieces of time, space, and language are locked in place. These Mexicans may find that they are far more comfortable living and working in a present-oriented environment and in an atmosphere of group dependence where the emphasis is on people. Typically, they feel the need to be close to their families and to be surrounded by those who speak the same language and share the same values. Satisfying these cultural cravings is sometimes far more compelling than amassing money for the future.

Sargent Navarrete's story illustrates why some young people want to return to Mexico. He earned U.S. citizenship serving in our Air Force. But, upon completing his tour of duty at age twenty-four, he took stock, and decided to move back to San Luis Potosí. There he has nice weather, family, money in his pocket, and opportunity. The area is beginning to boom. He speaks English fluently, and is well positioned to work for a non-Mexican company. And all the things modern young people want—wine bars, discos, and Internet cafés—are just an hour's ride away in León. Why live in Peoria?

A Mexican gentleman I met on the road a few years ago also fits the template above. He reminds me that many Mexicans who have immigrated to the United Sates prefer to return to Mexico. He also helps me see how, amidst the wave of American economic investment in Mexico, I must not slip into the mind-set of the typical gringo, assuming that *I* am there to help *him*. From his cultural perspective, I'm in his country and he can help *me*.

I had been asked to look at the town of San Luis del Rio Colorado in the northwestern corner of the state of Sonora to determine if it was a suitable place to install an industrial park. Here the Colorado River empties into the Sea of Cortez, creating an agricultural oasis in the middle of desert salt flats and the rugged steep mountains of Baja. While in San Luis, I stop a local to ask him about his community. He is carrying a kilo of tortillas and is headed home. "I'll give you a ride," I offer. On the way to his place, he tells me all he knows about what foreign companies have plants there, where workers come from, and how life in general is treating the locals. "I can't complain," he says. "I worked in Los Angeles for five years, but I prefer to live here. I had a good job, but I would rather come back to where I started and work in the tortilla factory." When I leave him off at his place—a wood door through a cement wall— he hands me a scrap of paper. "Here's my phone number," he says. "Please let me know if I can ever help you."

◈ ◈ ◈

CHAPTER

SIXTEEN

Across the Social Spectrum

In the remote suburb of Ciudad Netzahualcóyotl, forty-five minutes by taxi from the heart of Mexico City, each row house has a tiny picket fence and a lighted number. Braulio and Cuca meet us at the door. Twenty-five years have passed since my wife and I last saw the entire family. Cuca's mother and father—Margarita, still beautiful, and Gerardo, now totally gray—have come the farthest, traveling sixty miles by bus from their hometown of Jojutla. We are also greeted by Braulio and Cuca's teenage son and by Cuca's half siblings—our "little friends" from the house where we once rented a room. All are there to see us.

The two-story structure—about twelve by thirty feet—has a crudely constructed stairway to the bedrooms above. There is a toilet under the steps, and in the back, a kitchen separated from the cramped living/eating area by an arch. This worker-class house isn't much, but it is theirs—a quantum leap forward from the single room where they once slept eight or ten to a bed.

For the most part, Cuca and Margarita stay in the kitchen. But they listen intently as Braulio tells us their story. The Peña family's printing business had fallen on bad times, Braulio begins, adding that after Señor Carlos died, his wife had taken over. I was aware that in the Mexican hierarchical tradition, when the father dies, it is *mamá* who assumes control over the family business—not the sons. So the señora had taken the reigns, and, as Braulio explains, had quickly run the business into the ground. What the señora did to Braulio's family next is a tragedy that all too often hits the lower class.

Wicked plots within

One Friday, the señora asked Braulio and the other four long-term workers in the print shop to come in and work on Saturday. They thought it was unusual that the doors were already open when they arrived, but they went about their business, finished, and locked up. The following Monday, when they returned to work, the police were waiting. The señora had accused them of theft and had all five of them thrown in jail. Braulio was handcuffed and put in the *juzgado* (hoosegow) with no right to even a phone call.

For lack of evidence, Braulio was soon released, but remained charged. He had also lost his job—all because of a diabolical cabal concocted by the señora. In Mexico, if someone is discharged without cause, the employer is required by federal labor law to pay a hefty severance package—one-month's pay for each year worked, plus three months' pay for separation, plus Christmas and vacation bonuses. The señora could no longer afford Braulio, but if she were to let him go, he represented a cost to the Peña family of about $25,000. Together, the five workers represented a liability of over $100,000 in separation pay. So, the señora had come up with a scheme to rid their family of this debt.

The incident had plunged a knife into the heart of Cuca and Braulio's family, wounding their self-respect. "Why would I steal petty cash after working there for thirty years?" Braulio asks. "Why couldn't they come to me like a human being. If they had told me that they had to let me go, and they couldn't afford my separation pay, it would have been much better. I would have accepted that. Maybe they could have helped me find other work."

Braulio and his family will survive, of course, but they have been royally screwed by their employers. Having known the Peñas and their children, I try to ask questions that might lead to a resolution. Braulio pours another round of rum. "What about Tia Tita?" I ask. Margarita said that she died. There was no emotion. "What about Oscar?" He went along with his mother on everything. "What about the daughter, Patricia?" She became a religious nut. She never did anything but go into the office and pray. "What about the oldest son, Carlito?" He went clinically psychotic. He beat his wife and was put in jail. He's living in Guadalajara now. "What about the youngest son, Willy?" He's the only cool one. He has his own business and seems to be doing well. "What about suing?" "They have very deep pockets," Braulio responds. "I don't think we can do anything with a corrupt system."

Without telling Braulio and Cuca, the following day I call Oscar and we meet for lunch in the Zona Rosa. I am secretly hoping I can find a way to ease the catastrophe, but I want to proceed cautiously. Oscar and I are the same age, and of all the Peña family, I have known him best. As he starts with a couple of before-lunch drinks, he gets on his cell phone and calls his mother—the dreaded señora. "I need for the chauffeur to come over here with some cash," he implores. He gets drunk.

During our lunch, I casually ask about the nice native family that had lived in the house with his aunt. "Does Braulio still work for you?" Oscar responds with a rapid no. "Oh really, why not?" "It's a long story," he replies, summoning the waiter for another margarita.

I offer, "Isn't it great that Cuca's little half sister, Silvia, has gone on to get a master's degree in psychology and is teaching school?" Oscar turns and faces me dead-on, adding derisively, "That's just in the CETYS system." (The reference is to a government-sponsored program for less fortunate people.) He looks at me as if to ask how I could have missed such an essential point.

The chauffeur arrives with money. "My cash-flow problem is incredible," Oscar complains, "what with inflation. My wife and I just built a new house. Every day the contractor is asking us for more money because his costs are going up. Despite it all, I manage to eke out enough to pay for a house in Cuernavaca for my former secretary. I had to buy her off somehow. She expected me to marry her."

It is clear that there is nothing I can do to help Braulio. His world and Oscar's are so far apart, and I am an outsider. As I see it, the Peña family is tumbling from glory toward an uncertain future, and Braulio—despite bumps in the road—will somehow pull ahead. I leave Oscar in a puddle at the restaurant.

Two years later, Braulio calls me in Michigan. He has saved up $7,500 toward the purchase of his own press, but the cost is $9,000. Like Oscar, he is on a treadmill of inflation. The price keeps going up, perpetually out of reach. "Would it be possible to borrow $1,500?" he asks. It was remarkable that, despite being cheated out of his longtime employment benefits, Braulio had been able to put aside this amount of money. He could not get a loan from a bank, so he had to find a way to avoid getting into debt with the man who owned the press, as this could lead to usurious practice. Somewhere in Mexico City, I own part of a printing press.

The next generation carries forward

The ascent from poor to lower middle class is not easy. Even when a degree of economic independence is achieved, entrenched social barriers remain. "The way to become white is to put on white man's clothes," goes the saying. The political and economic center of gravity is with the *mestizos,* but there is great social cachet to being whiter. Oscar made a commitment to maintaining white skin by marrying Julie, an American. *Güeras* (white women) are sought after. Maybe Braulio and Cuca's son, Miguel, who graduated from Mexico's best engineering school, will break through the barrier. But who knows? One problem remains: Miguel is still a bit browner than Oscar Peña. He still goes home to his worker house. Maybe *his* kids will make the jump to the next social class.

This is another contradiction in Mexican society. While people can advance politically and economically by getting an education, changing social class is more difficult. Your social class *is* your context, and you carry it with you everywhere you go. Race remains an issue with regard to social class. As Mexico modernizes, class distinctions will be the last bastion of tradition to change.

Consuelo's and Luis' struggle

"Can you take a small package of money to my mother?" Pablo asked. It was 1985, and the earthquake that devastated Mexico City had so disrupted financial transactions that the only safe way to send money from the United States was to have it delivered in person.

I met with Consuelo and her son Luis—Pablo's mother and brother—in the lobby of the elegant Hotel Maria Isabel. Pablo had left Mexico fourteen years earlier. He attended college in the States and got a job in the computer department at Norcom, Inc. He was doing extremely well, and, like so many Mexicans in the U.S., sent money home to his family.

Consuelo and her family are solidly middle class. They are proud *mestizos.* What distinguished them from the lower class is their economic struggle and not their skin tone. True, the lower classes tend to be browner and the upper classes tend toward whiteness, but most people in Mexico, whatever the social class, are *mestizos.* Consuelo's family had been middle class for generations and were comfortable with city life. They would never live on a *rancho,* nor would they feel particularly comfortable living in luxury and being domineering over servers at the ritzy industrialists club. They are fully inculcated with middle-class values, which are defined in economic terms. Self-improvement in their case means having a professional son working alongside American management in the United States. Self-respect for Consuelo and her clan is a function of advanced education, professional status, and the ability to travel internationally. When they can, they will join a sports club, go to the symphony, and meet groups of friends at a nice restaurant. Unlike the American middle class, there is no drive among their group to show that they are common, nor do they aspire to having luxuries that they did not work for.

The problem with being middle class in Mexico at the time of my visit in 1985 was that all the political swings from the left to the right, and the concomitant economic crises, affected the middle class first and more deeply than other classes. Things people depend on to maintain a middle-class lifestyle slip out of reach or are simply unavailable for a while. They have to live in a middle-class neighborhood and pay a middle-class mortgage, but their income drops in value every six years as the government devalues the peso. They can't afford their house, their car, or even toilet paper. Their son has to drop out of Rice University. They have to give up on their dream for a condo on South Padre. They are lucky to hold onto their house.

Consuelo thanked me in exquisite English. Her proficiency as an English teacher had helped launch Pablo on his career in the States. For Consuelo, the *dólares* I delivered from her son represented a hedge against inflation. She told me how they recently had to sell their car. The payments had gone through the roof, so to speak. In Mexico, all loan contracts are adjusted for inflation, usually according to a stock market index (*Cetes*) or the official fiscal adjustment rate. To make matters worse, in an inflationary economy, employers naturally want to delay pay increases. Given that there are so many more people than jobs, they dare not complain if they are lucky enough to be employed. So, the middle class soldiers on.

There are numerous ways in which economic crisis hits the middle class. Let's say you are a restaurant owner with a significant investment in your facility. What do you do in times of economic bust when you have few customers and can't meet payroll? You may have to cut off your waiters from their minimum wage. The waiters, for their part, have no choice but to continue serving; that way at least they get tips. Similarly, the middle-class lawyer, businessperson, or security alarm salesman also absorbs part of the economic shock simply to keep a job. He may have to take a client out to lunch at his own expense, provide his own stamps to send a brochure, use his car, and pay for his own parking—all without reimbursement. If he fails to comply, the owner will get someone who will. The lower-class person may depend more on such price-controlled commodities as beans and tortillas. He can also go back to the village. These are not options for the middle class. The middle-class Mexican would no longer know what to do in a village. He wouldn't know how to farm or slaughter chickens. The middle class often does not have reserves to fall back on in hard times.

Constant struggle with finances is what defines the Mexican middle class. There are perpetual worries over money. Inflation can have more of an effect on Consuelo and Luis—the established middle class—than on Braulio and Cuca. For the worker class, the price of meat goes up and workers' wages don't. But many of the most basic needs—eggs, workers' home mortgages—cost little or have price controls. The cost of these items rises at a rate less than inflation. Also, when Braulio loses his job, his mortgage payments are suspended, but Consuelo has assets such as her middle-class house, and she is in danger of losing it if she cannot make payments. By contrast, the really rich guy complains a lot about the economy, but he does so in all the best restaurants.

The middle class also struggles to compete with the incursion of foreign capital. Many middle-class businesspeople own the wrong assets in the wrong places—outdated equipment in factories that can't grow in old, congested industrial areas. This is particularly true in Mexico City, where the only true value such businesses may have is in real estate—the factory and land. If an owner wants to relocate, he has to pay the mandatory separation fees to his employees. If he has fifty employees, this can amount to a million dollars. Either way, the owner feels the pinch. Again, the middle class is the most susceptible to economic swings. The workers don't have this problem. They can go where the jobs are. And the rich can take care of themselves no matter what.

Moreover, much of the middle class has little confidence in government, the legal system, or the police. Crime in the street is a constant worry. I saw Consuelo again recently. She had contracted Parkinson's disease but was doing well on herbal remedies. Luis was another story. He was approached on the street by a couple of thugs. When he refused to turn over his money, they stabbed him. He bled to death in front of his mother's house, waiting for the ambulance to arrive.

Señor Sanjuan's silver boxes

Señor Sanjuan has lots of *pesetas . . . y tiempo para gastarlas* (money . . . and time to enjoy it). The wealthy son of Spanish immigrants, he lives in Lomas de Chapultepec—the upscale hills of Mexico City.

My wife and I were on a little pilgrimage on behalf of our American friend, Marci, who thought we would enjoy seeing the house where she had grown up. Her father had been president of Pan American Airways de Mexico in the 1950s. She was especially interested in finding out what Señor Sanjuan had done with the house, and any news he might have about her prior servants.

Remembering Marci's family, he is pleased to receive our call, and we are graciously, if a bit cautiously, received. The conversation quickly turned to his distress that the TV company, being too cozy with the PRI and having a virtual patent on all broadcasts, has put up an antenna and spoiled his view of Mexico City.

After lighting a cigarette, he shows us the house, pointing out where his architect created an opening between two rooms, and how he has added to the servants' quarters. No, he doesn't know what has happened to Marci's service crew. The sense of his removal from day-to-day concerns is palpable. He appears to have little feel for what is going on outside his haven of luxury.

Most of all, this upper-class gentleman is proud of his antique silver boxes. He has Irish silver and English silver. These are his passion. Although he is aware of the provenance of his boxes, in fact, he is oblivious to poignant aspects of his own history.

Eighty percent of the silver above ground level in the world today was mined in Mexico during the Colonial Period (1519 to 1820). At the time, Spain's kings demanded their royal fifth. For this reason, many of the mines and inns in Mexico bear the name, *Quinta Real*—or "royal fifth." While the Indian peasants worked for pajamas, the *corregidores,* governors, entrepreneurs, and viceroys all got their shares of the silver proceeds. Back in Spain, the gentlemen and gentlewomen spent their windfall silver on silk finery and expensive wines from other countries. During this period, the Spanish squandered money on a mind-boggling scale. By contrast, the British and Irish turned the precious metal they received in return for goods into handsome Sheffield services and domestic pieces that were bought around the world. They reinvested their profits in land, factories, and machinery to make fabrics and other trade goods that built the wealth of Great Britain. The French put their silver craftsmen to work making watch fobs and buttons for the men and bouffant hair ornaments for the ladies. While the British were building an empire, and the French establishing themselves as the masters of style, the Spanish wasted a fortune. Mexican workers slaved on, sometimes hijacked on public roads by gangs who sold them to mining companies that needed cheap (meaning free) labor.

That Señor Sanjuan, of pure Spanish descent, prides himself in collecting the artifacts of Mexico's exploited past seems strangely ironic. His boxes are beautiful, but they are also empty. Offering us sherry, he lights another cigarette and talks about possessions, not family, and annoyances, not problems. His position in Mexican society is undoubtedly secure. He doesn't have to worry about the day-to-day fluctuations of the *peso*. He has enough to carry him through, without risk of having to sell his boxes. He has *peseta* and dollar accounts in the bank, and plenty of offshore savings accounts.

Unlike Señor Sanjuan, most Mexican upper-class families are sharply aware of their history and the consequences of Mexico's domination by the Spanish. They are descendants of *criollos,* or Creoles. Creole is a term that has nothing to do with race or ethnicity, and has no pejorative implication in Latin America. Creoles were so called because they were of pure Spanish blood, yet born in Mexico. The Spanish looked down on them as second-class citizens, and the Creoles have not forgotten it. They are Mexican, proud, part of the upper class, and feel fraternally related to all other Mexicans. They may have even picked up a bit of native blood along the way. As these Creole descendants are likely to say, "We either brag about our native blood, or we are damn liars."

One of the reasons for this relatively positive attitude toward color or race is that race was overemphasized during the colonial era. There were thirty-two recognized and legally restricted racial categories. If your father was white and your mother was native, you were considered white. However if your father was native and your mother was white, you were *indio.* The term *indio* became derogatory because if your mother was white and your father native, you had no choice but to live in the Indian village, and were therefore stigmatized and doomed to being uncivilized. Other categories described black, white, and native mixtures, tracing your registered lineage for five generations. This era produced such terms as *mestizo, mulato,* and *salta-atrás* (a term that means literally "a jump backwards"). The category "other" was sometimes applied to people who were racially all white, but who had no social status—castaways, orphans, and ex-prisoners, for example. Therefore, they could not stay at "white" inns. Such racial distinctions were overthrown along with the Spanish yolk. As a result of their history and their drive for self-respect and its corollary, respect for others, Mexicans are aware of, but do not categorize by, race. Imagine how different our culture would be if we knew that everyone in the United States had at least some black blood.

The Casa Gonzalez

In one of Mexico City's faded-glory neighborhoods near the U.S. Embassy at Rio Sena number 69, the Casa Gonzalez offers a pleasurable oasis. Here, the outside world meets a culturally fluent Mexican family whose boarding-house operates according to traditional class structure. The Gonzalez family established their popular B and B in the 1930s, pulling four houses together into a compound. With twenty-three spotless rooms and excellent fare, they have a staff of five maids. Anita is the inside boss. With mixed Aztec and Spanish blood, braided hair piled on top of her head, and erect posture, she looms tall and dominant. She is chief cook and also entrusted with the reser-vation book. Enriqueta, one of the maids, is a full-blooded Indian, with a face that would crack if she ever stopped smiling ear to ear. She is chatty. She goes on and on, but while I nod appreciatively at every phrase, I'm never sure what she is saying. I don't know if the problem is her Spanish or mine. Luz is serious and serves dinner. Modesta basically doesn't want to be a maid and shows it. Clara has been employed the longest and works very hard.

All these women have been coming in from a village in the state of Hidalgo, north of Mexico City, for a long time. They have their toehold, and any time the opportunity presents itself, they cycle a new woman in from the country. They aren't paid much, but they have food, shelter, and the tips they earn from the boarders. It's a lot more than most people from their village make, and they are able to send cash back to family members in need.

The maids know they are maids, but they are fatalistic. They know that being a maid is universally recognized as being subservient. They have no doubts about their status and do not wish they had been born the Duchess of Vergara. They are reconciled to their condition, so long as their children can go on to school. That satisfies their quest for self-improvement. They work for the long term and know that in their case moving up will take more than one generation. The maids are patient. They remind those who know Mexican history of what the Spanish priests said of the natives—that they are wonderfully obedient people—when you tell them to stand up, they stand up. When you tell them to sit down, they sit down.

Clara's daughter lived with her at the Casa Gonzalez long enough to complete school. Today, she's an architect. It pleases her to no end when I refer to her as *arquitecta*. But in keeping with the social delineation, the *arquitecta* still eats in the kitchen with the womenfolk from the village. These women are among the luckier ones. They came into the city in the internal migration wave before 1985 and landed in a house whose owners could not have been more welcoming and helpful.

The Casa Gonzalez was run for years by Señor Jorge Ortiz Gonzalez, the son of the founders. He was born in an upstairs bedroom of the main house. Most visitors, being foreigners, called him Señor Gonzalez instead of Señor Ortiz. He would shrug, smile, and answer to whatever they called him. Señor Ortiz died suddenly in 1999. The air in the heart of the city is terrible and there is a high incidence of lung cancer and heart disease. Because of pollution, employees of the U.S. Embassy around the corner are rarely assigned for more than two years, but for those to whom Mexico City is home, there is no such relief.

Today the eldest son, Jorge Eduardo, oversees the operations, welcoming guests in at least three languages. In his early thirties, he is a university graduate engineer, but his duty to the family business comes first. Jorge Eduardo's English is more like his father's than his American mother's. He speaks in a clipped accent and well-enunciated tones, unlike a slack-jawed gringo. He also speaks French and has studied Italian. His sister Antolina has a Ph.D. in philosophy. The younger boy wants to be an aeronautical engineer. All attended the French *lycée* in Mexico City. Antolina, who raises money for street urchins, put her education to work writing a book about street musicians in Mexico City. Their mother prepares meals from the B and B's leftovers each week, delivering them to a home for unwed mothers. But she's American. Señor Gonzalez used to complain that those girls should not have gotten in trouble in the first place.

By Mexican middle-class standards, the Gonzalez clan is doing very well. Their assets are earning a livelihood for the family and allowing the younger children the leisure to pursue their dreams. They enjoy their work, protecting their clientele like family, cautioning them where to go, where not to go in the city. They arrange for taxis to take their charges to see the pyramids or to concerts. "But don't take the subway from the Palacio de Bellas Artes after dark," they warn. "Our business is greatly affected by Mexico's reputation for crime," Jorge Eduardo laments, "but the perception is unfair, because the crime rate here is lower than in Chicago."

Outside the Casa Gonzalez

I first noticed the woman in native Huichol dress about ten years ago. She was outside the Casa Gonzalez, putting on a sullen face while extending her palm for a handout. The little girl and the baby brother sharpened the image of poverty. As a child in Colombia, my parents had told me that it was best not to give money to beggars—it only encourages them. But I had learned differently in Mexico. I observed that the Gonzalezes would pass the woman a taco every now and then and would not discourage roomers from giving her alms.

A year later, she was still there. This time, I was not so rushed. At the market next door, I bought a toy guitar about six inches long, with a tiny crank for playing music. When I asked *mamá* if I might give the little instrument to her daughter, she raised her head to nod assent. It was then that I saw that half of her face was paralyzed, most probably from a stroke. In a land where people outnumber jobs by so much, she had *zero* chance of finding steady work.

Months later, I saw the familiar trio across the Avenida Reforma in the touristy Zona Rosa. When I asked if they remembered me, the little girl replied, "Sí!" Their eyes told me that they did. Why were they here instead of in front of the Casa Gonzalez? "We go there on Wednesday," she replied. I gave them forty pesos.

Come Wednesday, these *pordioseros* (godforsaken people), as they are compassionately called by the Mexicans, did not show up at the Casa Gonzalez. Had they gotten rolled because they had that much money? On the contrary, they appeared on Thursday—mother, daughter, and baby son, scrubbed and beaming. The little girl was wearing a freshly ironed and starched white dress. Clearly, they had access to laundry facilities, and when time and money permitted, they preferred to be clean and starched than rumpled and dirty.

Antolina was familiar with the family. "These beggars are organized," she told me, explaining that they come to the outskirts of the city from their villages. The mother is from a Huichol village and can't even speak Spanish well. Enterprising men—*coyotes*—rent them a tarpaper shack with running water and minimal bathroom facilities on the outskirts, and others organize their begging stints. They are shuttled into the city at dawn and back to the barrios at night, paying the pirates a portion of their begging proceeds. For everything else, they are on their own. "The better they do, the better corner they get," Antolina said wistfully, adding that some continue for years, while others go back to the country. She also explained that *all* Mexicans have a sense of obligation toward the natives. "We feel a sense of duty to protect them," she told me, "because they cannot protect themselves." From Antolina's perspective, they may share some of the same blood, and what has befallen *los indigenas* (the indigenous ones) is not their fault. Those who can, must help provide for them. Her attitude is akin to the political elite's commitment to the ideals of the revolution. We will give them their land back or see that somehow their needs are met.

Several years later I happened across the threesome back in the Zona Rosa. *Mamá* was on her feet, speaking Huichol to a gaggle of her friends, with a display of rag dolls spread across a blanket on the sidewalk. She had accumulated enough cash to buy product directly from the factory. Now she is a businesswoman, aided by the kids, who still beg from those not buying a doll. When resources permit, they would rather be in business than begging. The drive for self-respect and self-improvement is constant. It affects upper-, middle-, and lower-class Mexicans, as well as these beggars who have come to the big city from the country for opportunity. For the beggars, the commitment to self-improvement will simply take several generations. They are not in a race. They just want to do the best they can. To them, there is no contradiction between being fatalistic and wanting to improve their status.

Frequently, women beggars are on their own with their children because they have lost their husbands to some misfortune. While many villages have free clinics, others do not, and these women can easily fall through society's cracks. Unless one of the members of the family has had a regular job, they have never been signed up for Social Security and don't qualify for hospitalization or retirement. This also explains why there are so many families among the poorer Mexicans in which a man may father two generations of children. If a woman dies, say in childbirth, an available man may pick up a second wife from among the widowed in his village. In rural Mexico, having many children represents an informal social security system.

Invisible social barriers

Across the spectrum of Mexico's population, certain social lines are sacrosanct. Individual Mexicans have no problem identifying themselves as coming from the lower class, middle class, or upper class, and they are careful to observe hierarchical distinctions. As generous as the Ortiz Gonzalez family is, it is inconceivable that they would let the beggar use a shower or even hire her as a maid. There is even a divide between this Huichol woman and the maids—the beggar wears native clothes and the maids wear uniforms. One is on the street and the others are in a house. The beggar never enters the gate. There is a clear spatial delineation. The distinctions are also attitudinal.

While the relationship of the Gonzalez family and their staff is close and affectionate, it is also separate. Traditional social patterns tied to class distinctions are well understood on both sides.

The guests in the Casa Gonzalez are middle class. But the *arquitecta* would never be invited to dine with the family or the guests, even though she is better educated than the machinist from Australia or the ice-cream store owner from Italy who are staying there. Her context is with her extended family from the pueblo. By the same token, middle-class Consuelo would never expect to be invited to the rich Señor Sanjuan's house for sherry. Nor would Braulio and Cuca be invited to Consuelo's house for a cup of coffee. There are no "whites only" or apartheid laws regarding crossing class lines, just self-imposed inhibitions on leaving one's past completely behind. There are also no politically imposed barriers to crossing social lines. Each class has a sense of self-respect that reinforces their class circumstance. Finding comfort within their group, Mexicans don't feel compelled to break down walls.

The formal and hierarchical nature of the Spanish language tends to perpetuate class distinctions in any Spanish-speaking country. In Mexico, differences between the classes are expressed linguistically through a series of unwritten understandings shared by members of the culture. Señor Sanjuan speaks elevated Castilian with a lisped soft *c* and *z*. He has a slight dental fricative or *shh* sound when he enunciates his *s*'s, extending his lips as if asking the listener to keep quiet as he speaks. Consuelo speaks Mexican Spanish and English, the languages of politics and commerce. Braulio and Cuca sing their sentences, such that *Eduardo* becomes a plaintive musical refrain.

The minute any Mexican picks up the phone, he or she knows a lot about the caller. There is a range of courteous ritual that people use on the phone. The upper middle class, the *bien educados,* are courtly. They come off as *muy culto* (very cultivated). A middle-class businessperson or government official may be more playful. He may say to the receptionist, "*No seas malita, pasame al jefe.*" (Don't be naughty, put me through to the boss.) The lower-class person is hesitant and overcompensates when he uses the phone. He is polite, but sometimes he stammers. He has little experience using a phone, and is somewhat uncomfortable with it. And the beggar lady who speaks Huichol and fractured Spanish stays on the street, maybe never to use a phone unless someone else connects her to a family member back in the village.

Progressions

Looking across the social spectrum of Mexico today, millions in the working class are bumping up against middle-class status. The middle class, for its part, is expanding slowly, and those within its ranks are evolving toward modern standards. Meanwhile, the upper class is shrinking and considers its alternatives—that is, whether or not to move to the United States or Europe to maintain a plush lifestyle.

In the midst of unprecedented economic mobility and conscious modernization, the reluctance to cross social barriers remains strong. The drive for self-improvement has more to do with economics than social class. Perhaps the hesitation to change class is related to the Mexican brand of fatalism or tradition. Or maybe it's a sense of hierarchy or group dependency with reluctance to break out of the group. Whatever the reason, it would simply never occur to Braulio and Cuca to put on their best Sunday outfits and go to the lobby bar at the Hotel Maria Isabel for a cocktail. That would be the American way, but not the Mexican way. Braulio and Cuca would think that a cocktail in the lobby bar was a waste of resources. They would be much more comfortable spending discretionary income on a soccer match or eating at a *taquería* in their own neighborhood. Nor would it appeal at all to Señor Sanjuan to go to a hardware store to buy the parts to fix a light switch. That would represent a failure. He wants to maintain the image that he has people to do that.

As the upper class clings to its dignities, the working poor, along with those in the middle class, remember their humble past. While holding to their social identity, these burgeoning segments of Mexican society know what they want for the future and are more willing than ever to adopt new modalities. Much of what Mexicans want is not money per se, rather the lifestyles they see on TV. They watch shows produced in the United States and see something we take for granted: offices with panels and modern seating, pantsuits, and lawyers working at desks dealing with important papers. Mexicans want to be modern.

The future of the middle class

The middle class is growing as evidenced by the cases of the *arquitecta* and Epifanio. Do they consider themselves middle class? Yes, when in their work spaces they do. When Epifanio is at his desk and the *arquitecta* is at her drawing board, the pride of work they manifest is unmistakable. *Es mi trabajo*—this is my work. It is also their new identity and their source of self-respect. When they go home, however, they trade their middle-class context for their lower-class sensibilities. Epifanio is a hero among his fellow villagers, but he is still one of them. Meanwhile, the *arquitecta* feels comfortable eating dinner with her family. The primary identity resides then with the nurturing group.

This is part of the contextual nature of Mexicans. Social class is very important in Mexico, whereas it barely exists as a concept in the United States. Mexicans can be economically middle class on the one hand, yet tied to family in the lower class at the same time.

One of the biggest mistakes Americans make is judging Mexico by our own standards, where our sense of class is related to economic success. Mexicans are accustomed to their stratified society, and those in the middle class are doing what they can to look after their own interests, whether Americans are in the country or not. One phenomenon may mislead us. Increasingly, they want *our* products. They drive our cars, buy our soaps, and watch our TV programs. But they retain their own values and views.

Modern Mexican youth do not feel that they have to break with tradition. There is no "rebel without a cause" syndrome, and little need to express independence. "Why would we do that?" Young people of Mexico assert their solidarity. Americans give lip service to family values, but here again is the giveaway that we don't follow through very well. Mexicans don't talk about family values, they practice them. And across the social spectrum, belonging to family is more important than belonging to a particular class.

Sifting Through the Finds

Just past the monument to the petroleum industry in Mexico City, the streets turn into splendid, tree-lined boulevards with mansions housing Mexico's elite. My taxi arrives in Lomas for my meeting with an architect. This is the first of numerous appointments for the week, and I have hired the driver to stay with me for the duration. But the circular street where the driver and I search for the offices is confusing. "I can't explain to myself," the driver says in Spanish, "how the numbers go up on the inside of the circle, and down on the outside of the circle!" This is the typical Mexican indirect way of saying that some bureaucrat screwed up. "I'll stop at the bakery and maybe someone there can help me."

Cheaper than a brake job

While he's checking things out, I hear a strange mumbling sound coming from across the street. At Mexico City's altitude, sound carries crisply. "That's the priest blessing a car," the driver tells me as he returns. Then he adds in a casual tone, "We do that in Mexico." As we watch the priest splashing holy water over the five-year-old four-door Pontiac, the devil prompts me, "And he throws in a free car wash as well, I see." Thinking I may have offended the driver, I append a quick, "Sorry, I shouldn't have said that."

"No. It's okay. I am not religious. I think it's funny. He's sprinkling the car with holy water. It won't do any good, but it makes the owner feel better. And it's cheaper than a brake job," he laughs.

"I worked in a factory in Ohio," he continues, now switching to English. "I worked with all kinds of people. I shared jobs with black people in the foundry. It was such dirty work that at the end of the day, we were all the same color." Then he tells me about going through the offices, and how everyone was so pleasant to him. "They would say, 'Good morning!'" He mimics perfectly a Midwestern nasal twang. When he speaks standard English, he sounds very Mexican; when he imitates Americans, he sounds like a Midwesterner. I wonder, "If he can mimic us so well, why does he retain his Mexican accent?"

As we circle the block again, he says he has a joke for me. "Do you know how to make holy water?" "How?" I oblige. "You boil the *hhhell* out of it!" comes the punch line, propelled on a guttural *h*. When the driver still can't locate the correct street number, I ask if he had found any help at the bakery. "No, the bakery was closed," he replies. "The sign in the window says 'open,' but the sign on the door says 'closed.'" Then, reveling in the humor of Mexican contradictions, he resolves the confusion: "I know what they mean—it is closed, but if it were not closed, it would be open." We have achieved a meeting of the minds. He knows that Mexicans can confuse Americans with their dance of the contradictions, and he appreciates that I too seem to enjoy the play.

Bits and pieces

As we continue in search of the architect's office, I think back on my early experiences in Mexico. While at the University of the Americas, my archaeology class assisted in digging the pyramids at *Teotihuacán*. We would find potsherds and try to fit them together to form a complete vessel. It was impossible to know what the whole looked like until we had all the pieces—an effort that required sifting our day's collections through fine screens. Even then, we could only guess at the nature of the person who might have used a particular object. There were no living souls to interview. No living guides.

But here I find myself in the company of a Toltec descendant who can help me understand how the pieces of Mexico come together. Because he's familiar with gringos, we can appreciate each other's context. Knowing we will be working together for several days, he relaxes, talks freely, and delights in surprising me. Just when I think I have him cornered about what he's thinking, he changes course, like a kid playing hide and seek.

A small price to pay

"There's a cop car," I point out. "Let's ask if they can help." "*Oye* . . . You know Mexico," the driver cautions. "Are you sure you want to do that?" "It'll be okay," I assure him. The policeman tells us that we are in Bosques de Cerezos, and we should be in Bosques de Ciruelos. He "volunteers" to guide us there. "This is going to cost you money," I chide the driver. "Me?" he laughs, glancing in the rear view mirror. "I hope you brought your money belt!"

We arrive at the destination. The cop gets out of his car and peers through the rear window, elbows on the sill. He is driving a brand new vehicle. He and his partner are wearing snappy new uniforms with shiny brass emblems, and carrying pearl-handled revolvers. "You know," the cop tells me, "I'm delighted that I could help you, but . . . gasoline costs money." I offer five dollars to compensate him for his trouble. He accepts with a polite, "Gracias, señor."

I'm not clear where we are. The address is correct, but I had expected a tall building, not a single floor. "No, this is it," the driver assures. "This is the new Bosques area. It's so new I don't know my way around yet, but this is right. We're on the lip of the canyon. The buildings go down from here."

He is right. The entrance to the building is on the fifth floor. This is the spot where, years before, I would sit with university friends flipping beer bottle caps into the void. In those days, Mexico City had its share of modern construction, but remained at heart a colonial city, deeply rooted in the past. Today the canyon is chockablock with new high-rises, health clubs, restaurants, and theaters—all built in the past fifteen years. Once inside, the buildings open up dramatically. Now from within, I am overlooking the barranca.

Crawling on our bellies

I meet with the architect—*arquitecto* Baillard—who has agreed to help me with a study of the commercial real estate markets in Mexico. He is a prominent professional and a student of people. His prestigious firm is part of the Barragán school of architecture. Their projects include the Camino Real Hotel and the acclaimed Renault plant in the northern state of Durango. These facilities stand as beautiful examples of what an architect can contribute to the residential, work, and leisure environment of Mexicans when sufficient capital is available. The signature features are massive walls, large open spaces, and splashes of bold colors—pumpkin, Maya blue, and sunflower yellow. The aesthetic effect is a stunning synthesis of pre-Colombian, colonial and modern influences. As our business concludes, I take advantage of the time to ask the architect about Mexico itself.

"Why is there virtually no design community outside of architectural offices?" This is true. There are no furniture designers and few interior designers. No jewelry or dress designers. No automobile designers. Nothing. There are avant-garde architects and world-class artists like Rufino Tamayo on the one hand, a huge gap, and then primitive crafts on the other. In contrast, Barcelona has couturier designers. Italy puts design into everything. Denmark designs cool pots and pans. The United States has an army of product designers in every field. But Mexico's furniture craftsmen have been copying the same old prerevolutionary designs for 100 years. Why does an intuitively artistic population seem so unconcerned with design today?

"It's hard to be design-conscious when you're crawling on your belly," is Baillard's emphatic response. "Most Mexicans assume that there is danger lurking around the corner. If they are eating today, they may be hungry tomorrow. When times are good, they must hurry to seize the moment. That's what drives them to make do—to be expedient. They see forces beyond their control. If it's not the Popocatepetl Volcano (just above Mexico City) it's a hurricane or some other calamity."

Most Mexicans, I concluded, are not like the architect, who has the resources to contemplate, design, and properly execute a civic masterpiece. Most Mexicans are like the team of workers who install the metal shutters, under pressure to get their work done according to someone else's schedule. They have to hurry up today, even though they may have no other work tomorrow.

Baillard has traveled and lived in the States. He is Mexican, but because his parents were European, he has the ability to see Mexico from an outsider's point of view. He has explained satisfactorily what I had never before understood. Unlike the architects in his firm, most Mexicans won't take the time to invent new design concepts. Nor will they take the time to calculate roof support stresses before suspending their cranes. Similarly, they won't take the time to think through their needs down the road for maintenance supplies. They borrow because it's expedient. They copy us because our designs enjoy more market currency. Otherwise, manufacturers fall back on reproducing past designs, colonial jewelry, and prerevolutionary furniture. If it works for now, go with it.

People rushing to stand still

The Mexican sense of urgency is tied to their awareness of the past and uncertainty about the future. The threats of a bad harvest or a natural disaster that plagued their ancestors have been replaced with new anxieties about jobs and inflation. Still, in the modern age, nature is in control. There is always the very real possibility of a drought, an earthquake, or an earth-crossing asteroid. Politics have changed. The economy has changed. But nature remains the same awesome and unpredictable force it has always been. There is plenty of impending doom to go around—enough to sustain a tradition of expediency. As in the past, today's Mexicans are generally too concerned with meeting the demands of the present to put their feet up and ask questions about trashcans, hat design, or "Where am I going?"

That Mexicans are a people in a hurry may seem contradictory at first. How does this fit with their patient disposition and circular view of time? Aren't Americans the ones who are always counting the seconds, champing at the bit, keeping one eye on the clock? Yes, but here's the difference: While Americans are charging forward on a trajectory to the future, the Mexicans are shuffling like mad on the treadmill of the present just to keep up. We see ourselves as individuals in control of our own destinies, competing to see who can get there first, or who can stay ahead. They continue to see themselves as part of a mass. They are not competing with one another. They will all get there together. Nonetheless, they are a people in a hurry, because slowing down for a minute would put them further behind. Now it is their fate to adopt American technology before the present runs out. They must do this for their families, for future generations. They are struggling to keep up while the time is right. This is more important than creating new designs.

The architect is one of the few people in Mexico who has the luxury of dreaming about shapes, planes, spaces, colors, and pleasing details. He does it with ample resources—including time—not afforded to the man in the street. The tradition of great public works is carried on by a privileged few. There is every reason to believe that the impulses that inspired great design of the past are still percolating under the surface and, when conditions allow, will find expression again. The man in the street, however, carries on the view of reality that at any moment . . .

Baillard is keenly aware of Mexico's long-standing tradition of creating and then abandoning great public works. The pattern can be traced to pre-Colombian times. Following periods of intense agricultural activity, while waiting for the corn to grow, laborers of the fields shifted their efforts to building. Colossal pyramids and massive cities went up, only to be abandoned in times of economic crisis. The Classic Maya broke all their minor idols and simply left their majestic public works behind. When the Toltecs fled Teotihuacán in A.D. 950, it was the fourth time the city had been deserted.

Having dug in a number of pre-Colombian archaeological sites, I have seen how one pyramid would be built directly on top of another. Sifting through the finds, I had marveled at the layers and wondered about the sameness. Yes, there were superficial differences in decoration and style from site to site, but why was it, I asked, that the underlying design never really changed?

"Pyramids are simple structures—the surest, fastest way of building the highest, biggest structure with the minimal amount of engineering," Baillard explains. I'm thinking *people in a hurry*. "Building pyramids was an expedient way of propitiating the gods." *Nature in control*.

At the pinnacle of the social hierarchy, with priests and princes, there were accomplished architects who conceived of temples, street layouts, waterworks, and pyramids five hundred feet high. These visionaries were the precursors of Mexico's architects today. Given the tumultuous history of the pre-Colombian period, there was little time for the average citizen to work out refined art or artisanry. After all, they figured, "When the next environmental calamity befalls us, we may well have to abandon these structures anyway."

Baillard agrees that there is no parallel to this pattern of building and abandoning within Western civilization or its antecedents. As far back as the Romans, Greeks, Sumerians, and Assyrians, the central challenge to civilizations has come from men. The self-referential Aztecs, unaware that other civilizations existed, saw themselves as fighting a lonely battle against nature. When they had a bad harvest, when the hurricanes struck, they abandoned their sites. "That attitude persists today," the architect adds. "Mexicans don't worry about arranging the pottery on the shelf, because *when* the earthquake hits, it will all break anyway."

Turning pyramids into cathedrals

For modern Mexicans, the final irony is that it was *man* who dismantled their last great city. A stunning reminder hangs on the architect's wall—an enormous, framed rendering of Tenochtitlán rising above a lake in a tree-lined valley. In the pure sunlight of the high altitude, the white stuccoed planes of massive pyramids decorated with brilliant splashes of blue, cinnabar, and maize are reflected in the clean waters. "This is how the *conquistadores* found it," the architect says. Then he adds, in a fatalistic tone, "It was the Aztec's fate that the Spaniards would take their city apart. In most of today's buildings there is only faded evidence of the impulse for the massive designs of the ancient past."

The architect reminds me that the Spanish knocked down the pyramids, reusing the materials to build Catholic cathedrals. The cathedrals were filled with wondrous, highly crafted statuary of stone, wood, and gold. The paintings were made of woven canvas, oil, and pigments that had taken the Spaniards hundreds of years to refine, depicting themes that represented centuries of their history and myth.

"Much of the Aztec culture was covered over," I lament. "But it never died," the architect clarifies. "You see, the stones of the cathedrals were the same stones that had built the pyramids. Underneath, little had changed. The Spanish conquered the Aztecs. But the Aztecs enveloped the Spanish within their culture. At the deepest level, the Aztec culture survived."

Walking, talking, and chewing gum

The next day, heading north out of Mexico City for a meeting in Querétaro with my driver and two American clients, we pass the statue to *La Raza* (The Race)—a celebration of the native blood that courses through Mexican veins. It is a sizeable model of the *Templo Mayor,* or "great temple," that was the focal point of Tenochtitlán. Around the temple are human figures with distinctly native facial features—the high cheekbones of the Aztecs and the sloped foreheads and round noses of the Maya. Much has changed in Mexico, but even in the center of congested freeways and busy interchanges— traffic honking and everyone on a tear—Mexico's past will not be forgotten.

As the driver fights his way through the snarl, my clients, fresh in from Minneapolis, are putting their challenge to me this way: "We want to open a machining operation in Mexico, but our operators are highly trained. Each operator runs three CNC (computer numerical control) machines and does his own in-process inventory calculations. Is this something we can accomplish in Mexico?"

I explain that I have contacted Grupo Desc, one of the largest conglomerates in the country, and set up factory visits and a meeting with the president, Emilio Mendoza Saeb, whom I had known from prior business dealings. I selected Grupo Desc for a tour because they had directors who also sat on Spicer, Inc.'s board, and Spicer's board shared directors with my client's board. "If you are serious about doing business in Mexico," I tell them, "you want to surround yourself with as many friends as you can find." We arrive in Querétaro for our first meeting with the management of one of Grupo Desc's stamping plants. During a tour of the plant, the Mexican production manager calls our attention to a poster-size copy of their mission statement on the wall.

In the United States, our companies put mission statements on their walls. We do it because it makes us feel better about what we really don't do very well. It might read, "Our mission is to work as a team to serve our client with personal attention so that we can grow our business by being the best at what we do." A reasonable analyst from Mars might read that as, "Our mission is to cover up the fact that we're a bunch of independent-minded crabs who have gotten too big to have a sense of the market, so we hide behind *big thinking,* and that makes us feel good."

Like Grupo Desc, many Mexican companies prominently display their mission statements. Many sound like ours. But what these statements are really saying is, "We have a mission statement on our wall because we are pretending to be a modern company like that American conglomerate you have been bragging about. If that is what you expect, then that is what we'll give you. We are a very agreeable people." But just because we can see through their smoke and mirrors—because we recognize they want to please their visitors—doesn't mean that we should fall into the trap of thinking that Mexicans are incapable of achieving world-class operations.

My clients are surprised by the sheer size of the plant, but they remain skeptical. They have a distorted picture of Mexican manufacturing, largely from television reports that focus on antiquated facilities dumping waste into nearby streams. But here, they arrive at an attractive, squeaky clean *Mexican* plant. Production is humming and so are the workers.

On the second part of our tour, the production manager demonstrates to my American clients that his plant is at least as efficient as theirs. There is no doubt about competence. The Mexicans are expert at what they do. As it turns out, the production department has its own motto—again, one that is not born of a need to motivate workers, rather of a desire to impress visitors. Their motto is the "four M's." The production manager explains to me that the four M's stand for *motivación, movilidad, mercadotecnia* (motivation, mobility, marketing expertise), and ... he can't remember the fourth. Being a wise-mouthed gringo, I can say anything, right? So to help him out, I say, "*meando y caminando para no hacer charco.*" That expression is equivalent to our "walk, talk, and chew gum," but literally it means, "pee and walk so you don't leave a puddle." Well, this is so irreverent that it blows his mask off. First of all, no one in a business suit would ever say "pee." He bursts out laughing, recognizing that I have uncovered one of the company's trade secrets—that they don't believe their mottoes any more than we believe ours.

I had coached the American clients a bit on intercultural communications: to be effective, be indirect. But later, interviewing the plant manager, one of my clients asks, "How much do you pay your CNC operators?" The plant manager obliges by saying, "You know, the market for operators varies around the world and is subject to many of the same forces you experience in the U.S. Compared to world rates, we find that we are competitive with China, for instance, because our operators are better trained. We find that globalization ... and furthermore. ..." The plant manager meanders all over to avoid answering a direct question.

As we leave the plant, the client observes, "Maybe I shouldn't have been so direct." "Next time, try this," I offer. "How much should *we* expect to pay CNC operators if we moved an operation to this region?" I assure him that this indirect approach is more effective. What's more, it's always best to put requests in context for the Mexican. In this case, the client would be hinting that his company is considering moving to the area.

Tweety Bird flies in Querétaro

Later, we visit another plant—as modern and impressive as the first. Here we watch as a lump of hot aluminum at one end of the plant is transferred by a bright yellow overhead robot up a long line of horizontally opposed machines, emerging as a piston at the other end of the line. We interview the plant manager. By now my American clients are so impressed, they are just about out of questions. But not entirely.

"How much would *we* expect to pay CNC operators if we moved an operation to this region?" my client asks indirectly. The Mexican plant manager responds, "A fully trained operator who does his own in–process inventory, after working in your plant for a year, would earn eleven thousand pesos per week. That's about one hundred and ten dollars. Plus, you would pay him thirty percent of the salary for federally mandated benefits, and another thirty percent for company benefits." A concise, accurate answer.

We return to Mexico City for our planned meeting with the president of Grupo Desc, Emilio Mendoza. The automotive division of the company owns a building in the new Bosques de Ciruelos area, which this time my driver has no trouble finding. It is twenty-six stories high, and Emilio's office occupies one half of the top floor. We have an illuminating meeting laced with stories of the latest manufacturing technology. Señor Mendoza, who has learned a great deal about Americans and achieved a high level of cultural fluency, insists that his American visitors call him Emilio. He knows that will make us feel more comfortable. He also knows that Americans like to break the ice with a joke. After exchanging greetings from mutual friends, Emilio delivers the following anecdote in perfect English. "What is the factory of the future?" he posits. "It will be operated by a man and a dog. The man is there to feed the dog, and the dog is there to keep the man from touching the equipment." He goes on to recap the Americans' impressions by adding, "And that yellow robot you saw? We call it *Piolín*. What do you call that in English? Tweety Bird, that's it."

My clients are further impressed as Emilio explains that one of Grupo Desc's automotive divisions has a 40 percent passive investment from Spicer in Toledo, Ohio. It gives Grupo Desc capital resources, access to new technology, and entrée to U.S. and foreign markets. The rest of the company is 100 percent Mexican. At the end of the discussion, the American clients are more than satisfied that whatever they dream of in the United States could be carried out in Mexico. The only proviso is that an American will have to find his own balance between being a gringo with all the answers and being a thoughtful, culturally fluent investor or operator.

At the end of the week

After five days together, the driver and I have become friends. We have shared war stories and observations about my American clients. After countless appointments and long conversations in unremitting traffic, my driver has revealed much about himself and about Mexico. All of the impulses of Mexico's past and present can be found in him. Like most Mexicans, he is more somber than his jocular attitude initially conveyed. While he is a "good time Charlie," he becomes deeply serious when he talks about his work and his family. He is more prone to accept contradictions than to demand consistency. He is not upset by the numbering system on the street, even though it complicated his finding an address—the only reason for having street numbers in the first place. Rather, he takes the burden upon himself to explain the problem, and is willing to ask directions.

He has trouble articulating how he feels sometimes. But he has no problem showing his feelings. "Do you mean that you think such-n-such?" I ask. "Yes," he says. Then, he turns it around. "Sometimes. And at other times, I think thus and such," is his second and only honest answer.

He is more accommodating than threatening. He will answer yes, but keep talking until he can come up with a polite way of changing his story. Conversely, if I had insisted that the numbering system was imbecilic, he would have agreed enthusiastically. If I had instructed him to turn left, he would have turned left—three times, until he ended up pointing to the right. Why? Because that would be a polite response to an agitated customer.

He understands how to deal with me as an American. He knows that I will appreciate his sense of the ridiculous. One of the endearing qualities of Mexicans is their ability to find humor in their often miserable condition.

Unlike his rural grandparents, the driver is a modern, bilingual, lower-middle-class, technical city dweller. He has spent considerable time in the United States, but he remains Mexican to the core. Nothing has really changed. Like his grandparents, he is fatalistic, practical, and hard working. While listening respectfully to the suggestions of foreigners, he will find his own solutions.

He is more like his ancestors than you would at first suppose, sharing their unchanging values for self-respect, self-improvement, and family. Despite discovering the benefits of *el norte,* he has returned to Mexico, able to earn twice as much as the average driver because of his ability to speak English.

My "friend" is coming from a very different context intellectually. The Yankee penchant for delivering the goods by Friday never rubbed off. The taximeter represents money, but it is no substitute for time. And just because he's got a tiny TV on his dash where he watches the Cubs, doesn't mean he has the same sensibility about life that we do. He is bilingual, but he thinks like a Mexican, not an Anglo white man or an African American man. He is flexible about his icons, because that is his way of surviving.

The driver loves Mexico and everything Mexican—even the priest and his rituals and the jumbled, unfinished, dilapidated neighborhood he lives in. He sees the mishmash of styles with uncoordinated motifs and colors, the cattywonkus business signs, the rusting Coke machines in front of shops, the broken windows and uneven pavement, and the emergence of opulence from a vacant cactus canyon. To him, these are the sum total of millions of microeconomic decisions made by people like himself doing what they can to survive and prosper. The chaos is beautiful and worthy.

Often, practices that seem questionable to Americans are viewed by Mexicans as necessary and benign. There is only playful realism behind the taxi driver's antireligious views. The used car owner will get a brake job—don't worry. The cop has to pay for his car, uniform, and gasoline, and the city can't afford the kind of police protection the rich clients expect. Ethically, Mexicans are doing all they can—praying, paying, and getting by.

The taxi driver on the street, the architect on the edge of the canyon, the plant manager on the factory floor, the corporate executive in his high-rise—all embody the mixture of Aztec fatalism and Spanish propriety. The archaeology of their minds makes them unique and self-referential. Many Americans are tempted to believe that if they simply adjust Mexican behavior a little bit, tweak their attitudes this way or that, we can all get along because our neighbors will finally have the same attitude toward business, education, or the universe that we do. This is not so. When we tweak, they change all right. What they change, though, is not their core beliefs. Rather, it is the way they envelop us in their culture.

Epilogue

When the juicer plant in Monterrey was completed, the construction company held a formal dedication ceremony. The mayor of Cienegas de Flores was in attendance with his entourage; a representative of the American Consulate paid a visit; and the industrial elite of the state of Nuevo León sat on the platform in suits and ties, listening to speeches in Spanish. The owner of the construction company—a prominent Mexican entrepreneur with many holdings—spoke proudly of his son whom he had placed in charge of the project. He finished his remarks with a flourish, hugging his son and giving him an affectionate kiss on the lips. This is fine in Mexico, but only between father and son, or members of the immediate family.

Sam, the Kansas businessman—the one who believed that "All those goddamn countries are alike. *I* know, I used to be in charge of Latin America!"—participated in his capacity as president of the American parent company. After two years on the project, he had fallen in love with the Mexicans and was eager to adopt their customs. When Sam's turn came, he spoke at length in English, congratulating the Mexican builders on their fine job. As he motioned the father and son to stand up, everyone clapped. A mariachi band trumpeted a fanfare. It was at this moment that Sam, in Dockers and a plaid shirt, gave the construction owner an *abrazo,* and then . . . kissed the old man on the lips.

The reaction was mixed. The Americans tittered. The Mexicans managed to hide their dismay, though a perceptive observer could see their backs stiffen slightly. What mattered was that a mission had been accomplished and the Mexicans and Americans were friends. As for the kiss on the lips, *we are all imperfect.*

Suggested Reading List

Mexican History and Culture

Castañeda, Jorge G. 1995. *The Mexican Shock: Its Meaning for the U.S.* New York: The New Press. Still valid though it describes the 1994 economic crisis, this book gives us insight into U.S. and Mexican political and economic relations. More importantly, it introduces us to Castañeda, an intellectual, sometimes critic of U.S. policy, who was foreign minister of Mexico under Vicente Fox.

Díaz del Castillo, Bernal. 1956 and subsequent editions. *The Discovery and Conquest of Mexico*. New York: Farrar, Straus and Cudahy. Díaz was there as one of Cortes' soldiers. His original account is more vivid than any number of modern recaps that followed.

Fehrenbach, T. R. 1973 and later editions. *Fire and Blood*. New York: Collier Books. If you read one history of Mexico, let it be this one. While not Mexican, Fehrenbach is a native of South Texas and has an affinity for Mexicans. His account is free of the social revisionism that characterizes much of today's "histories."

———. 1985. *Lone Star*. New York: Collier Books. A useful companion to the above book, with useful insights into border issues.

Grayson, George W. 1988. *Oil and Mexican Foreign Policy*. Pittsburgh: University of Pittsburgh Press. Grayson is an acknowledged expert on Mexico and his insights are worthwhile, especially in current economic and foreign policy spheres.

Kandell, Jonathan. 1988. *La Capital: The Biography of Mexico City*. New York: Random House. This is an excellent read especially if you are assigned to or visit Mexico City.

Katz, Friedrich. 1981. *The Secret War in Mexico: Europe, the United States and the Mexican Revolution*. Chicago: University of Chicago Press. If you want realism, deep understanding, critique of U.S. foreign policy done evenhandedly, Friedrich Katz is excellent.

Knight, Alan. 1996. *The Mexican Revolution*. Vol. 1 and 2. Lincoln, NE: University of Nebraska Press. If you have time to read through 1,200 pages of text, this set will tell you all about the revolution. It is free of ideology, which is a rarity in today's Latin American studies, which are replete with Marxist rantings.

257

Krauze, Enrique. 1997. *Mexico, Biography of Power: A History of Modern Mexico, 1810–1996*. New York: Harper, Collins. There are a host of Mexican historians and authors who contribute to our understanding of Mexico. Krauze is an essential read.

Lafaye, Jacques. 1974. *Quetzalcóatl and Guadalupe*. Chicago: University of Chicago Press. The author explores the melding of the Spanish and Aztec mentalities during the colonial period.

León-Portilla, Miguel. 1988. *Time and Reality in the Thought of the Maya*. Norman, OK: University of Oklahoma Press. Authoritative and informative.

MacLachlan, Colin M. 1988. *Spain's Empire in the New World*. Berkeley, CA: University of California Press. This is as good a description of the role of ideas in institutional and social change as exists. It addresses the conflict within the Catholic Church as to the humanity of indigenous peoples.

Reavis, Dick J. 1990. *Conversations with Moctezuma: The Soul of Modern Mexico*. New York: Morrow. Reavis discusses the conflict between the native and Spanish mentalities.

Teichman, Judith A. 1988. *Policymaking in Mexico: From Boom to Crisis*. London: Allen & Unwin. This is a useful analysis of the economic crisis of 1982, with implications for Mexico's political and economic strategies.

Womack, Jr., John. 1969. *Zapata and the Mexican Revolution*. New York: Alfred A. Knopf, Inc. This book gives good insights into the revolution and Zapata, and also gives insight into how the Mexican mind works.

Popular Readings about Mexico and Mexicans

Doerr, Harriet. 1984. *Stones for Ibarra*. New York: Penguin Books.

Esquivel, Laura. 1993. *Como agua para chocolate*. New York: Doubleday. A modern novel.

Fuentes, Carlos. 1991. *The Death of Artemio Cruz*. New York: Noonday Press.

Hamill, Pete. 1997. *Piecework*. Boston: Little, Brown and Company. His Section 3, titled "Mexico," helps the reader build context with Mexicans.

Márquez, Gabriel García. 1970. *One Hundred Years of Solitude*. New York: Avon Books.

Morrison, Terry, and Wayne A. Conaway. 1997. *The International Traveler's Guide to Doing Business in Latin America*. New York: Macmillan Spectrum. An "airport book rack" checklist of dos and don'ts.

Paz, Octavio. 1984. *One Earth, Four or Five Worlds*. San Diego: Harcourt, Brace, Jovanovich. One of Mexico's leading writers' most popular and instructive novels.

Pindell, Terry. 1996. *Yesterday's Train: A Rail Odyssey Through Mexican History*. New York: Henry Holt & Company. This is a good read and illuminates today's Mexico torn between its past and modernity.

Riding, Alan. 1985. *Distant Neighbors, A Portrait of the Mexicans.* New York: Alfred A. Knopf.

Ryan, Alan, ed. 1995. *The Reader's Companion to Mexico.* San Diego, CA: Harcourt, Brace and Company. This is a compendium of writings by authors who have been impressed by travels in Mexico, including Katherine Ann Porter, Langston Hughes, D. H. Lawrence, and John Steinbeck.

Trujillo, Charley. 1990. *Soldados: Chicanos in Viet Nam.* San José, CA: Chusma House Publications.

Readings on Culture in General

Geertz, Clifford. 1973. *The Interpretation of Cultures.* New York: Basic Books, Inc. This is a seminal book explaining Geertz's sociological approach to acquiring cultural information. He calls it "thick description."

Hall, Edward T. 1959. *The Silent Language.* New York: Doubleday. Anthropologist Hall shows how cultural factors influence the behavior of individuals without their knowledge.

———. 1976. *Beyond Culture.* New York: Anchor Press. The anthropologist looks at Japanese behavior.

———. 1983. *Dance of Life: The Other Dimension of Time.* New York: Anchor Press/ Doubleday. Hall shows how time is an organizer of activities. He compares Americans and Japanese.

———. 1987. *Hidden Differences.* New York: Anchor Press/Doubleday. Doing business with the Japanese. These books are interesting for their observations and methodology, though it is up to the reader to make the connections with the Mexican context.

Hampden-Turner, Charles, and Fons Trompenaars. 2000. *Building Cross-Cultural Competence, How to Create Wealth from Conflicting Values.* New Haven, CT: Yale University Press. This is a brainy text written for three people within a corporation, or for professors at Wharton. Its five-dollar words will leave the average reader perplexed. Its contribution is that it uses copious research to deliver conclusions about cultures on a macrolevel.

Harris, Marvin. 1974. *Cows, Pigs, Wars and Witches: The Riddles of Culture.* New York: Vintage Books. Anthropologist Harris debunks stereotypes we form about other cultures. Why are cows sacred in India where everybody is starving to death? Cows aren't sacred. Indians do eat hamburgers.

———. 1977. *Cannibals and Kings: The Origins of Cultures.* New York: Vintage Books. Harris shows how cultures develop in response to environmental changes.

Hofstede, Geert. 1994. *Cultures and Organizations, Intercultural Cooperation and its Importance for Survival.* London: HarperCollins. Hofstede did an extensive survey of IBM employees around the world. His work is authoritative and groundbreaking. However, it is mostly theoretical and does not pretend to direct the soldier on the ground.

Quigley, Carroll. 1979. *The Evolution of Civilizations*. Indianapolis: Liberty Press. Analyzes culture within the framework of civilization; describes how civilizations form, peak, and retreat into history.

Storti, Craig. 2001. *The Art of Crossing Cultures*. Yarmouth, ME: Intercultural Press. All authors bring their own experience to their work. In this case, Mr. Storti concentrates on the culture shock of being assigned to a foreign country. He helps you cope.

Trompenaars, Fons, and Charles Hampden-Turner. 1997. *Riding the Waves of Culture, Understanding Diversity in Global Business*. New York: McGraw-Hill. The same authors of the previous book published the results of the above-mentioned research here first. It is helpful in dividing cultures into work and behavior typologies. Again, it is academic.

Books on Mexican Business Culture

Condon, John C. 1997. *Good Neighbors, Communicating with the Mexicans*. 2nd ed. Yarmouth, ME: Intercultural Press. This is a succinct work about the differences between Americans and Mexicans on the cultural level. It touches on many valid points. It clearly states differences and alerts Americans to the Mexican perspective.

Kras, Eva. 1994. *Management in Two Cultures, Bridging the Gap between U.S. and Mexican Managers*. Yarmouth, ME: Intercultural Press. This is a succinct work that examines the differences between Mexicans and Americans and their ways of doing business. As in the case of *Good Neighbors*, it helps Americans realize the differences in American and Mexican perspectives.

Other Good Reads with Implications for Mexico

Diamond, Jared. 1997. *Guns, Germs and Steel: The Fates of Human Societies*. New York: WW Norton & Co. Among other examples, Diamond explores the true factors behind the Spanish conquest of Mexico.

Soto, Hernando de. 2001. *The Mystery of Capital: Why Capitalism Triumphs in the West and Fails Everywhere Else*. London: Black Swan Books. This economic treatise helps us understand the particular historical economic problems of Latin American countries.

Teresi, Dick. 2002. *Lost Discoveries: The Ancient Roots of Modern Science—From the Babylonians to the Maya*. New York: Simon & Schuster. This is a popular book that extols the brilliance of Maya mathematics and calendrics.

DATE DUE